KILLING THE BUTTERFLY

KILLING THE BUTTERFLY

A Cuban Memoir of Democracy's Demise

GUILLERMO
MARQUEZ-STERLING

SANTOS BOOKS
EVERY STORY SACRED

First Printing, 2025
Published by Santos Books, Elizabethtown, PA
ISBN:9798992412802

"The deeper the wound, the more beautiful the art."
Jose Marti (1853-1895)

To my mother, who provided light and joy at all times.

For a family tree and other information, please visit our website https://www.killingthebutterfly.com.

CONTENTS

CHAPTER 1

Olga

April 2020
    South Florida

The psychiatric wing at the hospital was modern and sterilized. The floor, a glistening polished marble, caused steps to echo against buffered walls painted a deep shade of ivory. Calming music filled the lobby as a muscular security officer wearing a black mask took my ID card while pointing to a sign with Covid-19 regulations, indicating I was to wear a mask while in the building. I complied, but not before taking out a stick of gum to chew on. Spearmint, my favorite. I twirled the wrapper in my fingers as I searched with futility where to place my disposal in a building lacking any movable furniture.

"Where can I throw this away?" I asked the officer as I showed him the small green, balled piece of paper.

He looked at it and then at my chewing mouth. "Gum chewing is not allowed. You'll have to spit it out."

He slid out a small plastic receptacle from under his table and held it in front of me.

"You're kidding me," I protested.

He stood silent, unwavering.

I rapidly chewed the wad about twelve times before spitting it out forcefully. It landed with a thud, followed by the balled up wrapper.

"Thank you," I said with a tone that was not grateful.

The officer held a sticky tag with my picture and name on it.

"Do people really look at the photo on these visitor tags?" I asked.

The officer didn't acknowledge my question.

"I mean, like, how would anyone know this was really me?"

"Sir, are you refusing to wear the visitor tag?"

"Refusing? No, of course not. I'll wear this. I just think the whole thing is a bit ridiculous. Especially the photo. I mean, look at it. Does it really look like me?"

"I think it does. I can see a smart-ass resemblance. Now keep your visitor tag under the left shoulder, wear your mask, and we won't have a problem."

"Yes, sir."

"Third floor. I'll escort you to the elevators, down the hall. You'll see the glass doors and the nurse's station on the other side. Press the intercom and a nurse will open the door for you."

I followed the officer, who used a key card to open the elevator. He stepped in to swipe the card again and pressed the button that would take me to where my mother was being held. At the third floor, the nurse's station was behind a pair of thick, glass doors. A young woman wearing pink scrubs and a matching mask approached me before I could press the intercom. Her tag read RN and her eyes revealed a smile.

"I'm here to see Olga Gutierrez."

"Yes, we were alerted by security. Come. Follow me."

The waiting room was separated by glass walls and furnished with small sofas, made from fluffy vinyl cushions. A table with four chairs was against the wall. Like the rest of the building, it lacked any item that could be deemed dangerous. My brother sat in one of the sofas, facing the patient wing. His small frame sunk into the cushions, and his crossed leg bounced with nervous energy. Normally, my brother would be friendly and funny, a trait we inherited from my mother's side of the family, but not on this day. As the nurse opened the doors, he leapt out of his chair to approach us and directed his ire at the young nurse, who stood about two inches taller than him.

"I've been waiting for three hours. When is the doctor coming? You told me he was here and that he would see me."

"Yes, sir," the nurse said while holding her hand out as if to stop his advancing charge. "Doctor Peck is in the building and he knows you're waiting for him. I'm sure he'll be with you as soon as he can. Please be patient."

"It's been three hours," he protested. "Longer, really. Three hours and twenty minutes."

"I'm aware how long it's been. Please step back and be patient."

"Can I at least see my mother while I wait for the doctor?"

"No. We've already been through this. Your mother is doing well, and all is good. You'll be able to see her if Doctor Peck allows it."

"Carlos, c'mon," I said to my brother and placed my hand on his shoulder.

He took several steps back while directing his angry stare at the young woman. She closed the glass doors and returned to the nurse's station.

"What are you doing?" I said to him, "You can't be picking fights with the nurses."

"I've been watching them for the last three hours, and they're dicking me around. They say the doctor will be here soon, but he's nowhere to be seen. Meanwhile, I'm stuck in a room that doesn't even have a TV, and Mom is probably freaking out."

"There's no TV?" I looked around to confirm his statement. "Why is that?"

"Cause it's a fucking loony bin. The people here are completely off their mind. There's a guy over there having an argument with an imaginary opponent. They let him walk around in a robe that's open in the back, and every time he turns, we can see his hairy ass. I bet you anything Mom's seen his hairy ass. She's gotta be losing it."

"Relax. It's going to be okay. Tell me what happened."

"What do you mean? I already told you."

"You told me she was Baker acted, but you didn't give me any details."

"As far as I know, she called the cops this morning, complaining about men who were going to confiscate all her belongings in the name of the revolution."

"What revolution?"

"I think..." he looked down and shook his head. "... she was reliving the early days of the Castro revolution. She may have overmedicated herself last night by mistake. Her voice was groggy when I spoke with her. I think she had a nightmare about Fidel Castro, and in the early morning she thought it was real."

"And, where were you?"

"I was home, getting ready for work when she called. The police officer was with her, and he told me he was taking her to the Emergency Room for a checkup, but I didn't know they were going to do a Baker Act."

"It's all so strange," I commented. "After all these years, why would she be dreaming about Cuba? It's been over sixty years. Do you mind if I take this mask off?"

"Is it safe? You're not coughing, are you?"

"I'm fine. I've been careful and staying away from people."

My brother lowered his mask.

"So, why would Mom be having nightmares about Fidel Castro?"

"I think she may have been triggered on Sunday," he said while looking down. "We were on Bird Road and saw a Biden rally get surrounded by Trump supporters, who were yelling and making threats. It was bizarre and pretty disturbing."

"Really? Was there a fight?"

"I don't know. I think so. There was a lot of chanting and name calling. We didn't stop. I didn't want to get caught up in the mayhem, but Mom got to see it all from the back seat. She said it was like Cuba when the Castro supporters harassed the people. I guess the scene stayed with her, setting the stage for the nightmare."

"So, in the morning she called the cops?" I asked.

He nodded.

"And you were able to talk to the policeman over the phone?"

He nodded again.

I sat next to him and looked around. Down the hall was the belligerent patient with a robe open in the back, his hairy rear exposed for all to see.

"We have to get Mom out of here," I said quietly.

"No shit!" My brother replied loudly.

"Dude, calm down. These people have the power and authority to keep Mom for as long as they want. Losing your temper won't help any."

"Don't lecture me. I've been here all fucking day. Where were you?"

"You know I was trying to get here as fast as I could. It's a four hour trip from St. Pete."

"Well, I'm the one that stayed to make sure Mom is okay."

"Are we back to that, really? I had to leave. It wasn't an option."

"Sorry, " My brother softened and looked down. "I'm glad you're here."

Forty minutes later a young woman wearing blue scrubs opened the glass doors for an older man with a graying and receding hairline. He was wearing small, circular glasses, a white robe and a black mask. The young woman followed him in, as we donned our face masks and stood to meet him. His two hands were behind his back, holding a notebook, a clear indicator that he did not want to shake hands.

"Hello, I'm Dr. Peck. Which one of you is Carlos?"

My brother took a short step forward.

"And you are?" He looked at me with a raised eyebrow.

"I'm Guillermo, Olga's younger son. How is she?"

"She is doing well. How do you spell your name?"

I slowly spelled out my name, as he wrote on his pad and smiled behind his mask.

"Do you watch late night, Jimmy Kimmel?" The doctor asked and looked up to make eye contact with me. "He has a sidekick, a Mexican fellow with the same name. Very funny."

I smiled politely, painfully aware that my name is uncommon, especially among non-Spanish speaking people.

"Is that a Mexican name, Guillermo?"

"No, it's from Spain."

"Hmm...." He then looked at my brother's sharp blue eyes. "And you... I never would have guessed you're named Carlos."

We stood silent, waiting for this doctor to finish with his unfiltered observations.

"You're not from Miami, are you, doctor?" Carlos asked.

The doctor looked down and ignored the question, "Do you have a list of the medications she takes?"

Carlos took out a folded sheet of paper with the names and dosages of nine medications. The doctor shifted his position to write words that were unintelligible to us.

"Indiana," he said without looking up. "I've been here for a few months. Interesting place. I thought coming to Miami would be exciting."

"And is it?" I asked.

"Well, there certainly seems to be a lot of excitement around here. A lot of flag waving. People do take their politics seriously." The doctor smiled and returned his eyes to the notes in front of him, "At first glance, I question the need for two of these medications, which should not be taken together. The other medications do have biological benefits, however, there might be some contraindications if taken for a prolonged period of time. But these two in particular... if your mother took them last night, it would explain the episode of disorientation and confusion."

He paused to look at us, and he must have seen two scared, grown children who only wanted to hear their mommy was going to be alright.

"Okay. Upon my examination your mother does not seem to present a danger to herself, but she explained that she lives alone and has been feeling lonely due to the forced isolation of the pandemic. For someone your mother's age, the forced isolation, the interruption of a weekly schedule and the combination of these medications can create a state of delusion and/or disorientation. With what frequency does she have contact with people?"

"I visit her on the weekends," my brother said, "and we talk on the phone every day."

"I live in St. Petersburg, but I call her every day," I said as the doctor looked down and wrote on his notes. "We have an aunt that visits her with regularity, and our mother has many friends and relatives with whom she speaks to on the phone on a daily basis, like..."

"Just a few more questions to confirm her story," the doctor interrupted. "It's a mere formality to separate facts from possible delusions. Please have a seat. Okay?"

We looked around and chose to sit at the table. The young woman remained standing.

"Your mother is Cuban, right?" He asked while looking at his notes. We nodded.

"She really is a delightful woman, very sweet and cute. I love her accent." The doctor smiled and looked at us for agreement. I nodded, but my brother remained stoic, waiting for information that could actually be relevant.

"And she left the island in 1959?" The doctor asked.

"Yes, um, what does this have to do with her state of mind?" My brother replied.

"Please. Let me ask the questions. Okay? She states she was married to the son of a famous politician, one Carlos Marcus Sterling."

"Marquez," my brother corrected.

The doctor looked at him, unsure what my brother was saying.

"You said Marcus, and it's Marquez," he clarified.

"Yes. That's neither here nor there."

I held my breath and glanced at my brother to see if he too was taken aback. Growing up, I always knew our last name was famous, bordering on sacred for the older generations. To hear this Indiana doctor so casually dismiss a name associated with Cuban history made me flinch.

"I'm trying to verify the story your mother narrated to see if any of it is fictitious," he continued. "She says your father was intimately acquainted with Fidel Castro. Is that true?"

I leaned forward to clarify. "What do you mean by 'intimately?' They knew each other, but I wouldn't say 'intimately.' That has a certain connotation."

"Agreed. Hmm..."

"But they knew each other from the university and the student union," Carlos added. "They definitely ran into each other many times."

"So, for some reason," the doctor continued without looking up, "she says that before leaving the island, she and her family were afraid for their lives. She described an environment that was hostile. Is that true?"

We nodded.

"If she did not support Castro, she was called a worm?"

"Yes," I answered. "It's what they called anyone who was against the revolution."

"Interesting..."

"What's so interesting?" My brother asked.

The doctor remained silent while writing a few notes. Carlos looked at me with widened eyes to see if I too was upset at the doctor's language.

"Okay," the doctor said while writing. "It seems the current political situation, and the Trump rally she witnessed the other day, triggered the traumatic memories from those days in Cuba. There seems to be enough similarities between the animosity we're living through and what your mother experienced when Castro came into power." He looked up and made eye contact with my brother. "That's why it's interesting. I know you're upset that your mother was brought here and that the police officer issued a Baker Act. I get it. Nobody wants to see their mother in such a place. I'd be upset too."

The doctor looked at me and then again at my brother. "Gentlemen, let me tell you what I'm going to do."

We held our breath as we waited.

"You look like good and caring sons. The fact that you're both here, worried for her welfare, speaks well of you and your family. Too often I am faced with patients similar to your mother who tragically do not have a single family member in this waiting room."

The doctor paused and tapped his pen on the notepad, like a metronome marking the rhythm for the music that was to follow. We leaned forward and held our breaths.

"I'm going to release your mother to your care..."

My brother loudly exhaled and silently mouthed, "Thank God!"

"... provided that you raise the question of her medications with her primary care physician."

"Yes, of course. Anything," my brother interrupted again.

"I also recommend she not live alone for the next few months, or at least until this pandemic subsides. Maybe she can live with a family member, or one of you?"

"Well, I guess I could move her into my apartment," my brother said while looking at me. "It would be tight, and I don't think she would want to live with us."

"I can take her to St. Petersburg to live with me," I offered.

"Those details are for you all to figure out," the doctor said with slight annoyance. "The point is to reintegrate her into a daily routine where people come and go, sit for dinner, and she can participate in face-to-face interactions. Okay? Do you understand what I'm prescribing?"

We agreed as he looked at us squarely.

"Good. I have to get going," he said as he stood up. "It was nice meeting you both."

"Doctor, before you leave, do you mind if I ask you a question?" I asked.

He paused and looked at me patiently.

"I just want to understand, and I'm hoping you'll be able to educate me," I continued as he stood silent, waiting for the question. "It's been over sixty years since our mother left Cuba. She has made it clear that she doesn't want to go back. She has a full life with family and friends, but this morning she was reliving experiences from very long ago. It doesn't make sense. Fidel is not even alive anymore. Do you see what I mean? Why now, and not forty years ago?"

"Because, nothing really goes away," Doctor Peck replied. "The human mind is amazing. It can store information, memories, conversations, feelings and ideas for an entire lifetime. There will be a moment in your elderly years when you will recall with vivid detail your first kiss, an event that was a lifetime away. Okay?"

The doctor looked at my brother and me as we sat at the edge of our seats, hanging on every word, pause and inflection.

"And maybe your mother did have traumatic flashbacks in the past. Who's to say? The difference is that twenty years ago she was younger and able to move on. Today she's taking a number of medications that have altered her ability to cope. Your mother had a chemically induced disassociation with reality, and re-lived a traumatic experience that, for all practical purposes, is engraved into her being. You can't put a timeline on trauma, nor can you place regional boundaries on it. What happens in Vegas doesn't stay in Vegas, and in your mother's case, what happened in Cuba followed her here."

He then looked directly at me with an intensity that was not hidden by his mask.

"Don't minimize the trauma your mother suffered just because it was sixty years ago. It's very easy to say she should get over it, but the mind doesn't work that way. The events of Cuba 1958 may have been a lifetime ago, but with all the recent political rallies, I would venture to say it's resurfacing today, more than ever. Okay?"

We nodded silently as he looked at us with inspecting eyes, assessing our ability to understand his words.

"It's common for people of your mother's age and condition to talk about their past, about the trauma they've lived through. Be patient with her. Okay? Anything else?"

"Can we go in to see her?" My brother asked.

"Oh no. Visitors are not allowed in the patient area. Wait here and when your mother is discharged, we will bring her to you. Have a good day."

Doctor Peck abruptly stepped away, clearly not wanting to shake hands, and waited for the young woman to open the doors for him. My brother and I looked at each other, fully aware of the new responsibility to take care of our mother.

Three days later, my mother sat in the backseat of the car looking out the window at the seemingly endless view of the Florida Everglades as we drove northward on I-75. Her hair, a bright, metallic shade of white, is what other passersby must have seen through the tinted window before noticing her pleasant face. My mother, at eighty-five, had aged into what the doctor described as "sweet and cute," words that at one time would have slightly offended this woman who often strived for elegance.

"And to think that Ponce de León traveled this land by foot," she said while staring at a horizon of uninterrupted glades. "We're doing it by car, and I can barely stand it. How many mosquitoes and snakes? No, no, no, no, no. Not even the promise of a turkey dinner at the Quaker Barrel would get me to walk on this crocodile-infested swamp."

My mother's mispronunciations made me smile. It felt like home when she spoke her Cuban version of English that pronounced a bowl of Quaker Oats as *Kwahker*.

"We'll be in St. Pete before you know it. And by the way, it's cracker, not *kwahker*."

"I know," she chuckled. "It's just easier for me to say it that way. *Pero*, Guille, you need to understand that my body can't handle these long car trips. If I have to go, I have to go. And I'm not going to have an accident here, in Maria's new car."

"Well, you're the one that requested Maria's car. Do I need to put a little pad under you?" I asked with a chuckle.

She caught my eye through the rearview mirror and smiled. "No, no, no, no, no. Can you imagine if I end up peeing in her car? *¡Que pena!* How embarrassing! Pad or no pad, I wouldn't be able to show my face. So, you better pull over... at a *Kwahker* Barrel or whatever."

"Mama, we just started this trip. Don't tell me you have to go already."

"No, I don't have to, but at my age you never know."

"Just don't think about it. We'll be reaching Naples in about an hour. If you really need to stop, there'll be other small towns and cities along the way."

Her gaze returned to the view of a blue sky adorned by cumulus clouds floating over the slow-moving river of grass. I increased the speed on my cruise control, determined to make the four-hour trip in three and a half. Over the last five years I had become familiar with I-75 as Maria and I packed our home of twenty-seven years in Miami and moved to St. Petersburg. We could have relocated to Seattle, Washington. I had an offer there, but we quickly dismissed the notion of living days away from our family and Cuban American community.

"Do you know what I hate?" my mother softly asked as she slowly returned from a daydream. "Cockroaches."

"Oh, God, Mama. Me too. Especially the ones that fly. I have to kill them right away."

"I can't even do that," her voice grew louder. "The thought of a cockroach running up my leg..." She nervously rubbed her arm to ameliorate the sensations she was re-living. "I think I would die," she laughed. "A heart attack on the spot. You know, when I was a girl in Cuba, I had a horrible encounter with roaches. Our house in Víbora Park, when we first moved in, had a nest of cockroaches in the kitchen drainpipe."

She moved to the center of the backseat to get a view of my face through the rearview mirror. A new energy filled her, and I smiled with anticipation at the story that was bubbling with her enthusiasm.

"The day before the movers arrived, *Mima* took me there along with a few other women to give it a cleaning. It was my job to give the kitchen a good scrubbing."

"What about *Tío?*"

"What about your uncle?"

"Didn't he have to help and clean the house?"

"No. Back then boys didn't do any housework. But stop distracting me. So, I was in the kitchen, trying to get that sink to sparkle. It wasn't stainless steel like the ones we have now. I had to scrub with a wire pad. You know those wire pads that are all bunched up?"

I nodded, completely unaware of what she was referring to.

"I finished scrubbing it, happy with how the stains had come off, until I looked at the drain. It took me a moment to figure it out, but there were these two long antennas, moving like this." She paired her second and third fingers and moved them slowly toward me.

"Oh God! Don't do that."

"Guille, it was the largest cockroach I had ever seen in my life. It came out of that drain and ran up the side of the sink. And behind it was an entire army of little roaches, *cucarachitas*, all of them running right at me. The strange thing was that I couldn't move. I was paralyzed. All I could do was scream. *Mira*, I screamed so loudly the entire neighborhood came to see what was happening. It was the loudest call for help I have ever done. A dozen people ran into the kitchen and started killing cockroaches."

"What about you?"

"I couldn't stop screaming because one of the roaches had crawled up my leg."

"No!"

"*Ay, mijo*. I thought I was going to die!"

"Were you wearing shorts or pants?"

"Pants. Back then girls didn't wear shorts unless you were at the beach or doing sports. No, no, no, no, no. I was wearing pants and the roach was..."

"Inside your pant leg?"

"*Mima* started to smack at the roach through the pants, but that only made it worse. So, I took off my pants and inside was the big cockroach, the first one I saw in the drain."

"What? The one you saw when you were cleaning?"

"That one."

"No," I said in disbelief. "How do you know it was the same one?"

"Because it was huge! Guille, you have no clue how large this roach was."

I started to laugh.

"Don't laugh," she said with a smile. "I'm telling you about my childhood trauma."

"Sorry," I said laughing, and recalling Doctor Peck's words. "So, *Abuela* rescued you from the roach?"

"No, she started to scream, too, because the roach ran toward her."

"So, what happened?"

"What do you mean?"

"Who killed it?"

"It was Manolín. He jumped into action."

"I thought you said *Tío* wasn't there."

"Hmm. I did say that, didn't I, but he definitely was there because he's the one that killed the roach. He stepped on it like a flamenco dancer. It became the joke in the family."

"What about *Abuelo*, was he there?"

"No. This was after the divorce. We had moved to Víbora Park and that house was part of the divorce settlement."

"So, back to the cockroaches."

"What about them?"

"Finish the story."

"No. Nothing. That was it."

"You didn't have any more roaches after that?"

"Where?"

"In the house, Mama. Did the roach problem in the house get fixed?"

"Well, Mima poured gallons of chlorine down the sink and I think it must have cleared the nest of roaches that was down there."

"So, a happy ending? You had a clean house with no more roaches."

"Happy ending?" she reflected and sat back in her seat. "There was nothing happy about that house," she said softly, staring out the window.

We drove in silence for several more miles. Highway driving always elevated my mother's anxiety. It was the reason why she sat in the back to minimize her chances of seeing the road ahead. I fought the urge to play music, knowing it would make her nervous. She thought a good driver never listens to music in the car, because it only distracts. My counter argument: "Yes, of course music distracts. That's the purpose." But, on this day, when her anxiety was already heightened due to her recent hospital stay, I decided to make the car ride as comfortable as possible, which meant not listening to my playlist.

A shiny, jet black Mercedes Benz SUV sped past us. It must have been going over one hundred miles per hour.

"¡Dios mío!" my mother gasped, startled by the sudden interruption of her trance-like state. "Look at that car. What could be so urgent for a man to drive like that?"

I nodded and held back a smile. The driver of that Mercedes Benz was a woman, but my mother's understanding of gender roles did not allow for a woman to be an aggressive driver.

"It is a nice car, don't you think? Those cars are made for highway driving... very comfortable, I imagine."

"Why can't you get yourself a nice car like that? Your cars always look like toys. I can see my grandchildren in a car like yours, but you? You should be in a car that commands respect, worthy of a man who dresses with a suit and tie. Instead, you have a little toy car, you dress in blue jeans, a protest shirt and Save-the-Earth pamphlets. No, no, no, no, no. How about a nice Cadillac, something worthy of the academic titles you've earned? How you fit in that little car is a miracle. Don't you dare take me anywhere in it."

"Well, that's why we're in Maria's car. I'll keep my Mini Cooper for city driving."

"Minnie... Isn't that the name of a Disney character, the girlfriend of Mickey Mouse?"

I laughed. I learned a long time ago to not take my mother's complaints too seriously or personally. It was her way of making conversation.

"It sounds childish. *Por favor.* You're a mature man, in your fifties. Get a real car, even if it's Japanese."

"What about an electric car?" I teased.

"Electric? Like a golf car? That would be the last straw." She paused and then with a nostalgic tone said, "I remember when your grandfather bought his first car."

"Which one, *Abuelo Manolo* or *Abuelo Carlos*?"

"Your *Abuelo* Carlos didn't drive. Not even when we left Cuba. I'm talking about my father, *Abuelo Manolo*. I was a teenager when he bought his first car. It was spectacular. Don't ask me what type. I didn't pay attention to car brands back then... still don't, but I know it was a big car, a convertible, worthy of a man who was successful. Back then, in Cuba, most people got around on a bus or trolley. To have a car was really something."

She paused and from the rearview mirror I could see she had wandered to a time and life only accessible in her memories. She was no longer on I-75, but on the streets of Havana, wearing a bright, flowered dress, sitting next to her father in his new car and giggling at the world around her. Although she knew she was in the car with me, her consciousness had crossed over to a land she had not seen in over sixty years.

"Your grandfather was a dashing man, you know," she said in a raspy voice and then attempted to clear her throat. "Do you have a *caramelito*, a lozenge?"

"No, I don't think so. Have a sip of water."

She looked at the bottle of water and sighed. "I need you to open it for me."

Like a contortionist, I reached behind me to retrieve the bottle. After loosening the lid, I slowly handed it back. She took a sip, almost spilling it, and then placed it down.

"Where was I?"

"*Abuelo*. You were telling me how handsome he was."

"He was more than handsome. He was debonair," she said with a smile. "He really knew how to dress, with the handkerchief in his pocket, like a dandy. And his car... What a car! It was an extension of his good looks. He was so attractive in it. I remember the women just looking at him when he drove by and me feeling like the most important girl in this world."

Another car zipped past us, startling my mother once again.

"Mama, do you want to talk about why you were in the hospital?"

"What do you mean?"

"You know, how you thought your home was invaded by Castro supporters?"

"*Ay mijo*, it's better to leave that alone. The doctor said it was a medically induced hallucination. Nothing more. Don't worry. It won't happen again."

We continued in silence as she stared out the window. I studied her through the rearview mirror and realized that in the span of a few years my mother had gotten old. She had always managed to retain a degree of youthfulness, a contagious laughter, and an encouraging attitude. Consequently, people addressed her as "Olguita," the diminutive of her name. "Olga" is reserved for matriarchs who command a household full of servants. Whereas "Olguita" is for the good friend, who serves you an espresso coffee while you share the latest chapter of your life, and together find something to laugh at. No, Olguita was not old, until now.

I'm not sure when it happened. Maybe it was after the third fall, or after the last bout of bronchitis that never really went away, but, somehow, she became fragile. Her voice and her hands trembled, her footing became unsteady, and in the deep corners of her mind an awareness crept in that something had changed. As difficult as it must have been, one day she announced she would no longer drive and she relinquished the freedom and independence younger people take for granted. Olguita had a way of joking about growing old while urging me to accept this inevitable part of life with an unnerving prophecy, "*Ay, mijo,* you'll get there too. You'll see."

And so, there we were, following Doctor Peck's orders in my wife's car, because mine was too small and unacceptable, when she said, "I need for you to pull over."

CHAPTER 2

Manolo and Tina

1 951
Havana, Cuba

He drove by the scenic *Paseo del Prado* in his new Plymouth Special Deluxe convertible with the top down, radio up, and his sunglasses on. Manolo was bursting with pride as people stopped to look at him in his new car, fresh off the lot. He always dressed well, but today he made the extra effort to look like the type of man who could afford a cream-colored Plymouth convertible. His hair was slick and his mustache pencil thin. His three-piece suit was tailor-made with a folded white handkerchief on the jacket's front pocket. His cologne was French, Guerlain, and his cigarettes American, Old Gold.

After several miles of cruising through the neighborhoods of *La Víbora* and *El Vedado*, where the homes were large, the yards manicured and the maids uniformed, Manolo drove to the home of his ex-wife, Tina, in the middle-class neighborhood of *Víbora Park*, where his children, Olga and Manolín, were waiting for him.

"Papá," his 10-year-old son screamed with delight as he parked the car in front of the house. "A new car? *¡Me encanta!* I love it!"

"Hop in, before your mother comes out," Manolo said with a smile.

"Papá!" Olga ran around the car to greet him with a kiss.

"*Mi niña*, jump in. Let's go for a ride."

She stood back, in awe, admiring the new car.

"*Vamos*. Get in."

19

Olga and Manolín were not yet seated when Tina emerged from the house with a scowl.

"Out of the car," she demanded. "Right now!"

"Tina, for the love of God," he complained. "It's just a ride around the neighborhood in my new car."

"Yes, lately, for you everything is new," she said, waving her arms around. "New car. New clothes. New girlfriend. Did you win the lottery?"

Manolo and the children sat motionless watching her.

"Out!" she screamed "You can take them for a ride on Saturday."

Manolo looked at Tina, who directed her children towards the house with a pointed index finger. He gave them each a kiss and secretly slipped a *peso* into his son's pocket. Manolín noticed the not-so-discreet gift and smiled at his father.

"Don't say anything," Manolo whispered. "This gift is for you."

Tina's stern look followed the children as they sheepishly walked to the house. As Tina returned her attention to Manolo, they stood on the front porch, anxiously listening for any hopeful signs of spending time with their father.

"It took you long enough," she reprimanded Manolo while keeping one hand on her hip.

"I meant to come earlier this week," he said, removing his sunglasses. His light blue eyes contrasted with his dark hair. When she first met him, it was his eyes that lured her. When she loved him - a lifetime ago - it was his eyes that beckoned her kiss. On this day, though, those eyes meant nothing. He had betrayed her by giving them to another. All she wanted now was the money the judge ordered. He leaned over and handed her an envelope. She took it, opened it, and quickly counted the bills.

"Ninety-five," he said.

"Is that all?"

"That's exactly what you need for her dress, photo shoot and the month's expenses."

"And not one penny more," she said sarcastically.

"What do you want? Your hatred does not inspire generosity."

"What? You want me to be happy that you left me for Jenny? She was but a little girl when we first met her."

"Stop it already. You didn't even know she existed. I understand you're angry, but don't turn the children against me. They should be able to see me without all this guilt."

"That's what Saturdays are for."

"Alright. I'll be back on that day for more guilt, and maybe I can see the dress, too?"

"Why?"

"Tina, *por favor*," he said with exasperation.

Tina looked away and curled her lips in contempt. Olga turned fifteen the previous year and did not get her *quinceañera* because she was away at a boarding school in North Carolina. Now that she was back for the summer, there were plenty of other social events where they could celebrate, even if it was late.

"I'll be going to the Boca Ciega party," Manolo said.

"Don't you dare show up with her."

"Sure," he sighed. "If it makes it easier for you to not make a scene."

"Make a scene? I'm not the one who's parading around in this ..." she said, looking at the car with disgust. "this... cry for attention."

"So, now I can't buy myself a car? I bought you this house and I agreed to everything your lawyer demanded. Can't I have a little something for me?"

"It's not the car, it's everything. I mean, look at you, all dressed up like a... Just who are you pretending to be? Cary Grant?"

"What?" He began to pull the car out. "As if you were Rita Hayworth!"

"Get out of here!" She tried to kick his car but missed. "*¡Cabrón!*" she yelled as he drove away. She turned around to see her two children standing on the front porch. Olga ran inside, afraid of a reprimand, while Manolín stood still.

"Mamá," Manolín said timidly. "Don't you like Papás car?"

"Get inside before I take that money your father gave you."

Manolín looked at his mother with injured eyes.

"Yes, I saw that. *Dale.* Go on, get inside."

Olga looked longingly at her departing father but was not upset because she knew how to visit him without risking her mother's wrath. While Tina, who worked as a schoolteacher, stayed late in the classroom every Tuesday, Olga hopped on the trolley to Old Havana and visited her father at the family business, "Fotograbados Gutierrez," known to them as "*el taller*," the workshop.

On that Tuesday, rain clouds hung over Havana as Olga stepped onto the trolley. All the seats were taken, and several passengers stood, conversing loudly. She looked around and decided to stand next to a group of seated women, who were discussing clothing costs at the department store, *Fin de Siglo*. Behind them were two men dressed in linen shirts loudly discussing the politics of Carlos Prío Socarrás, Cuba's president.

"Prío is a coward," one man accused while the other prepared a counter argument. "He's afraid of the gangs and meanwhile the corruption is out of control."

"You're just repeating what Chibás is saying on the radio."

"But it's true!"

"Not necessarily. Chibás is crying because he lost the elections to Prío, and now he is constantly flooding the radio with this complaint."

"Open your eyes. Do you think the corruption will just go away on its own, magically?"

Olga was blankly staring at the floor when she saw a small cockroach crawl onto the edge of the man's shoe. She gasped and stiffened.

One of the women seated by her looked at Olga's change of posture. They made eye contact.

"There's a *cucaracha* over there. By that man," Olga whispered.

The woman smiled, dismissing her concern and returned to the conversation.

Olga was unable to relax, keeping watch over the insect, until the trolley arrived at Calle Sol, where she quickly got off and walked one block to the building that housed *el taller*. It was one of the older buildings in the oldest part of the city, leading her to reach a new realization: "There's probably roaches in there too."

"Olguita," her Uncle Angelito greeted as she walked into the front office. He was at his desk, reviewing artistic sketches that were to be printed in a magazine. Her other uncle, Pedrito, sat a few paces away at his desk, smoking a cigarette and studiously looking at the accounting books. Olga walked up to Angelito, who smiled and tilted his face for her to kiss him on the cheek. Behind him were several cameras that had been dismantled, with their parts strewn about.

"I hear you're going to be the runner-up at the Boca Ciega party *and* you're getting a new dress," he said to her with a smile.

"I was hoping to be queen this year, but Tita sold more tickets," Olga replied. She walked over to Pedrito to kiss him on the cheek. He tilted his face without lifting his eyes off the books.

"*Niña*, how are you?" he asked while exhaling cigarette smoke.

"*Bien*. Are you going to the party?"

Pedrito shook his head without losing sight of the accounting.

"I'll be there," Angelito said cheerfully. "Taking pictures of you in the new dress."

"I don't have a date," Olga frowned.

"I would be surprised if your mother allowed you to have one. You're only fifteen."

"But Elenita, Dora and Carmen will have dates."

"And how old are they, seventeen, eighteen?"

"So!"

"Just because you have friends who are older than you doesn't make you older. You do know the difference, right?"

Olga pouted playfully and then spun around.

"*Tío*, how many cockroaches do you think are in this building?"

"How many?"

"Aren't you afraid they'll come out and crawl on your leg?"

"You don't have to worry about the cockroaches. They're behind the walls, too afraid of the sunlight. And if they come out, you know what to do."

"What?"

"Call your brother and have him dance the flamenco." Angelito laughed.

"I have to go. Papá is waiting for me." Olga walked toward the door that led to the back of the business, where the workers did the engraving.

"*Oye*," Angelito called out to her. "Bring me a *café* from El Chamberí."

"Me too," Pedrito said quietly.

Olga returned and opened her hand. "You don't expect for my father to pay for it, do you?" Angelito laughed and placed a few coins in her hands.

"El Chamberí is not cheap, you know." She kept her hand out.

Angelito smiled and placed another coin in her hand.

"He probably doesn't have a dime left to his name after what he paid for that car." Pedrito looked up, flicked his cigarette on the ashtray and commented, "Foolish!"

"I love his car," she said and turned around. "I think it's great."

Angelito smiled as he watched his niece exit.

"You know she's keeping those coins?" Pedrito said softly.

"I know," Angelito replied with a wistful smile. "Allowing her to cheat me out of some coins is a small way to make amends."

Pedrito glanced over at his brother and rolled his eyes in disbelief.

As the youngest of nine siblings, Manolo did not have a high status in the family. He was forced to drop out of school in the eighth grade and learn the trade of the family business, one his mother, Concepción, tried to protect him from. She coddled him, no doubt because he was the baby of the family, but for her it was about the chance to be the mother she always wanted to be. This created some rivalry as the siblings noticed the special treatment he received. Some argued their mother loved him better because of his blue eyes, a physical trait shared only by one of the sisters. Some argued it was because of their father, an Andalusian roisterer who managed to return home in the late hours of the night more often than Concepción liked, and still some others argued that it was because he was born to aging parents who had gotten soft with age. Regardless of the reason, Pedrito knew there could be no room for special treatment at a time when people were dying from tuberculosis and a third of the island was unemployed. The final straw was when he heard the news that his little brother was going to a country club to play tennis.

"Tennis, for God's sake!" Pedrito argued in a raised voice with his mother. "It's a game for pampered Brits. Just who do you think we are? Where do you think we live?"

"You don't understand," Concepción tried to explain. "You were born during the War for Independence. We were too busy not getting killed while Spaniards and Americans shot at each other. Your father, who came from Spain a few years earlier, had to give all his earnings for the new Cuba or else be accused of sympathizing with the crown. Do I need to remind you how bad it was, the mud you played in because I couldn't buy you any toys?"

"Mamá, you don't need to tell me. I ate bird food because there was nothing else, which is why Manolo can't pretend to be a child of royalty."

"One day, life got better. We now have a steady flow of money. Why can't we give him what I couldn't give you? He knows we're not descendants of royalty. He knows life is hard and he'll have to work. Let me be the mother who gives her son a tennis racket for his birthday. What's wrong with that?"

"The kid has received more schooling, more new clothing and more cuts of steak than any of us. It's time he learns how to earn it and how difficult life is. It's a lesson I'm going to give my children, and my children's children."

Pedrito marched out of the living room, and saw Manolo timidly standing on the front porch with the tennis racket in his hand. Having heard the argument, he knew his brother's intentions and retreated several steps.

"¡Ven acá, mojón!" Pedrito reached over to grab him.

Manolo jumped out of reach and began running. Pedrito, who smoked a pack of cigarettes a day, ran after him for a whole block before giving up the chase.

Manolo was at the workshop the following day, only after hiding the racket. He worked hard and eventually became a talented engraver. Yet, it was not enough for Pedrito to have prevailed. Manolo was treated like a common employee and not given an equal share of the profits. He quietly accepted the inequity, telling himself that Pedrito was teaching him a lesson.

In his eighteenth year of life, Manolo met a young woman from Güira de Melena, a small country town south of Havana. She was in the city studying to be a schoolteacher. Tina, named after her mother, was attracted to the young tennis player, and it wasn't long before they agreed to marriage. They began their family in a small, rented home, enjoying the growing economy of the blossoming island-nation. All was going well for the young man who still held on to his dream of becoming a competitive tennis player, when for unknown reasons, he began to suffer from incapacitating migraine headaches. When this malady came over him, there was no analgesic that could alleviate it. The pain pushed from the inside, driving him to retreat into the darkness of his bedroom and suffer for several days until it somehow released him. Other than placing ice on his head and balsam on his temples, there was nothing Tina or his children could do. On many occasions, Concepción came to sit by his side, while Tina and the children went to their classes. Nobody understood the recurring affliction, but it was Concepción who argued the family pay the expenses for a medical treatment. To her surprise, Pedrito agreed, and he sent Manolo and Tina to seek a cure in Rochester, New York. Unable to speak a word of English, translators helped them communicate with the medical team, who were amazed that a Cuban man with "dark" skin could have clear blue eyes. Decades later, recalling the details of that trip, Tina described how it felt to be looked down upon for the very first time in her life.

"We wanted a diagnosis, and they kept asking about Manolo's blue eyes. He was still grumpy from the lingering effects of the previous headache, and he lost his patience. We didn't know it was racism. We didn't even know that word, 'racism,' but now, after all these years, I tell you that's what it was."

After two days of tests, the doctors prescribed brain surgery as their course of treatment. It was Tina who told him it was okay to doubt the wisdom of doctors, alerting him to the possibility of the cure being worse than the illness. In an action that did not require the help of translators, Tina and Manolo fled Rochester and returned to Cuba where a group of local doctors suggested a less draconian treatment, the removal of teeth pushing against the temporomandibular nerve. Manolo, now in his early thirties, was willing to trade his smile, but not his brain, for the possibility of relief.

In an effort to cover all the bases, Tina found a healer, Emma, who prayed to the saints, lit candles and recited liturgical chants to invoke the healing power of the Spirit. Manolo thought her to be a strange and peculiar-looking woman. Her facial tick, which almost disappeared when she prayed, did not instill confidence. The first time Manolo sat in her living room Emma explained that a malignant spirit was causing his headaches. Certain she had the power to banish evil spirits, Emma waved her arms and chanted invocations while smoking suspicious herbs.

Manolo sat dumbfounded, wondering why he ever agreed to this nonsense. He leaned forward, determined to leave, when Emma placed her index finger on the top of his head. An electric sensation vibrated on his scalp and swept down his extremities. Most likely it was a jolt of static electricity, but the shock was enough for him to surrender to her incantations. Minutes later he opened his eyes to find Emma's daughter,

Jenny, standing in front of him. She had none of her mother's peculiar traits and all the beauty of a twenty-year-old. Jenny smiled at him and a new motivation propelled Manolo to continue with the prayer sessions.

Decades later, while living as an exiled refugee, Manolo considered the possibility that the sulfuric vapors at the workshop could have been the culprit of his malady. His doctors did not look into the effects of toxic fumes, but their post-surgical instructions stated he discontinue working as an engraver. On doctor's orders, Pedrito reassigned him to the darkroom for film processing, and the headaches became a distant memory. Until the end of his life, Manolo wasn't certain if his healing could be credited to the oral surgery, the prayers of a healing woman or the change in his work conditions. What was certain and irrefutable was the departure of the headaches, and the spirit that caused them.

Feeling strong, healthy, and free of headaches, Manolo decided life was good and worth enjoying. He bought himself a new tennis racket and returned to the game he loved. To his surprise, he had several consecutive victories on the court. Encouraged by those victories, he stood up to his eldest brother and demanded a raise with full partnership rights. To his surprise, Pedrito agreed and gave him the long-awaited standing. Empowered by that victory, he confessed to his wife his love for Emma's daughter, Jenny. To his surprise, he learned Tina had one hell of a backhand. After chasing him out of the house with every available dish and ornament crashing all around him, she hired the most powerful lawyer in Havana, the honorable Carlos Márquez-Sterling.

"I want the beach house in Boca Ciega. We bought it so we could have vacations there. I'll be damned if Jenny gets to parade in it."

Her lawyer took notes.

"I want a new house for me and the children. No more renting."

The lawyer continued to make note of her requests.

"And I want to live in a nice neighborhood. *El Vedado*."

The lawyer looked up at her and raised an eyebrow.

"Okay, maybe not there, but somewhere nice."

"How about *Víbora Park?*" the lawyer offered.

"Yes. That's nice enough. There. That's where I want the house. And why do I have to keep on working as a schoolteacher? I should be able to stay home and take care of the kids without having to worry about money. I want a monthly income that covers all my expenses."

"You're going to quit working?" the lawyer asked.

"No, I love my job, but I want the option."

"I agree. He should pay for all your expenses."

"Thank you, and any future expenses. He wants a new woman, fine, but he's going to pay. I want every penny... and custody of the children, too."

"What about visitation?"

"None. He can't see them."

"That's not going to be received well."

"Okay, once a month."

A disapproving silence hung between them.

"Once a week?"

"Better," the lawyer returned his gaze to his notes.

A week later the lawyer returned with the good news that Manolo agreed to the terms of the settlement. Eager to move on with his new life, he decided to give Tina everything she asked, but it was the fight that she truly wanted, not an easy victory. So, she instructed the lawyer to restrict visitation to a few hours on Saturdays. It made Tina smile with satisfaction but forced Olga to lie and sneak on Tuesdays. To Olga, it made her father seem more like a victim than a perpetrator. In the divorce settlement, Manolo may have lost more possessions than he should have, but he won something a lot more valuable, the adoration of his daughter. This became obvious when Olguita showed up on a Tuesday afternoon, unannounced, at *el taller*.

"What are you doing here?" Manolo asked her on that very first visit. "Is everything okay?" He was wearing his sweat-drenched work clothes.

"I just passed by to see you," she said with a smile.

"But... you're not supposed to be here."

"Says who?" Olga challenged.

"Your mother and her lawyer. I'm supposed to visit you on Saturdays."

"Did they say I'm not allowed to visit you?"

Manolo paused, not sure of the legality of her argument.

"I can do whatever I want. And you can't stop me from coming here, or from sitting with you at the Chamberí."

Manolo smiled.

"Wait here. If we're going to the Chamberí, I need to change out of these clothes. Talk to your Uncle Pedrito for a while."

Pedrito lifted his head and made eye contact with Manolo.

"I mean, Angelito. Talk to your Uncle Angelito."

Pedrito relaxed and returned his attention to the accounting books.

After several weeks of Tuesday visits, they developed a pattern. Manolo would be washed, wearing a clean shirt and ready to leave the moment Olga stepped into the building. They walked to El Chamberí, sat at their favorite table by the window and enjoyed a cup of coffee and flan, or a whole meal if they wanted to splurge. Olga's non-sanctioned visits were precious to Manolo. He treasured them, not only because they skirted around the court-ordered restrictions, but because she lifted his spirits. She was in that phase of adolescence when every day made a difference, and she would be slightly less childish than the day before. It was obvious to everyone that with every passing day Olguita became more beautiful, more womanly, and, he feared, more vulnerable to the corruptions of the world. Consequently, these weekly visits were his last opportunity to be the father the divorce was keeping him from being.

At the restaurant, Olga observed her father as he placed the order. He seemed beaten, overworked and unappreciated. The work of photoengraving was unpleasant and unforgiving. It exposed him to suffocating heat, burning chemicals and cutting machinery that scarred his fingers, tattered his clothes and exhausted him to levels she would never know. So, when he donned a three-piece suit on Sundays to drive through the city in a cream-colored convertible, she knew it was his hard-earned reward.

"Papá," Olga asked as she ate a spoonful of flan.

He looked at her as he sipped from his espresso.

"Why are you making me return to the boarding school?"

"You know why."

"It's good for me," Olga sighed, "and it will keep me away from Mima's anger."

"I don't want you listening to her deranged stories. It will poison your mind and you might start believing them. I'm getting married in a few months and I know she'll use you to get back at me."

"So, why isn't Manolín in a boarding school?"

"Because I can't afford to send the both of you, and he's very attached to your mother. Otherwise, I would. Now, don't be sad. It'll only be for a little while. You'll be back once it's all over and your mother calms down."

They ate another spoonful of flan in silence.

"And you're learning English," he said to her. "You're the only one I know who can speak it. C'mon, say something. Teach me your favorite word."

"Hmm..." Olga thought with a smile. "I like the word, 'wonderful.' It has a good flow."

Manolo tried to repeat it but failed.

"Won-der-ful," Olga said, a smile still on her face.

"Guan-der-fool."

"When people look at your new car, they think 'how wonderful!' Get it?"

Manolo smiled. "Teach me something else, a phrase."

"Well, I learned this in my first few weeks of being there. 'Everything is upside down.'"

Manolo laughed wholeheartedly and asked Olga to repeat it several times.

"It sounds so funny. *Ebrree ting ees op-sad doun.*"

Manolo roared with laughter while Olga thought about the ironic truth of that phrase, and her eyes filled with tears.

"*Ay, mi niña*," he reached for her hand. "Why are you getting sad?"

Olga wiped away her tears and forced herself to smile. Manolo pushed aside the empty plates to hold her hand.

"Tell me about the dress your *madrina* is ordering for you. What color is it? Where did they take you, *Fin de Siglo*?"

"No. We went to Ultra. It's white, Papá. You know, because I'm a virgin and summer."

"*Bueno*, I'm going to the Boca Ciega party. I've asked Angelito to take pictures, and I'll show them to everyone so they can all see what a pretty daughter I have."

"Papá, *por favor*. Nobody cares. Besides, you have a pretty girlfriend now."

Manolo looked down, grabbed the cloth napkin and wiped his mouth.

"What does Jenny have to do with this?"

"Sorry," Olga apologized. "I shouldn't have said that."

Manolo took out several coins from his pocket and placed them on the table. He pushed back on the chair to leave.

"Wait. Not yet," Olga said. "Let's stay here a little longer. Besides, we have to order coffee for Angelito and Pedrito."

They sat in silence as they waited.

"Papa?"

"*Si?*"

"Who is Chibás?"

"Eduardo Chibás? He's the political leader of the *Ortodoxos*."

"A man on the bus was saying that this man, Chibás, was crying on the radio because he lost the election. Is that true? Did he cry on the radio?"

Manolo began to laugh. "No, *mi niña*. It's a figure of speech. Chibás is always complaining about the corruption and he's on the radio a lot, denouncing the president."

"Oh," Olga nodded. "He had a cockroach on his shoe."

"Chibás had a roach on his shoe?"

"No, the man on the bus. It was small, but I was worried it was going to come at me."

Manolo looked at his daughter and thought her to still be childlike.

"Do you think they have roaches here?" Olga asked.

"Why do you ask?"

"Ever since the roaches came out of the drain, I can't stop thinking about them."

"I heard your brother danced a flamenco and stomped them to a mush," he laughed, but Olga didn't think it was funny, leading him to use a more empathetic tone.

"It must have been a scary moment for you."

"*Ay, Papá*, I screamed so loud."

"I wish I could have been there to protect you from those bugs."

"I don't know why they rushed out. Angelito says roaches stay behind walls and don't like to be in the sunlight."

"This island is full of them," he said, taking out a cigarette and lighting it. "They're everywhere. Even in the cleanest of places, behind the walls, inside the drains. You watch, one day they'll come out from their hiding places and take over."

"Why is that? Did God make them to torture us?"

Manolo looked at Olga and became pensive as his eyes drifted to a remote thought. "I've wondered that too. Why would God make roaches, or anything for that matter? Yes, it's a good question. More importantly," he flicked the ashes of his cigarette into the empty cup and looked at his daughter, "It's a grown-up question. It shows you're becoming a young woman with a mind of your own. So, why did God make a creature like the cockroach?"

"I don't know. It's just that... they're so.... The thought of one crawling on my skin makes me want to cry."

"Do you really want to know what I think?"

"About cockroaches?"

"About 'why?' I'm not sure you'll understand me. This is philosophical, you know, and maybe you're still too young."

"*¡Ay Papá, por favor!*" Olga protested. "You're beginning to sound like Mima."

"Oooh! That hurt."

"I hate it when she says I'm too young."

Manolo shifted his body in the chair, took one last puff from his cigarette and, while extinguishing it, said, "Why something happens is sometimes just a matter of history, and we study history to help us understand, but you asked something different. You want to know why God does something."

"Why did God create the cockroach?"

"Yes." He took out another cigarette and held it in his fingers without lighting it. "From my point of view, God made the cockroach and every ugly thing out there because they have something to teach and we have something to learn. I know why I have a brain, but I don't know why I was getting headaches. Do you see where I am going with this?"

"I think so."

"Because it's the same direction your question was headed."

"About the cockroaches?"

"Just listen for a moment. I've been thinking about this for some time."

Olga leaned forward, smiling with eagerness.

"We all have our share of cockroaches swarming out of the drain, but for me it was the headaches. I want to know, why did God afflict me like that? And now that I no longer have those headaches, I think I've figured it out."

"You have?"

"I needed to experience headaches in order to understand life better. It's the bad moments in life, the ugly moments, that help us build a good life."

"I see... but I don't know if we're talking about the same thing." Olga shook her head. "I don't want to learn anything from those bugs. I just hate them."

"You're not listening. I'm trying to tell you that there's a lesson here for you."

"What?"

"I don't know. It's your lesson, not mine."

"That's not fair."

"It's totally fair. You know why?"

"Why?"

"Because *Ebrree ting ees op-sad doun.*" He stood up and smiled, "C'mon let's go."

******

Tina was standing in the living room with four suitcases by her side, watching the news report on the television about Eduardo Chibás shooting himself during a live radio broadcast.

"I just don't get it," Tina said to herself.

"What?" Olga asked as she approached and looked at the screen with curiosity.

"Why would this man shoot himself?" Tina looked on, almost in a daze. " He had such a promising future."

"*Mira*, Papa is here," Olga said with excitement.

"Your father?" she replied with surprise.

"Papá!" Manolin screamed as he ran to open the door.

Outside, Manolo stood next to his cream colored convertible. He greeted his son with open arms and a hearty laugh. Olga ran into them and joined in the hug.

"And what are you doing here?" Tina asked from the front door.

"I'm here to take them to Boca Ciega. *Vamos*, go get your bags," he said to his children, who quickly ran back inside for their luggage.

Manolin jumped with excitement and ran inside.

"You could have told me you were coming," Tina complained. "I made plans for my brother to take us."

"Well, I thought it was obvious. I'm going and I have a car and..."

"It's okay. Don't worry. You can take the kids."

"Really?" Olga exclaimed with glee.

"Yes," Tina said and stepped aside for Manolín, who was trying to get through with two large suitcases. "It's okay, this one time."

Manolo looked at his ex-wife and perceived a sadness in her demeanor.

"Are you okay?" He asked her.

"Of course, I am. Why?"

"I don't know. You look a bit sad."

"Oh. I was just watching the news about Eddy Chibás. I can't believe he shot himself."

"Yes, I heard," Manolo said while opening the trunk of his car. "But he's still alive. They're trying to save his life."

"Do they think he'll survive?"

"Who knows. By the way, there's room for you," Manolo said as he loaded the luggage. "And there's room for the dress too."

"I don't think so. I'll wait for Mario, and I'll keep her dress with me, just in case."

"In case of what?"

"In case I don't trust you with the dress," she snapped.

He stepped back and closed the trunk. The children stood still, fearing she might change her mind.

"The party is at seven," Tina said, "I need Olga to be early, so I can do her hair."

"What about this *renacuajo*, tadpole?" Manolo placed his hand on Manolín's head and tousled his hair. "Doesn't he have to get his hair done?"

Manolín laughed.

"Seriously, be on time." Tina said before she stepped back.

"Help me bring the top down," Manolo asked his son, who was already rotating the crank and studying how the top retreated into its compartment.

Tina stood at the front steps of her home as the car sped away. Her brother, Mario, arrived minutes later. He was a joyful man who knew how to laugh at the mishaps of life, but he also carried a six-inch knife and was not afraid to use it.

"Did I see the star tennis player drive out of here with the kids?" Mario asked.

Tina laughed. "I'm glad you're here, you know," she said with a wry smile.

"Whatever you need." After loading her bags into his trunk, he turned on the car radio. *El Manisero* was playing. It was a song about a peanut vendor who sexually insinuates himself to a young woman through the sale of a peanut cone. Tina, eager to be free of the dark mood that had marked her for days, began to sing along. They listened to song after song, without once talking about her feelings or his troubles, a perfect way to begin a weekend at the beach.

The two-lane road to Boca Ciega, a beach on the northern coast of Cuba, cut through miles of wild palms and open land, with small herds of grazing cows every few miles. The music made the ride seem shorter, and within an hour, they were at the entrance to the beachside complex. Rubio, the neighborhood manager, stepped out to greet Tina.

"*Buenos días,*" Rubio said as he approached the car. "It's good to see everyone arriving."

"*Que tal,* Rubio," Tina said. "Yes, I think we're going to have a full neighborhood this weekend. It should be fun."

"And where's Olguita?"

"She's coming later with her father."

"*Sí, sí...* of course," he glanced at Mario and smiled.

"Rubio, this is my brother, he's going to be joining us."

"I am?" Mario asked, surprised.

Tina shot him a look.

"That's right, I am. Yes, I'll be here for the weekend."

"You might as well. This is the weekend of the big party." Rubio said, leaning closer to Tina. "So, Olguita is coming later? You have such a special girl there, always smiling."

"Thank you. Thank you," she replied while turning away.

"Do you know who bought a plot of land this week?" Rubio asked.

Tina and Mario looked on in silence.

"Manolo, your ex. I guess he couldn't stay away." Rubio placed his hand on the car.

"I heard," Tina rolled her eyes. "I hope it's not too close to mine."

"I don't think so. Besides, the rest of the Gutierrez clan is here," Rubio said and laughed. "I can throw a stone in any direction and hit a Gutierrez."

"The same thing happens in Güira with our family," Mario said with a chuckle. "There's an Oliva on every block of that town."

"Oh, you're an Oliva?" Rubio said to Tina and touched her shoulder.

Tina recoiled. "We need to go. Thank you."

"My mother's cousin married an Oliva," Rubio touched her shoulder again.

"Let's go," she ordered Mario.

Rubio kept on talking about his family as Mario pulled the car away.

"Don't encourage that man," Tina said to her brother. "He gives me the creeps."

"I saw him looking at you, but I didn't think... I mean, you're an attractive woman."

"That's not the point. The moment that man heard about the divorce he was all over me."

Mario nodded and slowed as he neared the beach house.

"So, I'm staying?"

"Of course, if you want. There's plenty of room. The kids can sleep with me, and you and Blanca can have the other room."

"Thanks. I'll see if I can spend the night. In the meantime, I'm going to look for a good game of dominos."

Mario walked to the beach while Tina stayed behind. She was in the process of making the beds when she caught sight of Rubio approaching the front door.

"Yes?" she said from behind the door.

"Tina, it's me, Rubio."

She opened the door and found him standing on the threshold.

"I came to see if you needed any…" he paused as he ran his eyes over her, "…help. Forgive me, I just…"

She examined him for a moment and thought him to be particularly unattractive, with a lower-than-average intellect.

"I'm wondering if you found everything working alright. It's been a couple of months since you last were here."

"Yes, Rubio. Thank you. Everything is good."

"Really? I can check the gas in the kitchen. Do you know if it's on and flowing? The Gonzalez family had problems with the regulator."

Rubio took one step forward across the threshold.

"No," Tina held her hand up. "You have to stop," she said as sternly as possible.

"What do you mean?" He retreated.

"You can't come in."

"I just thought that with Manolo…"

"He'll be here soon. He's bringing the children."

"Yes, of course. The children. You know, I think Olguita is so special. She's going to break a lot of hearts in a few years."

"Look," Tina said, lifting her eyes toward the road. "Here they come."

Rubio turned to see Manolo arriving. "*Oye*, is that a new car?"

Manolo had not finished parking in front of the house when Manolín jumped over the door and ran into the house.

"Rubio," Manolo called out. "Come, help me with the bags."

"New car, huh?"

Olga stepped outside while Manolo opened the trunk. He gave Rubio one suitcase.

"How much does a car like this cost?"

"Plenty. There's only five of them in Havana." Manolo carried two suitcases. Rubio was right behind him.

Olga followed, yawning.

"*Hola*, Olguita," Rubio said.

Olga glanced his way but did not acknowledge him. Rubio, still carrying a suitcase, followed Olga inside.

"Leave that suitcase here," Tina said to Rubio, stopping him from entering further.

"Yes, of course," he said, putting the suitcase down and stepping out.

"Mima, can I go to the beach?" Manolín yelled from the bedroom.

Tina followed Rubio outside.

"If you need anything, don't be afraid to call," he said as he walked away.

She smiled a tight-lipped smile.

"Rich people," Rubio mumbled.

Tina heard his grumbled comment and closed the door. She returned her attention to Manolo who was in the second bedroom, kicking off his shoes.

"I'll take Manolín to the beach while you and Olga get ready for the party."

"That's a good idea. Be back by six."

Manolín jumped with excitement.

"Put on your swimsuit," Manolo said, rubbing his head.

"What's that?" Tina pointed at a third suitcase.

"You don't expect me to be in the same outfit all weekend, do you?" Manolo's voice revealed a layer of surprise.

"And where are you planning to stay?"

"Really?"

Tina rolled her eyes.

"I promise you won't even know I was here. I'll get ready after you're at the party. It means I'll be late, but at least I'll be clean."

"Alright, but you can't sleep here," she conceded while walking toward the other bedroom. "I'm sure Angelito can make room for you at his house. And I don't want you using the bathroom, either."

Manolo and his son could hear her mutterings through the wall. They looked at each other and emitted a restrained laugh. The father and son were eager to enjoy the crystal blue waters of the beach, just one block away. Several other families were there, filling the air with laughter and playful screams. Manolín ran excitedly toward them, while Manolo approached a group of men playing dominoes under a coconut tree. The sound of clicking tiles greeted him.

"Manolo," they called his name in unison, extending the final vowel for several seconds until the remaining "o" was hanging in midair, like a coconut waiting to fall. Manolo responded in kind, pulling a bottle of rum from his portable cooler.

"I'll share my rum if I can rotate in," he said as he stood by the table.

"*Coño*, just in time," Eduardo, one of the first homeowners in the neighborhood, said. "We ran out of rum about two sets ago."

"Who wants ice?" Manolo asked with a proud grin.

"And he brings ice, too?" Mario, Tina's brother, said loudly. "Juan, give the man your seat, you've been playing like a cross-eyed drunk."

Juan complained, defending his skills and sobriety.

"The day you bring ice and a decent game is the day you can keep your seat. Manolo, come over and sit."

Juan stood reluctantly under the coconut tree, but as soon as the tiles were being reshuffled, he left toward the water, cursing, "*Vayanse pa'l carajo.*"

Manolo chuckled and made eye contact with the fourth player, Brown, an "*Americano*" from New Jersey who years earlier had bought most of the empty lots and was reselling them to interested buyers. While everyone else returned to Havana on Sunday evenings, Brown lived in Boca Ciega. He had a firm body, a tan darker than most natives and an intimidating look. Rumors surrounded *"El Americano"* and his connections with the American mafia.

"I don't get it. If everyone thinks Prío is corrupt, why did he get elected?" Brown asked while examining his tiles.

Manolo placed a tile down, a double two.

"Dos. El niño, the boy," Mario liked to announce the categorical name of each number, a tradition linked to superstition that influenced lottery playing and other forms of gambling.

"We think every government official is corrupt," Manolo answered. "It's just the way of politics here."

"There's corruption that's under the table," Mario said, "and then there's in-your-face corruption. Grau, our last president, was in our face."

"Did you see the gun battle in Orfila?" Eduardo asked and placed his tile, two and six.

"Seis. El perro," Mario said and speedily placed his tile, six and five.

"I saw it on TV," Brown commented. "I had been here maybe a few months, and the news showed a gunfight in the middle of a neighborhood, like Chicago and Al Capone."

"To answer your question," Manolo said. "Nobody had any hopes that Prío would clean up the rampant government corruption, but at least he should put a leash on it, move it to the back of the house and away from the streets."

"And who is this Chibás character who shot himself?" Brown asked, took a tile from the pile and rapped the table with his knuckles.

"Chibás is an overly dramatic sore loser," Mario said. "He's been on the radio every night saying he had proof of Prío's corruption, and then when he couldn't produce it, he shot himself."

"That's a bit much," Brown commented. "Don't you think?"

"Exactly," Eduardo said with annoyance. "Are you going to play or sit there all day?" He challenged Manolo, who was looking at his tiles with a smile.

Manolo placed a tile, double five. He was down to one tile.

"*Eres un cabrón*," Mario protested. "You're locking the game."

Manolo took a sip of his drink and laughed.

Eduardo rapped the table with his knuckles, and so did Mario.

"Guys," Juan called out, running toward them.

The men turned in his direction. Juan was out of breath.

"There's *un marijuanero* on the beach.*"*

Manolo stood up in anger. Brown looked at him, clearly not understanding.

Manolo translated with hand gestures.

"A pot smoker on this beach?" Eduardo asked, surprised.

"Where?" Brown asked.

"Behind those palm trees," Juan pointed.

Eduardo stood. "*¡Hijo de puta*! I can smell it now, that son of a bitch."

The men began to walk in the direction of the palm trees, but Brown, still sitting, called them back. "What are you going to do, make a scene in front of the children?"

"What do you want, pretend the drugs are not there?" Juan said, visibly frustrated. "Go and scare him away, but don't start beating up on the man," Brown said. "You have to be calm about these things or somebody can end up dead."

Manolo nodded. The men looked at him with approval.

Mario extended his knife to Manolo. "Here, take my knife."

"I don't want your knife," Manolo said

"Stop being a pretty boy and take the knife," Mario said.

"We're not going to kill the man," Brown raised his voice. "Keep your knife. Eduardo, you go with Juan. The two of you should be enough."

Juan and Eduardo walked toward the palm trees. When the pot smoker saw the two men heading toward him, he collected his bags and started walking away, as if nothing were wrong. Juan and Eduardo picked up their pace and the pot smoker began to run. Brown laughed and returned to the domino game to flip over Manolo's last tile, five and blank.

"Look at that, you had the winning move."

Manolo smiled and started to put the tiles back in their box.

"What?" Mario asked. "Game over?"

"I want to go in the water," Brown said. "Manolo, what about you?"

"After I finish my drink," he replied, sipping from his cup.

Mario raised his eyes to look at Eduardo and Juan, who caught up with the illicit smoker and were slapping him around.

"Look at them. They think they're so tough," Mario commented. "What's Eduardo, a bookkeeper? And now he's the guard, on the look-out for funny weed."

"He's protecting our neighborhood," Manolo said while taking one final sip. "We don't want those types of people here."

"Well," Mario smiled, "a little weed here and there..."

Manolo and Brown raised their eyebrows, not sure what to think.

"Maybe if you had smoked a little weed," Mario joked, "your headaches would have been cured."

"I dare you to talk that way with your sister present," Manolo said playfully.

"*Caballeros*," Brown said, kicking off his shoes, "while you discuss the dangers of marijuana, I'll be in the water."

"Me too." Manolo stood up. "You staying?" he asked Mario while removing his shirt.

"Yeah, I think I'm going to enjoy this shade and drink some more from your bottle."

Brown slapped his hands together in anticipation and took off his shirt. Together, he and Manolo walked to the shore, increasing their pace as they neared, until eventually they were running like teenage boys.

******

Manolo woke up to the sound of Mario singing in the shower. The distant sounds of the neighborhood party entered through the open windows. Manolo knocked on the bathroom door, eager for Mario to finish.

"*Oye*, don't take long in there. We're already late."

Minutes later Mario emerged with a towel wrapped around his waist.

"I love this house of yours. It has good water pressure."

"Well, it's not mine anymore. It's your sister's."

"Right. Did she leave you with anything?"

"A smart-ass brother-in-law who takes long showers."

Manolo knew the water pressure was good, and it gave him pleasure to think he had bought a well-engineered house. It wasn't *Varadero*, the beach for famous baseball players and politicians, but just as enjoyable. When Manolo came out of the bathroom, Mario was gone. The mirror reflected his sunburnt face and a wardrobe designed to impress: blue linen pants, a white guayabera and white cloth shoes that didn't require socks.

Close to one hundred people were at the party. Word had gotten out that a band from Cienfuegos was playing. By the time Manolo arrived the party was full of couples dancing and children running. Olga was seated with a group of teenage girls, who were pairing up with boys too afraid to talk. Manolo paused to admire the beauty and charisma his daughter radiated. People were drawn to her smile, laugh and effervescent personality.

"Olguita! Olguita," Angelito called. "Come stand over here with your mother. I want to take another picture."

Olga skipped toward him, the white dress flowing with her limbs. Tina was wearing a flowery summer dress, one Manolo had seen many times before, yet to his surprise, she looked ravishing in it. The mother and daughter were posing for the photograph when they caught sight of him.

"Papá," Olga shouted with glee. "Come, I want you in this picture."

Tina's face hardened with a scowl as Manolo approached to get in the picture..

"I see that you finally woke up from your rum-induced nap," Tina said.

"Yes, what a joy it was to sleep through your barks and jabs."

"*Vamos*, on with it," Angelito said. "Smile for the camera."

Tina looked away, refusing to smile. Manolo barely managed to slant his mouth toward a pleasant look, while Olga smiled from ear to ear. Angelito had Manolo posing alone with his daughter when a teenage girl came and took Olga away.

Laughter, music, rum drinks and plenty of dancing filled the air. While the band played the "Cha, Cha, Cha" Manolo searched for a friendly face. He caught sight of a few women looking at him appreciatively. Soon after he was enjoying the rhythmic beat with women, whose inviting smiles led him to forget they were married.

Tina was watching him from a distance. She was angry at herself because she could not stop the jealous rage swelling within. Every time Manolo placed his hand on a woman's hip and exchanged silent insinuations, she wanted to rip his blue eyes out.

"Look at Manolo, making every husband in the room nervous," Brown said to Tina from behind.

She turned around to find the handsome *Americano* offering her a drink.

"Thank you." She accepted the drink and smiled.

"Your ex-husband doesn't have headaches anymore, I'm told, but I think he lost his common sense, dancing with married women like that."

"He does seem to have a newfound confidence. He never danced like that when we were married."

"Shame on him. And how come I haven't seen you on the dance floor?"

"Me? No, not tonight. What about you? I'm sure there are plenty of women here who would like to dance with you."

"I have an excuse. I'm a foreigner and this beat doesn't flow to my hips."

"I have an excuse too. I don't feel like it. Now, if you'll forgive me. I have to see why the food ran out."

Brown reached for her arm and pulled her back. Tina was offended by his unwelcomed touch, but saw he was looking across the room.

"Do you know that man?" he asked with a concerned tone.

Behind the multitude of people, hidden by the dancing and the carousing, toward the back of the room, stood Olga listening attentively to a man.

"I can't see who it is."

Tina stepped forward for a better view. The man had Olga's hand in his. He was pulling her away from the people and to the backyard. Olga smiled, but Tina could tell it was out of politeness.

"I don't like the looks of this," Brown said.

"Neither do I." Tina started walking toward her daughter when she realized the man luring Olga away from the party was Rubio. She turned to Brown with a panic-stricken face.

"Go. I'll get Manolo," he said to her.

"Mario," Tina yelled for her brother.

Olga thought it was strange for this man, whom she barely knew, to have a gift for her in the backyard. He seemed friendly enough, and just a few hours earlier he had been at her house so she felt it was alright to be led away by him. To her surprise he placed his hand on her waist and whispered in her ear, "You are now a woman and it's time you understand how you inspire the man in me."

Until that point, Olga had no awareness of a man's desire. He pulled her closer. She tried to pull away, but his strength kept her in place. His breath was on her, compelling her to turn away, close her eyes and hold her breath. She did not want to smell him, nor hear what he was saying. She blocked everything out, not wanting to admit something was happening, when Tina pulled Rubio's hand from Olga.

"What?" Rubio was surprised.

Manolo ran in, leapt around Tina, pushing her to the side, and punched Rubio in the face. Rubio fell back. Manolo landed on him, swinging furiously, while Brown and Mario joined in the beating.

Tina regained her balance and ran to hold Olga, who in fear was turned toward the wall with her eyes closed. The music came to an abrupt halt, and people screamed, startled by the commotion. Mario had taken out his knife and was pressing it against Rubio's face, who pleaded for mercy. Olga, still immobilized, felt her mother's hands and began to breathe once again. The darkness receded and her vision focused on an insect within an inch of her face, a cockroach on the wall, rubbing its hairy feet. Olga spun around and threw herself into her mother's arms, while Mario, Manolo and Brown dragged Rubio outside, banishing him from Boca Ciega forever.

It would be many years before Manolo would see Rubio again, a man who held a grudge against him and the class of professionals who disfigured his face. Olga, however, was able to forget Rubio and effectively blocked the violation from becoming part of her memories.

******

Decades later, while recounting the party, it was the cockroach on the wall that my mother remembered. I knew there was more to the story, because years earlier my uncle, Manolín, remembered it as the only time his father had been violent. Yet, on this day, under the shade of an oak tree in my home in St. Petersburg, my mother didn't say a word about Rubio and the violation.

"I met your father at that party," she said to me. "He arrived late, I think."

"He was six years older than you, right?" I asked.

"He was already in law school."

"So, how was it that he came to the party?"

"He came because he used to be friends with my cousin. The two of them would play billiards and hang out at the bars in Havana."

"And did you and he do much talking, or dancing?"

"Your father didn't dance. No, no, no, no, no. I don't understand how a man who grew up in Havana, a city surrounded by music, didn't dance."

"Strange, right?"

"Well, that's who he was, and your father never tried to be someone else. You know, when I first saw him, I was on the front porch of that house, the music was playing, and he was really listening to the music, all the instruments."

"Hmm..." I nodded.

"I introduced him to Elenita Santiago. She wanted to dance, and he said to her, 'Maybe later.' From that day on, Elenita and the girls called him, 'Maybe Later.' The jokes they said about your father..." My mother laughed. "Here comes 'Maybe Later.' Will you be going out with 'Maybe Later?' Want to kiss? Maybe later. Want to... you know what? Maybe later."

We laughed.

"So, is that all you remember from that first encounter with Papa?"

"It was funny, because I remember him standing next to me. He looked like he wanted to dance, tapping his feet, almost singing along with the music. So, I told him we could dance if he wanted to, and you know what he said?"

"Maybe later."

"Yes," she laughed again. "But your father looked at me, and he could tell something was wrong. He asked if I had been crying."

"Had you been?"

"Crying? Well, yes."

"Why?"

"Why what?"

"Why were you crying?"

"I don't know. I think it's because I saw a *cucaracha*. You know I had an experience with a roach that went up my pants."

"I remember you telling me about it."

"What struck me about your father was that he noticed. He didn't know me, but he saw I was upset. That's when I told him I had seen a cockroach on the wall. He must have thought I was a silly little girl. He then said something I didn't understand at the time, but I thought it was so smart and true."

She paused and I could see her mind drifting.

"What did he say?"

"Oh, I don't know. After all these years, all I remember is thinking that I had never heard anyone speak like that. The men I knew were really boys, if you think about it, and not one of them spoke the way your father did. Maybe you should have asked him."

"I think I did, as a matter of fact."

"You did? When?"

"Oh, some time ago. He was telling me about the first time he met you."

"Hmmm..." she replied and then she slowly looked up at the tree branches, allowing her gaze to drift with the memories, and for a moment I saw my twenty-one-year-old father reflected in her nostalgic eyes.

"Guille, you have to cut down these branches. They're too close to the house."

"Yeah, I know," I replied and then said with a smile, "Maybe later."

CHAPTER 3

Carlitos

April 1985

South of Nashville, somewhere on Interstate 65

He sat on the passenger seat of the twenty-foot U-Haul truck as I drove him, and the remaining contents of his life, down to Florida. He was escaping the harsh winters of southern Illinois and moving to a warmer climate where his heart could pump blood without the stress of fourteen-degree weather. After forty-plus years of smoking and never curbing the ills of a combative, Type A personality, my father developed coronary heart disease, which led to three heart attacks in his fifty-eighth year of life. The cardiologist prescribed a handful of meds, a leafy green diet, a complete cessation of smoking and a milder climate. This was his second and last attempt at establishing a life in Florida, but instead of moving to Miami, once again, he decided on Panama City Beach.

"No, Guille. *¡Qué va!* No way! It is unbelievable that at this stage in my life, after a lifetime of sacrifice and hard work, I would not have a place to call home. I thought I could do it in Miami. I tried. I really did, but that city spat me out and rejected me. I cannot live there."

He examined his pack of spearmint gum and counted the remaining sticks.

"I think I can make this one last longer," referring to the wad of gum in his mouth that curbed his urge to smoke.

My father could be quiet. I have many memories of him sitting in silence with his thoughts, but when Carlos Márquez-Sterling II decided to grace you with his insight, there was no stopping him from dominating the conversation for hours on end. The only escape was to find a fictitious reason to excuse yourself from the endless monologue, but on this road trip there was none. I was locked in from Carbondale to Panama City Beach.

"I'd stay in Carbondale, if I could, but it's too cold. My heart can't take it. Believe it or not, I like it there. I understand the people. They think I'm a strange version of Mexican, but, for the most part, they're honest, hardworking and reliable. *El Americano* from that part of the country is like a simple piece of artwork, easy to interpret. You know what he means and where you stand. I can't say that about Miami. No, no, no, no, no. Miami is like one of those paintings from the guy that likes to splash paint, and when you look at it you ask, *¿Y esto que carajo es?'* What the hell is this? But you know, Miami wasn't always like that. *Oye*, Guillermo, Miami was a small country town when we first got there. You don't know what a downgrade it was for us. We came from Havana, a city comparable to New York or Paris. Havana was alive twenty-four hours a day. No matter where you went there was music playing. People talk about Miami like it's a great city, but you don't know a great city until you visit Havana... *antes de Fidel,* of course. Everything I tell you is before that son of a bitch stole our country and our life. He turned Havana into a Third World ruin. *¡Una mierda!"*

He began to recite his favorite love poem, "Everything Was Better in Cuba." The sky was a deeper shade of blue, the sun brighter and the greenery greener. The tomatoes, eggs and beef tasted how God intended them to. The beaches had softer sand and crystal clear water. The women had better legs, and the men... well, here is where I think my father made an exception. The men all had to be *unos cabrones,* shit heads and scoundrels, that allowed for things to get so bad that the creation of a beast named Fidel Castro was inevitable. We were well into the second half of that recital when my father decided it was time to stop and take a break.

"Get off at the next exit and slow down. I think your brother is *comiendo mierda*, not paying attention. I've been watching him sway all over the road like a drunk trying to piss inside the bowl."

My brother, Carlos Francisco, was given the task of driving behind us in my father's car, a 1956 Studebaker Sky Hawk that my father personally rebuilt. It was his prized possession.

There is an overabundance of men named Carlos in my family, consequently most of them are called by their first and middle names together, or a nickname. My father was Carlitos, and at times *Gordo*, due to his stocky build. My brother is Carlos Francisco. My cousin is Carlos Manuel, which is also the name combination for my father and a pseudo cousin nicknamed Charlie. My grandfather was the first Carlos, and my mother called him *El Viejo Márquez*, Old Man Márquez, but never to his face, because he would have objected to the ageist modifier. You'd think having so many men named Carlos would be a problem, but it wasn't. The upside to family squabbles is that we never had a reunion with all the Carloses in attendance. Decades later, both my brother and I succumbed to tradition and named our sons Carlos, of course.

As my father observed through the side view mirror the zigzag driving of my brother, I heard him mumble a common reprimand using his first and middle name.

"*Ay*, Carlos Francisco, Carlos Francisco...."

Not only did my brother have the important task of driving our father's reconstructed Studebaker, but his passenger was my father's second wife, Mariana, along with their dog, Celia. Mariana and my father were the unfortunate victims of a head-on collision that shattered my father's ankle and left her mentally and physically impaired. It had been a decade since that accident, but the damage inflicted on their bodies and psyches remained a continual obstacle to the smallest of chores. It was the worst tragedy in the latter half of my father's life, because Mariana's cognitive and motor skills were permanently impaired. To add insult to injury, the doctors of that era (circa 1975) had little pharmacological data to warn against the side effects of the many pills they prescribed.

Ten years later, Mariana barely functioned and was further crippled by a combination of medications not yet understood.

"There," he said. "Pull into that McDonald's. Let's see if we can stretch our legs. Do me a favor, take care of Celia. Your brother might end up losing her."

I stood outside with Celia, a wire-hair fox terrier, the only breed my father would ever own. Like most dogs of that breed, she was energetic, difficult to manage and eager to snap, characteristics my father respected. As I shivered outside the doors of the McDonald's, my brother came out looking upset. Clearly, my father had told him his driving wasn't any good.

"I don't know where he gets the idea that I was zigzagging," my brother complained. "I was right behind you the whole way."

I nodded with indifference. Too cold to care. My tropical, Miami blood was not used to the April temperatures of Tennessee. All I wanted was to get back in the truck and make it to Panama City before it got dark. Mariana came out of the McDonald's with food stuck to the side of her lip. We didn't say anything. My father's zipper was unzipped. We didn't say anything about that either.

After carefully maneuvering the large truck out of the lot, my father pointed to a teenage girl skipping around with another little girl, presumably a sister.

"You see that girl?" he said.

"Which one?"

"The older one. *Bueno*, she reminds me of your mother when I first met her."

"Really?" I said in a surprised tone. The girl didn't resemble my mother, or at least the person I thought she would be at that age.

"Your mother was prettier, of course. Much prettier, but that girl, playing the way she is, and those cheeks, that was your mother at age fifteen."

"Hmmm…" I was more interested in getting on the highway than looking at some random girl.

"When I first met your mother, she had a smile and a way about her... I just couldn't stop looking at her. I knew she was too young, and she was going away to boarding school. So, I made it a point to find her the next summer, at a party."

"Was it at the beach?"

He didn't acknowledge the question.

"She was dancing on top of a table to Spanish guitar music that played on the phonograph. She had the whole outfit, including the castanets."

I asked again, "Was this party at the beach house?"

He looked at me and nodded.

"She had control of the whole room. When she laughed, everyone laughed along with her. She stole my heart that night. I remember she wanted to dance, but I didn't really dance. She insisted, and I surrendered. How could I not?"

He smiled at the road ahead, remembering a life long gone, but still present in his mind.

"Back then, Havana was buzzing with life. No matter where you went, there was music playing and strangers reciting poetry. No other city in Latin America was like it. Even the homeless were different. Mind you, we didn't have too many homeless people. It's not like here in this country, where every city has people living under a bridge."

A golden-colored, convertible sports car sped past us.

"Look at that car," my father said, momentarily distracted by it. "An Alfa Romeo Spider. That car is for racing, you know. If you try to buy one, it'll cost you *veinte mil cocos*."

"Twenty thousand?" I exclaimed.

He laughed at my reaction.

"*Pues sí*, Guille, as I was telling you. Havana was one of a kind. There was a homeless man called *el Caballero de París*. He was mentally ill, but he knew poetry and recited verses for entertainment, and then people would give him a few coins. Imagine that. A homeless man who was a poet. You don't see that in Miami, do you? No, no, no, no, no. Only in Havana would a person like him exist."

He paused, lowered the window and spat out the wad of gum. A blast of cold air filled the cabin, but it didn't seem to bother him.

"Papa, raise the window," I asked.

"¿Tienes frío?"

I nodded and he laughed.

"You don't know cold until you have to shovel the driveway at seven in the morning, and everything is frozen solid. Shit, this is nothing," he said while manually raising the window. "Your brother knows that early morning cold. If you had come to Carbondale, like you were supposed to, you would know it too, but you escaped and joined the Navy. Smart move, I have to say. It was the fastest way to become your own man and deprogram from the brainwash of the Gutierrez clan."

He made a buzzing sound and a goofy face when he said "deprogram" as if I had been connected to a machine. I laughed in a manner that made him laugh, so he repeated it.

"You knew deep down inside you didn't want to be a Gutierrez, so you took the one step none of them would ever take. When I heard you joined the Navy, I have to confess, I was impressed. Pleasantly surprised."

He paused to place a new stick of gum in his mouth.

"Are you feeling the urge to smoke," I asked.

"It never goes away. If I don't have a cigarette in my hand, I feel like a dog without his tail. But don't make me talk about it because it only gets worse. Where was I?"

"You were talking about me going into the Navy and before that about the madman who recited poetry and how wonderful it was to grow up in Cuba."

"Sí. Sí, of course. You know, when I think about Cuba it's almost as if it was an enchanted island. No, no, no, no, no. I don't know how to paint that picture for you, because life here is so different. Your life, in particular, is so different from mine."

"How so?"

"*Mira*, Guille. It's everything, down to the way you were educated. This is a different culture and a different time. Your mother did a good job of raising you. I have to give her credit. Quite frankly, I was pleasantly surprised to see how well you turned out despite having been raised next to the Gutierrez clan, but..."

He slapped my knee and I braced myself.

"*Estás comiendo mierda,*" he said angrily. "You're wasting your life. I understand a young man's drive to have fun. I had my share too, but by the time I was your age, I was certain I had to get my life in order, because I knew much was required of me. Do you think you can dance your way through life?"

I watched his anger grow as he described his disappointment. His eyes widened. His rate of speech intensified and his hands began to move forcefully.

"This also applies to your brother. Don't think you're alone in this lack of... purpose. Your brother lives in some fantastical land where he thinks everything he wishes for will just be granted. Poof!"

He paused to feverishly masticate his gum.

"It's not your fault and it's not your brother's fault. The two of you didn't get taught anything different. Sure, you joined the Navy to get away from it, but you can't cleanse yourself of it until you come face to face with it. No, no, no, no, no. In this life you better be ready. Pay me now, or pay me later, but pay you must. Nobody escapes."

He paused to breathe and to calm down from his rant. I focused on the road ahead and didn't say a word, hoping that the worst had passed.

"Pay me now or pay me later." It was a phrase he used often to highlight the consequences of our actions. Whenever he said it, I would secretly roll my eyes. I didn't care about world affairs, which for my father was a deadly sin. I knew enough history to follow along in his conversations, but don't ask me who the Secretary of State was, what battle tactics Ulysses S. Grant used against the Confederate Army or why Puerto Rico was still a colony. Yes, my father's assessment was correct. I preferred to live for the joke, the drink, the surfable wave and the romantic interlude. Isn't that what life is for? I almost offered the counter argument but he didn't want to hear it. And then he slapped my knee, once again, this time with affection.

"But you'll find your purpose soon enough," he said softly. "Life has a way of putting it right before you and there'll be no getting around it. That's what happened to me. Cuba was in so much turmoil, and the men running the island were such *hijos de putas*, that my purpose grew out of my natural reaction. In the face of such blatant mediocrity and corruption, it was impossible to not have a purpose."

Several cars ahead was a red truck with a milk advertisement on its rear door.

"Get behind the milk truck. He's driving at a good speed and it'll make the drive easier. He's probably on his way to Birmingham."

I switched lanes and got behind the milk truck. My brother, who had been behind us, didn't follow.

"What's he doing?" my father asked.

"I don't know."

We watched my brother speed past. Mariana smiled and waved at us through her passenger window. My brother seemed upset as he got in front of us and moved to the right lane.

"He's getting off at the next exit," my father warned. "Something must be wrong."

He got off the highway and sped through a small town to the nearest strip plaza and pulled into a Hardee's parking lot. My father got off the truck to approach the Studebaker while I found a suitable space to park.

As I locked the truck, I could see my father carrying a small suitcase and leading Mariana into the Hardee's. Her small, rapid steps and erratic hand movements were indicative that her nervousness was peaking. She tugged at the back of her pants while he led her inside. A clump was sitting in her rear, staining her pants.

"Here," my brother handed Celia on a leash.

I instinctively accepted it.

"Did she shit her pants?"

"Oh my God! It was the worst. She was farting and laughing."

"Oh no," I grimaced, fully aware of how bad her farts were.

"I was signaling you for at least two miles." He was angry at me. "Couldn't you see my flashing lights?"

"Sorry. Papa was talking."

"Yeah, I know," he said loudly, almost yelling at me. "I even drove up and honked at you. You guys were oblivious."

"It was that bad, huh?"

"And then I saw her do it." He looked down as if traumatized. "I saw her face and I heard her grunt. The smell got... concentrated."

"Did you lower the window?"

"Of course, I lowered the window! I was freezing my ass off, but it was useless. It was useless. The smell stuck to the back of my throat." He seemed to be on the verge of crying. "Guille, man, I can still taste it."

"Oh, man, I'm so sorry. Go inside and get yourself a milkshake or something. Don't worry about Celia. I have her."

"And I honked at you, over and over again, but you were just laughing away with Papa." He looked at me with eyes that revealed hurt feelings. "What were you laughing at?"

"I don't remember now. Go and get yourself something."

He walked to the Hardee's with his head down. It affirmed, once again, that I was right to join the Navy straight out of high school. My brother did as he was told and studied at Southern Illinois University, where my father taught, but I chose differently. I knew I couldn't live with a stepmother who no longer functioned, and with a father whose anger was out of control. My father thought I was escaping the Gutierrez clan by joining the military, which may have been partially true, but in reality I was avoiding him and daily situations like this one.

"It's your turn to drive with her," my brother yelled. "I'm going with Papa in the truck."

"*¡No jodas!* No fucking way!"

Twenty minutes later, Mariana and my father emerged from the bathroom. She wore another set of pants that was of that mid-seventies polyester style. From the safety and warmth of the truck, where I sat to guard my seat, I watched my father tenderly care for his second wife. He was counting pills and administering a pharmaceutical cocktail to a woman who was a mere shadow of her former self. I grew impatient, too young to understand that level of care.

We continued our journey in silence. I was doing the math, calculating our estimated time of arrival. Papa remained silent. I didn't want to look at him, because I sensed he needed a moment. I caught a glimpse of the blue Studebaker through the side view mirror. My brother was zigzagging in his lane and Mariana was blankly staring at the road with her mouth wide open.

"Look," I pointed enthusiastically at a red milk truck in front of us.

"It can't be the same one," he said, "but get behind it. His pace is good."

I patiently waited for traffic to allow me in. The effort to maneuver our truck into position jolted my father from his exhaustion. Still, he was quiet, and it worried me. I preferred to have him talking and working through his emotions than sitting in silence and stewing.

"So, Papa, how did you know you wanted to marry Mama?"

"What?"

"Yeah, like you were dating Mama when she was a teenager, not yet eighteen. When you proposed to her, didn't you think she was too young?"

"No, not really. Back then most women were married before they turned twenty."

"Yeah, I've heard. But how did you know she was the one you wanted to marry?"

"Are you going to marry Maria?"

"I think so."

"Why?"

"Well," I smiled. "We're good for each other and I think I love her."

"You think?"

"I know," I quickly corrected. "I know I love her."

"Good. You should be certain, and that's my answer too. It's the answer of any young man who is looking to take that step, and I was no different."

He took out a stick of gum and folded it in his mouth.

"Listen, your mother and I were like any young couple you see today. Just because we were from a different era doesn't mean we didn't feel the same attractions you and Maria have. The world may change, but the human condition remains the same."

I bit my lip with regret, fearing he was going to lecture me on sex.

"When I first started dating your mother, I wasn't sure I wanted to be a lawyer. I was second-guessing who I was and why I was on that path."

I relaxed and breathed easier.

"And then, little by little, as I held her hand during walks and she would pull me in close, it started to make sense. That's when I realized I had found the right woman, the one to marry. To answer your question: you'll know if Maria is the one to marry, when you're next to her and everything seems right. Yes, your mother was young, but I knew I found a diamond in a pile of coal. I just happened to be the lucky fellow who picked her out, and together, during those first few years, we lived a life worthy of a romance novel."

He lowered his window a little and looked at the horizon while crisp cool air tingled our cheeks and noses.

"Don't tell Mariana, but your mother was with me during the best years of my life. Your grandfather was running for President. I was running for Congress. Everywhere we went it was simply electrifying. We were the generation that was going to set Cuba on the path to become the nation it deserved to be. We were full of hope, and with your mother by my side, I felt like nothing could stop us. And then, well... *mierda le entro al piano*, and everything turned to shit."

He paused for a moment and I realized he had taken another dark turn. It was inevitable. Everytime he spoke about Cuba and the politics that led to Fidel Castro he would smack his lips.

"Batista ruined it. *¡Ese cabrón!* He just couldn't step down. Your grandfather begged him to do the right thing, but there was too much money influencing every layer of politics. We had our problems, sure we did, and they would have been faced if only we had been given a chance, but the people lost their patience. That's when the violence escalated, and Batista grew stubborn, but what really created *el hijo de puta de Fidel*, was that nobody had the balls to admit what was happening, except for your grandfather. He called it, but once Fidel arrived there was no return. We had to leave. Correction, we had to run. We came to Miami and I, a man who was perfectly groomed for legislative life, and who won a congressional seat, well... I had to drive Coca Cola trucks for a living."

His urge to smoke must have been strong, because he took out another stick of gum and began chewing furiously.

"We moved into a little apartment over by the Orange Bowl and when that first winter hit, we thought we were going to freeze to death. You know those windows that have long rectangular pieces of glass?" he asked with a smile.

"Jalousie windows. Abuela still has them in her house."

"*Si*, jalousie. That winter was so cold we had to use newspapers to cover the space between each glass. When the wind blew, we could feel the cold air like pins and needles." He started to chuckle. "That winter every Cuban refugee conceived a child. You'd think there wasn't a single television set in the whole city." His chuckle became a loud laugh. "That's when your brother was born. It should have been the best years of our life, but I didn't know we were broken. *Ay*, Guille! Leaving Cuba damaged us. Damaged me."

"I should have seen the divorce coming, but I didn't. I came home one day to find your mother had packed my bags. You were a newborn and your brother was in the playpen. I didn't know it then, but now I realize we had one fight too many. Still, I didn't think it justified kicking me out of the house. It was your grandmother, Tina, who pushed for the divorce. Your mother and I could have worked out our differences, but your grandmother..."

"Where did you go?" I redirected his story, not wanting to hear a recital of complaints I was all too familiar with.

"I went to New York to see your grandfather. I thought that maybe he could help me, but that didn't work either."

He smacked his lips, a clear indication that he was deeply immersed in a bad mood.

"No, that didn't work either," he repeated and stared out the window. "I used to think he was invincible. Your grandfather survived assassination attempts, a bomb on our front porch. He escaped from prison in *La Cabaña*. The man was fearless, but on that day in New York, as he closed the door on me, I saw him defeated. I had nowhere to go, but he just closed the door on me. I might as well have sat in Central Park and traded poetry for quarters."

He looked out the window, lowered it some more and stopped talking. It was at that moment that I had an epiphany and it became clear why he wanted to sit next to me on that truck.

During the first two decades after Fidel's revolution and the massive exodus from the island, my generation became the unofficial facilitators of dinner table conversations where our parents tried to make sense of what had happened, why, how, and who was to blame. This was especially true of my father, who after suffering three heart attacks, knew time was not on his side. All those summers I spent with him in southern Illinois as an arrangement between divorced parents, all those times when my brother and I would visit the man we fearfully called "Papa," we had no clue why he raged the way he did. He must have known I never understood him, not even partially, and this trip to his final resting place was his last effort to explain himself. In those moments of silence, somewhere between Nashville and Birmingham, I opened the door to the halls of his mind and asked him to let me in.

"Where was your mother, my grandmother?"

The question startled him.

"Your grandmother?"

"You don't really talk about her. Where was she?"

"She stayed in Cuba. That door was closed when she and your grandfather divorced. You know, she wasn't well. Today, there might be a diagnosis and possibly a treatment, but back then, well, back then all we could do was duck and run. She had a temper like you've never seen, but she did like your mother, especially in the beginning. They went shopping together and my mother was determined to polish her, but at some point, she gave up. I'll never forget a gathering at the house, it was a Who's Who of Havana's high court. Your grandfather was trying to unite the party against Batista, and your mother decided to charm the women in the room, but instead it backfired. Your grandmother, Silvia, came to me and said I better clean your mother's mind and remove her bathroom humor, or else she would never be invited to another event."

"What did she say?" I asked with a laugh that appreciates bathroom humor.

"I don't know, and back then I didn't care. I took your mother to every gathering in Havana. She was going to be a Márquez-Sterling and it was up to everyone to get used to her, not the other way around. When I tell you that we went places, I am telling you that four nights a week we were out. You name it, we were there. We were living during historic times, experiencing something special, and I didn't want to miss any of it."

My father smiled, took out the third stick of spearmint gum and held it in his hand.

"I think she recited a dirty poem," he chuckled, "the kind you learn as teenagers but never share with your parents." His chuckle became a laugh. "It was shocking."

He paused, let out a nostalgic sigh and said, "*Ay, Olguita.*"

I raised an eyebrow, thinking, "Did he just say what I think he said?"

My father always referred to his first wife as "your mother," and to hear him call her by the endearing diminutive reserved for an inner circle of friends jolted me. It was proof that once upon a time love existed between the two people who brought me into this world. I never had the benefit of watching them live together. For better or for worse, most likely better, they divorced before I learned to walk. I accepted what every adult told me, "You are the second son of Olga and Carlos," but was I really? They were so different, diametrically opposed in just about everything, that it was impossible to understand how they ever married in the first place, until that road trip twenty-two years later, when he sat next to me, transported by the memory of a bride he held a lifetime ago, and called her "Olguita."

CHAPTER 4

El Caballero de París

March 10, 1952
Havana, Cuba

José María López Lledín was not known by his name, but rather by his title, *El Caballero de París,* The Parisian Gentleman. He had been anointed so because of his gentle demeanor, mysterious past and formal attire, which included a long black overcoat he wore with dignity, despite the stains of lost love and squandered dreams. His graying hair was unruly, often competing for attention against a shaggy beard and benevolent bearing. Poetry was his currency. A homeless man, he wandered the streets of Havana reliving suspended fantasies and trading rhymes for alms. Often, *el Caballero de París* could be seen staring into the distance, silently drifting through cloud-like layers of perception, greeting magical beings who accepted his poetic and philosophical quips in exchange for some needed sustenance.

Early in the morning, as the moon held on to a graying sky, *el Caballero* held on to his portfolio of inscribed cards, which he distributed to conjure the good will of creatures he believed would otherwise devour him. As he walked on *La Rampa,* a street that led to the city's seawall and esplanade, his black overcoat reflected beads of scarcity, which caught the early morning rays, bestowing an aura of saintly wealth. With every step he left a neighborhood whose quiet stirrings receded to the approaching frenzy at the intersection of L street where the building, Radiocentro CMQ, stood.

Modeled after New York's Rockefeller Center, Radiocentro CMQ was the hub for political talk and entertainment. The ten-story building and its courtyard dominated the intersection. All other structures became neglected spectators of commentaries narrated from the studios of CMQ. It was there, in its courtyard, where a political and intellectual class of Cubans sipped coffee, ate their *pastelitos* and discussed the island's failing democracy.

El Caballero walked with the slow gait of a madman, painfully aware of the new reality he was entering, one filled with disrupting noise and needless talk.

"Where am I?" he said to himself as he approached the courtyard. He turned and looked back at the sleepy neighborhood he awoke from. There was no food back there. He had to move forward and face the dangers of the intersection ahead. A bird cried in the distance and the smell of blood pierced his perceptions.

"I am entering a jungle where four-legged creatures walk upright. Half human, half beast. Part ferocious, part civil."

Near the street, a lion and a wildcat, both dressed in a suit and tie, spoke animatedly, their paws moving through the space between them. He recognized the lion, Carlitos, a young lawyer who liked to exchange verses and at times gave him something to eat.

"*No comas mierda*, you imbecile. Batista is not the solution," the lion said to the wildcat. "That man loves power and it's the only reason he's there."

"He's here to save us from the mess," the wildcat replied.

"We are weeks away from an election," the lion said, showing his teeth, "and everybody knows he is losing. So now you find it acceptable for him to take control of the army and declare himself President?"

"Absolutely! Would you allow Prío, a man tainted by corruption, to continue leading the country down the drain?" The wildcat slanted his ears and moved his whiskers.

El Caballero approached slowly, wondering if it was safe for a timid poet like himself to be near such ferocious beings. The discussion became increasingly louder as the half human creatures talked over each other, uninterested in listening to a counter argument.

"I would allow for democracy to continue..."

"A man who gave free reign to the mafia and gangs..."

"...without the elections we fall into..."

"...to run their illicit business through the treasury..."

"...civic apathy and a collective fantasy..."

"...*come mierdas*, will be each and every one of us."

"...that cripples the courts and we'll stop being a republic."

"You might as well elect this *loco*," the wildcat pointed at *el Caballero*.

The lion paused and turned to look at *el Caballero*, who froze in fear.

"Because that is what we're doing if we continue with these sham elections. At least with Batista we have a chance to clean the house and start over."

The lion stepped towards *el Caballero*.

"This *loco*," the lion said, "can see more clearly than you and all the other Batista supporters. All you're doing is masturbating to the sound of his voice."

"*Vete pa'l carajo,*" the wildcat said. "Go to hell," he yelled as he threw his arms up in the air and stepped away.

"Hell is where we will all be," the lion roared angrily. "So, go clean your butt hole, because we are about to get fucked!"

All chatter in the jungle ceased. Silence lingered heavily in the air as the words echoed against the building. Every creature in the courtyard turned in shock to look at the pacing lion, who was eager to pounce on his retreating opponent but began to grumble to himself.

"*Cretino*," said the lion in a low roar.

"Please tell me, Mr. Lion," *el Caballero* said meekly, "is it safe to be near you?"

The lion looked at *el Caballero*, as if for the first time, and then turned to look at the wildcat, who was entering the building.

"*Imbéciles*," he said.

El Caballero stood silent. The lion smacked his lips, not a good sign.

"Batista led a coup d'état early this morning. The army generals and the police chiefs are all in support. We might as well bury the constitution in the cemetery."

El Caballero remained silent, unsure of how to respond without further contributing to the agitation of the fierce being before him.

"Come, let's get some coffee," the lion said in a softer voice.

El Caballero relaxed. The lion faded and the image of a young lawyer returned.

"You must be hungry," Carlitos said as he pivoted toward the café just a few yards away.

El Caballero smiled, reaching out to touch Carlitos' arm. "Just remember:

> *In this duplicitous life*
> *nothing is true nothing is false*
> *Everything depends on the color*
> *of the lens through which we look.*

"Hmm... Campoamor," recalling the poet. "Very good. Very good."

El Caballero stood silent, waiting for the lion's usual reply, another poetic quote.

"I don't have a response. I'm too angry!"

Carlitos and *el Caballero* walked toward the café on the courtyard. After a few steps, Carlitos turned and recited a verse by José Martí,

> *I know when fools are laid to rest*
> *honor and tears will abound,*
> *and that of all fruits, the best*
> *is left to rot on holy ground.*

Other men gathered around the café, like wilderness creatures at a watering hole. They were curious about the new King of the Jungle,

Batista, and how he managed to pull a coup d'état weeks before the election. Quietly, at the side, stood the hyena, observing the young lawyer. *El Caballero* noticed him, an American scavenger named Brown, who reached forward with a couple of coins, seemingly to buy him a pastry. *El Caballero* looked in his bag for a magical card to offer in exchange. Carlitos pulled him back and shook his head in disapproval.

"Not him," he whispered.

El Caballero stepped back and the hyena returned the coins to his pocket.

"He's mafia," Carlitos quietly warned.

The hyena smiled. "Have a good day," he said and stepped away.

Carlitos watched Brown as he walked down La Rampa toward the Hotel Nacional. On the opposite sidewalk was his father, Carlos Senior, engaged in conversation with Goar Mestre, owner of the radio station CMQ. Unlike his own heated discussion, heard by most passersby, his father's conversation was almost imperceptible. As always, his father was the disciplined statesman, who did not allow emotions to interfere with argument. He stood straight as an arrow, with a briefcase in one hand and a raised index finger in the other, his usual gesture for emphasis.

Carlitos placed his hand on the shoulder of *el Caballero* and quickly retreated it as if punctured or burned.

"You're wet," he said with surprise.

El Caballero gave him a shy smile.

"*Chico* you should probably take this off before you get sick."

El Caballero nodded, "When I get to the *Malecón*. I have a spot there."

While sipping coffee, Carlitos watched his father cross the street with Goar Mestre. They walked with the urgency of men who knew time was against them. An assistant to Mr. Mestre quickly approached him in the courtyard with a pad and pencil in hand, while Carlos Senior altered his direction to approach his son.

"Where is your secretary?" Carlitos joked with his father.

"Where is your pad and pencil?"

"Do you want a coffee?" Carlitos offered.

"No, thanks. I've been up since early and I've had several." He lowered his briefcase to the ground and then looked at *el Caballero*. "*Chico*," he whispered. "What are you doing with this crazy man? His smell will stick to you."

"You sure you don't want a coffee?"

"I don't have time for that, with everything I have to do."

"This morning, I would argue, it's a bit late for any of it."

"Would you rather we surrender to the lunacy?"

El Caballero observed Carlos Senior. He had golden wings, like those of an eagle. Carlos Senior spoke with the wisdom acquired from a lifetime of studying the horizon.

"I have to get inside and give an interview," the Golden Eagle said. "They're waiting for me. From there I'm going to the Capitol to see how we manage this."

"Manage?" the lion asked sarcastically.

"What do you want? Batista has the upper hand in this power move. Somehow we have to convince him to allow the democratic process to continue."

"There's no management here. We have to get Batista out before he starts thinking the island is his own personal possession." The lion began to pace as the eagle remained still. "Papá, you are very popular. I watched you campaign, and the people love you. All the polls indicate you would win the senate seat by a landslide. If you were to say in public that we must fight against Batista, the people will follow."

The eagle looked at the lion and exerted dominance. The lion ceased pacing and momentarily became submissive, almost childlike.

"Have you not learned anything? If we make a call to arms, it's the fastest way of getting hundreds or thousands of people killed. You want that blood on your conscience? I know I don't. No senate seat is worth that. We're not revolutionaries. We can restore the democratic process peacefully. *Óyeme*, I need you to listen carefully. Go to *el bufete*, the firm, and handle all my appointments at the office. I left instructions with the front desk."

The lion smacked his lips, a habit the eagle recognized as an indicator of annoyance.

"Today is not a day for your antics," the eagle ordered as he picked up his briefcase. "Do as I ask and don't create any problems. Because when you shout in this courtyard that we are about to get fucked, it reflects directly on me."

Carlos Senior walked away, swiftly gliding into the building with the ease of an elder statesman who never reveals the desperation in his heart. His son smacked his lips again, and looked back at *el Caballero*, who smiled innocently.

"Here," he said as he placed a coin on the counter. "Get yourself something to eat. And take off the wet coat."

"Where will you go?" *el Caballero* asked.

"You heard my father. He wants me to do his bidding."

El Caballero stepped forward and held up his finger.

> *Look at the river, born from time and water*
> *and know time to be its own river.*
> *Like the river, we are lost*
> *and faces will pass like rushing water.*

"Lope de Vega?" Carlitos asked.

"Borges," *el Caballero* said with a smile.

"The Argentinian fellow. Hmm... I have to go. Today is no day for me to linger."

El Caballero stood still, watching the young lawyer hurry away.

"And don't forget to take off that coat," Carlitos called out without looking back.

El Caballero walked slowly, like a man with nowhere to go and twelve hours to get there. His stride was in sync with the rotation of the Earth. Unaware of time or distance, he eventually found himself in front of the Hotel Nacional. Young men in servant uniforms bustled about, carrying luggage for arriving guests. And there stood Brown, the hyena, greeting a group of fellow hyenas dressed in matching black suits with black ties, laughing in unison at the blood around them.

"Peculiar talk," he thought to himself, recalling portions of the English language he learned when he used to wait tables. Across the road was the city's sea wall, *el Malecón*, his favorite meditating site. There he sat, took off his overcoat and set it to dry. He gazed at the deep waters of the Caribbean, searching for images lost in the horizon of his mind. A mermaid swam up to him. She had beautiful blue hair and verdant breasts that glittered.

"*Caballero,*" the mermaid said. "Come in and make love to me."

"I'll drown," he countered.

"The joy of our love will be more powerful."

He laughed at the suggestion.

"What?" She rose over the waters to playfully entice him with her beauty. "Don't you want to make love to me?"

"I do. I do. I also want to hold a star in my hands, but I know its brilliance would consume me. Let me ask you *sirena*, you who have sung to many a man, tell me, why do men chase powers they can't control?"

"Men are creatures from a savage jungle who pretend to be something different," she said, floating on the water, tempting him with curves he had not held in many years. "But not you. You know what you are. Come, be true to your nature and swim with me."

A wave splashed against the wall and the mermaid dipped beneath it. He could still see her, smiling at him, as he followed her into the depth of the sea.

Cristóbal Díaz Ayala saw *el Caballero*, dripping wet and seemingly suspended in time, staring blankly at the street and the currents of moving people. The catatonic lunatic stood like a rock, bifurcating traffic, staring open mouthed at images not visible to anyone. Indifference surrounded him, but Cristóbal was moved to assist the madman.

"¿*Caballero?*" Cristóbal stood in front of him, in an effort to get his attention.

El Caballero turned his eyes from the dancing movement of the swarming bees, to focus on the horse before him.

"*Caballero,*" the horse said again. "Can I help you?"

"Oh, thank you," *el Caballero* smiled. "I can use a stallion like yourself. I need safe passage to the *escalinata*, the staircase. Perhaps, if you could be so kind, you might allow me to ride on your back."

"Here, hold on to me. I'll get you there."

Cristóbal placed the hands of the passenger on his shoulder, as if he were blind, and safely guided him through the moving crowd. They halted at the end of the street, where the staircase to the university welcomed them. *El Caballero* smiled at the guiding horse, who slowly morphed into his human condition.

"Oh, you're a student," *el Caballero* said, recognizing him.

"Yes, we've traded poetry before."

"Well, thank you. I'm not sure I could have crossed by myself."

"It was my pleasure to be of assistance. Besides, I have to be here," pointing to the top of the staircase. "Members from the F.E.U. are meeting to discuss Batista's coup d'état."

El Caballero looked up to see a gathering of colorful animals and birds standing behind the statue of the Alma Mater. He looked back at his guide with amazement, and saw him transform into the shape of a stallion, rapidly ascending the long staircase. *El Caballero* took interest in this assembly and slowly made his way to the top of the staircase where he could listen to the furtive plans of jungle animals.

"We were less than three months from the election," a large Bengal tiger said, displaying the enormity of his teeth.

"The Army generals cannot be part of the solution," the black panther whispered. "To them it always is about domination."

"They think they can stop the corruption," a peacock commented while fluttering its feathers, "while doing a corrupt act."

"Ha!" Flocks of green parrots laughed in unison. "Ha, ha, ha!" They perched themselves on the statue.

"The corruption will only get worse," the black panther whispered.

"What the country needs is a stronger court system and a corps of inspectors to keep a watchful eye over the departments and agencies," the stallion said.

"So, what do we do?" the Bengal tiger asked.

"Metaphor," the lion said. "We cannot get in the way of Congress. It's their work that must prevail now. We can only dabble in metaphor."

The animals remained silent, waiting for a clarification.

"I got the idea today while arguing with *un come mierda*. Let's bury the constitution in the cemetery."

The animals stood in silence, not yet assimilating his vision.

"Batista, with the coup d'état, has effectively killed the constitution. So, let's give it a funeral and bury it in a prominent location."

"Ha!" the green parrots hackled in unison. "Ha, ha, ha!"

"I can get a dozen crying women dressed in black," the peacock said to the tiger.

"Let's have eulogies and lamentations," the tiger replied.

"She was so young! Why did she have to die?" the horse neighed.

"We'll read excerpts and then cry some more," the chimpanzee said while laughing.

"We'll cry out for justice!" the panther paced. "Call Batista a murderer."

The lion stepped back, pleased with the energy his idea had created. He caught sight of *el Caballero*, who was standing to the side and listening with amazement.

"Do you want to be a part of this, write us a few verses?" the lion asked *el Caballero*.

"I ..."

"We can even have a mock procession," the chimpanzee jumped over to the lion and interrupted. "With a casket draped in black."

The animals were now talking excitedly among each other.

"And a sign that reads, 'Here lies our Constitution.'"

"… 'killed in her prime.' Marvelous!"

"… and the crying women behind us."

"People will come out to see what's happening!"

"They'll join us."

"Let's put it in the obituaries."

"Flowers. We'll need flowers."

The lion stood tall among the other animals and with his silent gaze called them back to order. He looked at them sternly. "We could be thrown in jail," he said.

"Most definitely," agreed the tiger.

"And beaten," the lion added.

The animals were all silent.

"How many of you are willing to suffer a broken jaw or be jailed with guards that have permission to be violent? Before we continue, you must know this may happen."

The group remained silent. From behind, the spotted leopard stepped into view. He hungrily entered the circle, as they looked at him with suspicion.

"Well, look at this. Everyone's here." The leopard looked around and caught sight of *el Caballero*. "Even the resident poet."

El Caballero stepped back, unsure of the leopard's intentions.

"Don't stop your plans because of me," the leopard said slowly, examining the other animals with piercing eyes. "I believe you were asked a good question. Is there anyone here willing to face jail? What do you think, Carlitos, is there anyone willing to do what it takes?"

"Fidel, you're no longer part of the F.E.U.," the tiger challenged. "You're not part of this plan or anything we might do."

"I've been listening to your little plan," the leopard said with contempt. "Metaphors, are you serious? A funeral? Play acting? It all sounds so childish."

"Fidel," the lion stepped forward, "you're not welcome here."

"I know," the leopard snapped and faced the lion. "I'm not welcome on your baseball team. I'm not welcome in this student union. I'm never invited to your little parties. Tell me, Carlitos, why do you dislike me so much? All I ever wanted was to be a part of university life, but wherever I go there you are, showing me the door."

The lion stood still, on guard, as the leopard resumed his pacing, stealthily moving toward the staircase.

"You might as well add another casket to your procession, for your father's political career," the leopard said with a smirk.

"What about yours?" the lion asked. "You were running for Congress."

"I was, but not anymore. I'm done with all this," the leopard said from the top of the steps. "Running for Congress is not going to change anything. The time for decisive action has arrived." The leopard looked at the other animals. "If anyone is tired of metaphors, find me. Soon I'll strike and change will come. I promise, and that's no metaphor."

The leopard nimbly raced down the stairs and disappeared into the street.

"What is wrong with that man?" the peacock asked.

"He's dangerous," the panther said.

"He's psycho!" a parrot loudly said, as the flock repeated it. "Psycho. Psycho. Psycho."

"The correct terminology is socio-path!" the horse amended, but the parrots weren't listening.

"Stop!" the lion roared. "We have work to do. We'll start our funeral procession here at four. That's in three hours, and we'll make our way to the capitol. Cristobal, get us several bull horns and contact your uncle's newspaper, *El País.* "

The horse nodded and departed.

"Rodolfo, get us the funeral casket and see if you can get a hearse, too."

The black panther leapt into a graceful stride.

"Antonio and Miguel, find the criers, at least a dozen dressed in black. And as many students you can recruit. We need hundreds of people."

The tiger and the peacock departed, as the lion continued to give orders and *el Caballero* quietly receded into the university campus, certain of his aversion to rallies and commotion. He continued to move from place to place, shade to shade, street to street, reciting poetry for coins and grateful for small blessings. When he gathered enough coins, he decided to eat at a small Spanish café, *El Baturro*, whose owner welcomed him without hesitation. It was one of the few places where the accents, music and décor reminded him of his hometown in Galicia. The walls were lined with bottles of Spanish wine. Wooden barrels randomly decorated the small establishment, to create an authentic Spanish atmosphere. *El Caballero* sat down to quietly enjoy a *caldo gallego* soup, when an exhausted laborer entered.

Manolo walked into the restaurant looking for a place to relax after a tiring day at the workshop. His clothes were clean, the second set after a days-worth of sweat. He entered the café with the familiarity of a man entering his home, happy to sit at his usual table, even happier to be served without having to ask.

The owner of the café greeted Manolo with a pronounced Spanish accent, a glass of red wine and a small tray of tapas. Soon after, the owner joined him with his own glass of wine. *El Caballero*, who was two tables over, dipping a chunk of bread into his bowl, saw Manolo's energy resurface after a few sips of wine and shared laughs with his friend.

"That's what I want," Manolo looked at *el Caballero* and then at the owner. "Can you bring me a bowl?"

The owner glanced over at *el Caballero* and stood up energetically.

"*¡Hombre!* I'll be right back with your bowl and chunk of bread."

Manolo smiled at *el Caballero* and lifted a glass of wine in salutation. *El Caballero* smiled in return.

A glass of wine in the midst of flowers
I drink alone, without companions or friends.
I lift the glass and invite the moon
with her and my shadow we three shall be.

"Rómulo," Manolo called out to the owner. "Bring a glass of red wine to this man."

El Caballero accepted and offered a toast with the glass in hand.

"Bravo! Bravo," Manolo exclaimed, clearly no longer as tired as when he first sat down.

"I've got one for you," Manolo stood with the glass of wine in his hand.

Long live wine,
long live bread,
and long live the cake
that you're going to bake!

Manolo, under the influence of the wine, laughed at his verse and sat down.

"Stop being so childish," the owner said to Manolo and slapped his shoulder with a dish towel. "Do you know who you're trading verses with?"

"Oh, am I in the company of an illustrious person?" Manolo asked with a smile.

"You are seated across *el Caballero de París*," the owner said, serving Manolo the bowl of soup with a chunk of bread. "So, keep your childish poems to yourself."

"¿*El Caballero de París*? I've heard of him," Manolo said, "of *you*," he redirected. "Finally, I get to meet you. How wonderful that it's in this manner, here. Tell me, what brings you to this corner of the city?"

"Good food and good company," *el Caballero* replied. "This is one of the few places where I can find both."

A momentary silence allowed Manolo and *el Caballero* to return to their meal. They were enjoying the soup when two men and a young woman entered the restaurant, commenting about a protest at the capitol.

"*¿Que paso?*" Manolo asked as they walked to their table.

"University students put on a funeral procession, accusing Batista of killing the constitution. It was quite a show," said one of the men.

"They had a casket, protest signs and several hundred people in the procession," the woman commented. "All of them chanting and making a commotion."

"The police were sent to break it up," the man said and pulled a seat for the woman. "It ended with everyone running out."

Manolo nodded and *el Caballero* stood.

"Thank you for the glass of wine," he said to Manolo. "It was the perfect completion to the meal. I must retire now. Have a good evening."

Manolo, who had a mouthful of bread, nodded and watched him leave. He was no longer in a celebratory mood. The news of the protest had him thinking about his daughter's suitor, the young Carlos Márquez-Sterling. Could he have been at the demonstration?

"Romulo, let me use your phone."

"Is it a local call?"

"*Hombre,* of course it is. I have to call my daughter. It won't take long."

Manolo was guided behind the counter to a black phone affixed on the wall. He dialed the number and after several rings, Tina answered.

"Tina, it's me. Is Olguita home?"

"Of course, she is. Why?"

"I need to ask her a question. Put her on the phone."

"What's this about?"

"I want to know if her boyfriend, Carlitos, is safe. There was a disturbance today, here, by the capitol, and I'm worried for him."

"Well, he's here now. They're sitting on the front porch."

"Oh. Does he seem like he's...."

"He got here two minutes ago," she interrupted. "Should I be worried?"

"No, I don't think so. But does he look..."

"He's fine," she interrupted again. "Do you still want to talk to Olga?"

"No, no. Listen, make sure they don't go out. It's not safe out there today."

"Where are you?" she asked with suspicion. "I hear dishes in the background."

"*El Baturro*, having some wine and tapas with Romulo."

"You shouldn't be out if there's trouble in the streets."

"I know. My point exactly."

"Go home," she ordered and hung up the phone.

"Everything all right?" Romulo asked Manolo as he slowly hung the phone.

"It's a crazy day, with all the political problems, you know. I was just calling to make sure everyone was safe at home. Especially Olguita. She has a boyfriend, and... "

"Really? How old is Olguita now?"

"Seventeen."

They paused and looked at each other for a moment.

"Damn, we're getting old!" Romulo pushed him playfully and they laughed.

Manolo stepped out of the café to see the half moon rising. The two glasses of wine he consumed, along with the friendship shared, left him feeling slightly elevated. He was standing at the bus stop, enjoying the breeze, when he saw *el Caballero de París* at a distance, sitting on a park bench, looking up at the swaying palms and talking to himself without a care in the world.

"How does he do it?" Manolo thought. "How does he not worry about today or tomorrow?"

The bus arrived and opened its doors for Manolo. He paid the nickel fare and saw the bus driver was a man of similar age and composure as he.

"Crazy day, right?" Manolo commented.

"How so?" the driver said with indifference. The doors closed and he stepped on the accelerator.

"Batista taking over the government must have created some turmoil, no?"

"Just another day in the life of a poor man."

Manolo waited for clarification.

"Everything is still running like it did yesterday. I showed up at work, got on the bus and I didn't know Batista had taken over until midmorning, when someone told me. Other than the student protest that blocked traffic on *Neptuno*, the rest of the city was business as usual."

"Oh, good to know. It's strange though, don't you think?"

"What?"

"That the military should take over the government a few months before the election and everyone is going about their business, as if nothing happened."

"Politics on this island is crazy," the bus driver said "Sometimes people are all fired up and ready to kill each other. Other times, people are indifferent and don't even notice what's happening. I think we're tired of the corruption. I don't trust any of them. They're all the same, these politicians. As long as I can work and get paid, I really don't care. All I have to worry about is providing for my family. A hungry child knows no politics."

"I feel the same way. I spent the day working, like always. And tomorrow I'll show up to work again. That's all I do. Who has time to think about these political games?"

"Where are you going?"

"*El Rosario, Arroyo Naranjo.*"

"Have a seat. It's about ten minutes away."

"You know, I have it pretty good. I go home at the end of the day to a new wife and a new house. I can't really complain, but I do have to work a lot for that pleasure."

"New wife and a new house?"

"Yeah."

"Good for you. Now, have a seat. And don't make me tell you again."

CHAPTER 5

Courted by Royalty

March 12, 1952
Havana, Cuba

Carlos Senior sat in a studio of the CMQ station, trying to focus on possible solutions. He knew that with Batista in power, he and the other candidates running for a political seat could be deemed a threat. So far, the coup had not been violent, but who was to say it would remain that way? He was silently debating different strategies, when the journalist, Héctor de Soto, began the interview.

"It's 7:45 and most of Havana is still getting used to the news that yesterday our democratically elected government was taken over by General Fulgencio Batista. I'm here with Doctor Carlos Márquez-Sterling, whose run for the senate was foiled by this coup."

Carlos Senior was frequently invited to be on the show because he knew time segments in radio were sacred, and he always respected the time allotted to them. Yet, on this day he was fully aware that rules and protocol no longer mattered. The island's political evolution toward a civil society took a huge step back to the days of "might makes right."

"Doctor," the journalist began. "President Prío-Socarras has left the presidential palace and taken refuge in the Mexican embassy."

Carlos Senior remained silent, waiting for a question.

"General Batista has announced his intention of establishing a provisional government and holding elections in two years. Many people have welcomed his intervention because the corruption has gotten out of hand, and they remember the good work the General did when he used to be president. My question to you, Doctor, do you think the island needs this type of intervention to instill order?"

"Your question has a simple answer, but it refers to a problem that is very complex," Carlos Senior replied. "Imagine a young woman who cannot use her hands because her fingers have curled and seized. She is taken to the hospital where the doctors do a full evaluation to determine a course of action. One doctor claims the fingers are immobile because of a neurological condition that is treatable. Another doctor says it's hopeless and he lifts a saw to amputate the patient's hands. If that patient were your daughter, which doctor would you prefer?"

The journalist remained silent.

"Assuming you want her to regain use of her hands," Carlos Senior continued, "the obvious answer is to treat the condition, but as a nation we are choosing to have our hands cut off. Yes, we have a problem. Nobody is denying it, but we also have a constitution, the means to remedy our problems. It holds the key to restore the functions of our island back to health. Batista is holding the saw that will cut off our hands. I want to jump across the table and stop him from doing irreparable damage."

The journalist smiled as Carlos Senior leaned back in his chair.

"It is a compelling argument," Soto said into the microphone. "Are you suggesting that General Batista does not have the welfare of the island in mind?"

"I'm not here to speak to his intentions. I'm here to speak to the consequences of his actions. He is creating an illusion of control and security. This might give the people comfort, but it is just an illusion. The very mechanism he is using to wield control will become uncontrollable, and just like our patient whose hands are in danger of being amputated, the institutions of civil society in our island are in danger of the same."

"We are coming to the end of our segment. Senator, what are your closing words?"

"I call on every elected official, regardless of political party, to stand against Batista. We have to be united for the good of the democratic process. Our republic is young, and our democracy even younger, but we can correct the corruption that has plagued us. Holding our country and constitution hostage is not the answer."

"Senator, your clear arguments remind us that we certainly could have used you on the senate floor once again."

"Hopefully, democracy will be restored and we both will have that pleasure."

"Thank you. It's always good having you on the show. You have been listening to Carlos Márquez-Sterling, here on CMQ. We'll be back after a word from our sponsor."

Carlos Senior moved his chair back and reached down for his brief-case. The journalist was looking at him strangely.

"What's on your mind, Héctor?"

"How many times have I interviewed you, Doctor?"

"*No sé*, several dozen." He smiled.

"I lost count too, but this is the first time I hear you speak so..."

"Straightforward?"

"No, that's not the word I would use. You've always been straight-forward. Alarmed is a better word."

"That's because I am alarmed. The future of our democracy is in jeopardy. It would be reckless to paint a picture of normalcy."

"Well, be careful. I can't imagine your words today won't have reper-cussions."

They shook hands and Carlos Senior walked out of *Radiocentro*. His car and driver were waiting for him at the edge of *La Rampa* to drive him to the Capitol, where he would convene with his fellow members of the Orthodox Party. As they drove up, police squad cars blocked the entrance.

"What's happening, Gabriel?" Carlos Senior asked his driver.

Several dozen police officers with batons in hand were blocking the entrance to the building, and traffic was being redirected.

"I'm not sure, Doctor. You may want to avoid the Capitol today. I'd hate for you to get arrested, or something."

"Let's go to the university. I have to teach this afternoon," he said while futilely searching for notes in his briefcase. "Nevermind, just take me home." he sighed in exasperation.

"Everything alright?" the driver asked while making eye contact with him through the rearview mirror.

"*Ay*, Gabriel, the thought of seeing the wife again..."

The driver remained silent and made a sharp turn to return toward *la Vibora*, an upscale neighborhood populated by large, Mediterranean style homes with courtyards and shade trees.

"You've seen how she gets," Carlos Senior clarified.

"Yes, sir, I have."

Silvia Dominguez O'Mahoney was a strikingly beautiful woman with dark red hair and a volatile temperament, both traits inherited from her Irish ancestors. Little is known about those Celtic immigrants other than the historical chronicle that they boarded a ship to Cuba in an effort to escape starvation and poverty.

"Why won't you take your cousin to the Department of Economics?" Silvia protested with a screech in her voice, speaking to her defiant son, Carlitos.

"He can get into the School of Economics on his own merits," Carlitos replied, "without leaning on my friendships to tip the scale."

She threw her arms up in the air and released an agitated objection. Carlos Senior walked in to witness the end of their squabble and the beginning of her tantrum. He knew his son was equally as headstrong as his wife, and in their battles for control, she lost more often than she could accept.

Manuel, her younger son, looked down at the commotion from the upstairs landing. He was a studious young man in his first year of law school. He was leaning on the banister, still in his pajamas. Silvia looked up at him for assistance.

"Don't look at me," he said with a book in his hand. "I am up to my eyebrows in Roman law. Besides, I don't know anyone in the School of Economics."

"Where are you in that history?" Carlos Senior asked.

"The Severan dynasty and the legacy of Ulpian," Manuel pushed his glasses up.

"You better know your Latin," Carlitos looked up at his brother and began to recite, "*Juris praecepta sunt haec: honeste vivere...*"

"*...alterum non laedere, suum cuique tribuere,*" Manuel completed the phrase and returned to his bedroom.

"There it is, he's more interested in Latin than in helping his cousin," Silvia protested.

"It's the Latin that provides the basis for my decision," Carlitos replied. He then turned to his father for support. "I'm doing Bernardo a favor, right Papá?"

"Quote all the Latin you want." Silvia's voice was reaching screeching levels. "All I know is that in his hour of need, you are turning your back on him."

"The basic principles of law," Manuel returned to the top of the staircase, with an elevated index finger to loudly proclaim, " 'live honorably, don't harm others, and render each his own.'"

Carlos Senior smiled and walked toward this study.

"You have turned them against me," Silvia accused her husband. "Are you happy now?"

"It's the part of Roman law that applies here, Silvia," Carlos Senior said. "Render each his own. Bernardo has to earn his own."

Carlitos followed his father to the study and closed the door behind him.

"I'm not going to help *el Canalla*, the Scoundrel, get into the School of Economics."

Carlos Senior looked at him with a prosecutorial eye.

"Where were you last night?"

"I had to keep a low profile after the protest, so I found refuge on Olguita's front porch."

"You got home late. Don't tell me you were up that late with her."

"Are you kidding? I can't go anywhere without a chaperone, and we can't even sit on the front porch without her mother looking through the window."

"Are you going to propose?"

"I think so, now that she's almost of age."

"Then you need to get your mother involved. She needs to meet Tina."

"What about her father, Manolo?"

"Tina is the one who rules in that family. Go with your mother and pay her a visit. Which means you have to make peace with her."

"What? And take *el Canalla* to the university?"

"Do I have to tell you everything? It's about making her happy, so do something she enjoys, like shopping. You know how much she enjoys buying suits and dressing you like a Hollywood star."

Carlitos looked down and smacked his lips.

"*Chico*," Carlos Senior recognized his son's annoyance, "is it that hard to spend time with your mother?"

"The island is going to shit, there's trouble in the streets and I have to play dress up!"

"There are worse things in life," Carlos Senior laughed. "Believe me." He then turned over a few stacks of paper and looked at his son with annoyance.

"Have you lost something?" Carlitos asked.

"My notes for class. I must have left them at the office." He grabbed his briefcase and started walking out with urgency. He stepped into the living room to find his wife's nephew, Bernardo, holding a secretive conversation with Silvia. They turned to face the father and son.

"Go ahead and tell him yourself," Silvia demanded in a shrill tone. "Tell him how you're not willing to help him get into the university. Do you have the face to tell your cousin he's not worthy of your care?"

Carlos Senior and his son stood momentarily frozen before their accuser, who had caught them off guard. A look of satisfaction swept over Silvia, who for once felt she had the upper hand over two men who did not respect her authority.

"Go ahead and tell him what your nickname is for him," Silvia continued.

Bernardo looked at her, surprised.

"Oh yes! They've lost all sense of loyalty here." She pointed her finger at her son. "He calls you the most awful *nombrete*. Tell him!"

Carlos Senior sighed in exasperation.

"Bernardito, *mijito*," Carlos Senior said to his nephew. "I cannot use my influence at the university for anything that might be construed as personal gain. My son is an extension of me. So, the same holds for him. Sorry. You'll have to get admitted on your own merits. And nobody here calls you by anything other than your name."

Carlos Senior looked back at his son and then stepped towards the door. Carlitos smiled at Bernardo and followed his father out.

"I call you *el Canalla*," Carlitos said with satisfaction as he passed by his cousin. "It's the closest I can get to a term of endearment."

"That's it!" Silvia screamed. "That's it! I'm done with all of you! That's my family you're treating with disdain. You hear me? My family!" She followed them to the door and then slammed it shut. Carlitos could hear her ranting and raving as he got into the car with his father. He looked up and saw his brother, Manuel, looking down from an upstairs window. He was clutching his book, petrified at the thought of having to deal with their raging mother.

"Why did you have to say that?" Carlos Senior admonished. "I'll never hear the end of it, and we'll probably come home to a pile of broken dishes. If you're going to have a political career, start at home. Learn how to get along with your adversary, especially if he's family."

"Papá, you can't stand the Dominguez family. They've done nothing but leech off your name and hard-earned money. I don't understand why Mamá puts them before us."

"My problems with your mother's family are exactly that – my problems. Don't make them yours. Your mother is not well. I've told you that before. Some screw has gone loose," he pointed at his head, "and her behavior is getting erratic."

"Doctor," the driver interrupted. "Where to?"

"The firm. I need to pick up something 'and then we'll go to the university."

"Gabriel, drop me off at the corner," Carlitos said. "I'll take the bus to Olguita's."

"Smooth this over with your mother."

The driver stopped at a corner that was full of people waiting for the bus.

"Carlitos, you hear me?" his father asked.

"Yes, yes. I hear you. I'll work on mom," he said as he closed the door.

Several minutes later, the driver dropped him off at his law firm on Amargura Street. It was an older building in Old Havana, requiring him to use the stairs. There, a trusted friend and campaign manager, Osvaldo Ruiz, greeted him. Osvaldo was a very large man, who served more as bodyguard than as political strategist, but nonetheless, his advice was always heard. The campaign was effectively over, but Osvaldo sat by the doors of the law firm regardless of the interruption imposed on a political future.

"I heard you this morning," Osvaldo said to Carlos Senior.

"You did?"

"The interview."

"Right, sorry. The day is moving so fast that it already feels distant."

"I like your analogy, with the woman whose hands are getting cut off."

"We'll see if the analogy translates."

"There's a young man here to see you."

"Who?"

"Don't know. He looks... poor. Maybe a student of yours."

"Osvaldo, give me a minute, and then I'll see what he wants."

Carlos Senior sat at his desk and found his notes on top of the credenza behind him. He was looking them over, to make sure they were complete, when a young man wearing a tattered shirt entered his office.

"*Sí*," Carlos Senior looked at the visitor.

"I've been waiting for you," the young man said.

"How can I help you? Do I know you?"

The young man was unkempt, with tousled hair, swollen eyes and puddles of sweat under his arms. He fidgeted and opened his mouth, as if to say something, but then changed his mind and bit his lip. Carlos Senior looked at him, puzzled. He was about to ask the visitor to sit, when the young man pulled out a gun and aimed it at him. The gun trembled in his hand and tears gathered in the corner of his eyes.

Carlos Senior jumped to the floor, behind the desk, and the gunman fired. He missed and hit the bookcase but continued to shoot frantically at the wall, unable to control his reflexes. Carlos Senior looked at the young man and made eye contact with him.

"Stop. You don't want to do this."

The gunman, now crying, threw the gun down and ran out. He was almost out of the building when Osvaldo Ruiz landed on top of him. Osvaldo, it turns out, was not afraid of jumping from great heights and threw himself down the staircase to apprehend the gunman. By the time Carlos Senior arrived, Osvaldo had constrained the gunman, who now limped and winced from having an oversized man land on him.

"I'm calling the police," Osvaldo said while tying the gunman to a fixture.

"No, wait." Carlos Senior ordered. "I want to talk to him."

Osvaldo stood aside as Carlos Senior interrogated the young man, who had very little information to offer. He assessed the young man to be desperately poor, and easily manipulated by those who offer cash. Somebody paid him for the act, but who?

"*Un Batistiano*," Carlos Senior said.

"The police should start a file on him," Osvaldo said.

"Let him go," Carlos Senior said.

"What?" Osvaldo was in disbelief. "He's going to try to kill you again."

"No, he's not. He's never going to do this sort of thing ever again. Right?"

"That's right, Doctor," the young man eagerly agreed. "If you let me go, I promise I'll stay out of trouble and I'll live an honest life."

Carlos Senior watched the young man rapidly walk away, while Osvaldo looked on with disapproval.

"If we call the police, we're sending him to his death. Don't you see?"

"Oh," Osvaldo nodded as he saw the bigger picture and rubbed his neck.

"Are you okay?"

"Me? I'm not the one who got shot at."

"Yeah, but flying down a stairwell is hazardous."

"Not for me," he chuckled. "The poor kid will probably have backaches for years to come, but I'm fine."

"He's lucky you didn't break his spine. I think you just earned yourself a permanent job." Carlos Senior laughed, gathered his notes and called out for Gabriel, who was parked down the street and unaware of the commotion. Once inside the car, Carlos Senior sat with the intention of catching his breath. His heart was still racing as he looked out the window at the passing scenery.

"Take the long way there, maybe down *el Paseo del Prado*, and drive slowly. I need to calm my nerves before I walk into the university," he told his driver.

He closed his eyes, cleared his thoughts and began his breathing exercises: inhaling for eight seconds, exhaling for twelve. He repeated the process for several minutes before opening his eyes. His heart rate and breathing were back to normal, his perception slightly improved. He could see the big picture, a nation manipulated by greed. People were walking on the shady promenade unaware how vulnerable they had become: the vendors trying to sell their wares, the young couples holding hands and there, on a bench, *el Caballero de París*, making paper butter-flies.

"How innocent!" he said to himself. "How very innocent of the crimes being committed against them."

******

Tina looked in the mirror, disappointed with the reflection. She had gained a few pounds, the kind that Manolo used to say were "in all the right places." This evening she resented the extra curves, which forced her to wear a dark blue dress in hopes of hiding her full figure. She reached for a pearl necklace and placed it on her neckline.

"What do you think?" she asked her daughter.

"Very elegant. I like it." Olga replied.

"Help me with it."

"I think I want a necklace like yours," Olga said while clasping it behind Tina's neck.

"You don't need one. This is for older women who prefer their neckline be the focus of attention. A pearl necklace on you would be lost. Nobody would notice it."

"*¡Ay, Mamá!* How can you say that?"

"It's true," she said, looking at Olga through the mirror. "The last thing any man will do tonight is look at your jewelry. Me? I am... what's the word? Matriarchal."

"Well, I think you look very elegant, especially with these pearls."

Tina turned around and smiled awkwardly, secretly wishing she could stay home, but her daughter had entered a new stage of life that required a chaperoning mother. Gone were the simpler days when Olga was a tomboy, playing ball on the street with the neighborhood boys, and her biggest worry was how to keep her scrapes clean. She and Manolo always knew certain changes would come as their beautiful daughter matured into a young woman, but Tina didn't anticipate getting divorced and having to face those changes alone. She didn't anticipate being invited to events above her station in life, with her daughter dressing like a debutante, eager to meet new friends with university degrees. Neither did she expect to find herself in front of the mirror expressing anxiety over a few extra pounds.

"Should we braid your hair?" Tina asked Olga, who sat in front of the full-length mirror.

"It's not the right place for braids. Marisa is never in braids and, besides, I look older with my hair like this."

"I've never been to a gala before."

"It's not a gala. Carlitos says it's a dinner party. You don't have to come, you know."

"Of course, I'm going. I'm your mother. It is not proper for you to go to these parties without a chaperone. Until you're married, you'll have to put up with me."

"Marisa isn't taking a chaperone. I think I'll be the only person there with one."

"You make it sound like I'm the one who invented this societal rule. I had chaperones, and so did every woman at that party. They all know these rules and play by them. For me to do otherwise would be considered unseemly. Is that what you want?"

"Mamá, go ahead and spray my hair. Carlitos is waiting."

Manolín's laughter was heard through the door.

"Your brother is keeping him company."

"That's a good sign, don't you think?" Olga looked at her mother through the mirror.

"What? That they get along?"

Olga nodded.

"Well, yes. I think it shows that regardless of how peculiar your boyfriend is, he's still able to get along with children, and that is very good. Close your eyes."

Tina sprayed a thick layer of hairspray on Olga, and then turned her around. Manolín's laughter continued to resonate through the door.

"Whatever he's doing," Tina said to Olga, who started to pick at her fingernail, "he's got your brother laughing."

Olga stood up energetically. "I can barely wait to see his house. I've never been inside one of those big homes in *La Víbora* or *El Vedado*."

"Remember what I said. The less you speak, the better. People are going to be interested to meet you, the fiancée of the young Márquez-Sterling. And if they ask questions about your father, refer them to me. I know we're different..."

"Very different!" Olga interrupted.

"What do you expect?" Tina looked at Olga through the mirror. "They practically live in the university. Whereas your father, and all his brothers, didn't make it to secondary school. We're bound to be different."

"I think that's what I like about him," Olga bounced. "He's so smart."

"*Bueno*, let's go." Tina examined her image in the mirror.

They opened the door to find Carlitos dressed in a tuxedo leaning over the coffee table with Manolín, playing with a pile of pennies. He stood, almost at attention, when Olga stepped into view. She was wearing a modest light blue dress that revealed her soft shoulders. Her neckline was decorated by a thin gold chain and cross.

"You look so handsome," she said.

Manolín seized the distraction to put the pennies in his pocket. Carlitos smiled, unable to stop himself from staring at her.

"You look simply..." His eyes were filled with adulation. "Not even Aphrodite, in all her splendor, could make my heart race like it is now."

"Afro who?"

"If I were an artist who painted freestyle, with my eyes I'd trace your profile, and call it a perfection that beguiles."

"Oh, *un piropo*. How nice," Olga blushed and looked at her mother for approval. "Did you hear that?"

"Yes, yes, very poetic."

Carlitos proudly extended his arm to Olga, who was still blushing, and walked her out to the car. Tina followed closely behind.

At the Márquez-Sterling home, a servant dressed in formal attire opened the front door to the foyer, where Silvia and Carlos Senior stood in formal attire, greeting the guests.

"Tina, welcome," Carlos Senior said warmly. "I'm so glad you could make it."

Tina smiled, slightly overwhelmed by the elegance. She then gave Silvia a slight nod, who smiled and greeted her just as warmly.

"Oh my God," Olga exclaimed. "What a house!"

Carlitos laughed and escorted Olga inside.

"You have such a beautiful home," Olga said to Silvia, "and a servant to open the door."

"Olguita, I'm so glad to see you here," Silvia said warmly. while extending her hand out to her. "Please come in. Carlitos' friends are in the back terrace. They arrived a short while ago."

"Tina," Carlitos said to his future mother-in-law. "Please make yourself at home. We'll be in the back, *en la terraza.*"

Tina wandered through the first floor of the home looking at the artwork. She found a large library where many men had gathered to smoke and discuss politics. The dining room had a chandelier and an elongated table, set for sixteen people. Servants hovered around it, making sure the candles were lit and the silverware in place. A separate table, in an adjoining space, was set for eight. Tina guessed it to be the table for the young people. The living room was furnished with antiques, most likely French, and had a separate sitting room with a display cabinet for glass figurines and miniature art. The women congregated in pairs or triads, conversing quietly while slowly walking between both spaces and sipping white wine. A servant with a tray of cocktail drinks approached Tina and offered her a glass. She accepted and noticed that the other women also wore dark dresses and pearl necklaces, assuring Tina they had more in common than she thought. Outside, in the back terrace, four young couples laughed with drinks in their hands.

"*Jóvenes*," Tina said to the group as she approached them. They paused their conversation and turned to her. She saw Olga holding a short glass with a rum drink.

"Olguita," Tina softly admonished while looking at her drink.

"I'll be fine, mother. It's not very strong. Carlitos prepared it for me."

"Tina, let me introduce our friends to you," Carlitos stepped forward. "This here is the Dr. Cristóbal Díaz-Ayala and his fiancée, Marisa."

Cristóbal stepped forward to gently shake her hand. "My pleasure," he said.

"A medical doctor?"

"No. Philosophy and law."

"The famous Marisa," Tina said while turning to his date. "Olguita never stops talking about you. She tells me you're graduating from the university next month."

"Yes," Marissa replied. "Olguita has become a good friend. She's so funny and cheerful."

"This is my brother, Manuel," Carlitos continued.

Tina marveled at their resemblance, with the exception of Carlitos being a good forty pounds heavier.

"And his date, Gloria Sanchez."

They nodded while Manuel said something nice about Olguita. Carlitos continued to introduce the remaining couple, Oscar Jorge and his wife Matty, whom Tina noticed to be exceptionally handsome, with a charming smile. Tina was impressed by Olga's new group of friends and their remarkable future as engineers and lawyers. Each man had intellectual depth and the women were equally as accomplished. It was new territory for Olguita, being among such learned people, but she navigated it well, thanks to Marisa, her new role model.

At the dinner table, Tina sat next to Gloria's parents, who also came to chaperone their daughter. The young people's table managed to be a boisterous group. Cristóbal seemed to be the storyteller, but it was her future son-in-law who spoke and laughed the loudest. Silvia had to walk over and quietly ask him to lower his voice, a request that went unheeded.

After the meal, the men went to the library while the women gathered in the sitting room. Tina sat with the matriarchs while the young women stood behind them. The conversation flowed through different topics, all of which Tina proudly contributed an opinion or fact. When the women discussed recipes, Tina had many. When they spoke about the youth, Tina offered her perspective as a schoolteacher. When they spoke about flowers, Tina, being a gifted gardener, also had something to say. Silvia was quite impressed and looked at Tina favorably, until one of the women commented on the coup d'état.

"Isn't it terrible?" a woman said while fanning herself.

"I don't know how we're going to restore the elections," another said as she also took out a fan.

One by one, the women took out their hand fans, an item missing from Tina's purse. They went around denouncing the self-appointed president and then looked at Tina expecting her to do the same.

"I happen to like Batista and I'm glad he took over," Tina said with a challenging tone.

"You do?" one asked in shock.

"Yes. Crime is out of hand. The gangs knew that Prío was useless. Someone had to do something. Batista has a firm hand. He'll establish order."

A deafening silence filled the sitting room. The women all looked at each other, not knowing how to reply to the minority opinion. Olga saw the disapproving look on Silvia's face and knew her mother had committed an unforgivable sin. Unsure of how bad the transgression was, Olga decided to step in and rescue the situation.

"I'd like to recite a poem," Olga announced.

"A poem?" a woman exclaimed with relief and continued to fan herself.

"*Ay*, how wonderful!" Silvia said loudly. "Marisa, go get Carlitos and tell him Olguita is going to recite a poem."

Tina looked at Olga, wondering if her daughter really knew any poems. Cristóbal and Carlitos came from the library and behind them several men, all curious to hear a performance from the new fiancée.

Olga entered the circle of women and stood before them with a big smile. They all smiled in return, delighted to see a young woman of education and culture. Olga cleared her throat loudly, as if for dramatic effect, and laughed. The women offered a short laugh. Cristóbal and Carlitos looked on with anticipation, Tina with dread.

> *Con un alambrito fino/ with a thin threaded wire*
> *te voy a coser el culo/ I'm going to sew your butt*
> *no te quedara bonito/ it may not look too pretty*
> *pero te quedara seguro/ but it sure will be safe.*

Silvia dropped her fan. Two other women followed and released theirs. Cristóbal was the first to laugh, and then Carlitos. They encouraged Marisa, who giggled nervously, while others emitted an authentic guffaw. Silvia recovered from her shock and thanked Olga for the amusement. Olga bowed and curtsied, unaware of the mixed reaction.

"Carlitos," Silvia said, "take Olguita and your friends to the *terraza*."

The women relaxed and some even chuckled while repeating the poem to themselves. Tina was pleased to see some of these "refined" women were not as pretentious as they appeared. When the evening ended, Carlos Senior and Silvia thanked them at the door. Olga leaned in and gave them both an unexpected kiss on the cheek.

Carlos Senior smiled, touched by her affection.

"That's quite a charming young woman," a departing guest said to Carlos Senior with a smile. Olga and Tina turned around to acknowledge the compliment.

"Such a breath of fresh air," the woman said. "It was what I needed, a little bit of laughter," she said to Olga, who accepted the compliment and moved on.

"Can we get some *churros*?" Olga asked.

"I know the perfect place," Carlitos replied. He drove to *El Paseo del Prado* where there was a churro vendor working behind a window of an open kitchen.

Tina yawned as the couple jumped out of the car and walked excitedly along the romantic promenade. She found a seat on a bench where she could keep an eye on them while enjoying the passing scenery of interesting people walking by. An older man, short in stature and smoking a cigar, sold balloons and spinning tops, while also ogling the women's posteriors. Tina hoped he would approach her, so she could call him a pervert. The opportunity never materialized as the balloon selling pervert moved further away. An older couple, in their sixties, walking very slowly, held each other with a closeness that was surprising to Tina, given their advanced age. She wondered if they were new to each other's arms or just more romantic than couples that age. Several young parents walked together, watching their children play and skip ahead of them. A gypsy woman with a deck of tarot cards approached passer-byes and offered to read their fortune. She was dressed in a bright colored skirt with a white bohemian blouse. Her arms were decorated with golden bracelets, her eyes painted with generous coats of blue eyeshadow, and her head adorned with a colorful scarf that weaved itself into her long black hair. As Olga and Carlitos neared her, the allure of the fortune teller could not be avoided, and Olga was staring at her like a child ogling a merry-go-round.

"A magical night for a beautiful couple," the gypsy woman said and approached with a dance-like leap. "I can read your future for a small price." She reached for Olga's hand, who was already offering it.

"Get away from us," Carlitos said and lightly pulled Olga's hand away.

Olga and the gypsy woman looked at Carlitos, both surprised by his rejection.

"Go peddle your nonsense somewhere else." He made eye contact with the gypsy as his tone of voice sharpened.

"*Ay, Carlitos, por favor,*" Olga protested.

"The *churros* are up ahead," he corrected his tone and lovingly tucked her hand inside his as the hypnotic sounds of Nat King Cole emerged from a nearby phonograph.

Tina watched the exchange between the gypsy woman and Carlitos, but did not think anything of it. She yawned once again, ready to go home, when a long-bearded man, dressed in tattered clothes and a black overcoat, approached her. He seemed to be oblivious to the people around him. Children ran from him, confusing his disheveled appearance for malice. Many pedestrians avoided him as if he were another inanimate obstacle in their journey.

"*Sirena*, mermaid," *el Caballero de París* said to her, "Do you like dry land?"

Tina froze, quickly formulating a plan if the madman were to sit next to her.

"These are not safe waters for you to swim in," he continued while remaining several steps removed. "Are you lost?"

A harmlessly loud group of young couples walked around *el Caballero*. They leaned on each other as they stumbled down the pathway. He turned and called out to them, in a voice that projected through the promenade,

> *Oh, Youth, divine treasure,*
> *How you flee, to never return.*
> *I can't seem to cry, when I need to,*
> *and cry, I do, when least expected.*

"*Oye*, Rubén Darío," a young drunkard called back to him. "I've never seen you look so poor," and laughed at his own joke. *El Caballero* innocently chuckled and returned his attention to Tina. He stood silent, waiting for her to speak. She was not inclined to demonstrate any interest, fearing he might get closer. She correctly deduced the madman would eventually move on if she did not engage him. After a few seconds of staring at Tina, he mumbled something inaudibly, bowed to her as if she were royalty and walked toward a side street in search of a soft corner to lie down.

Tina got lost in her thoughts, isolated from the activity surrounding her, as she watched *el Caballero* disappear into the night.

"Do you feel pity for him?" Carlitos said to her in a quiet whisper. The air of his voice touched her face, startling her. She turned, unaware of his proximity.

"It is a sad thing to watch. Lost potential. A life derailed. How great would this man be if his mind were slightly more balanced?"

Tina shifted her position to face her future son-in-law. She wondered why he was sitting so near. This was not their usual interaction. The authority and respect awarded to her position as mother had always kept him at a distance. She leaned back. Carlitos was not looking at her, but at the fading image of *el Caballero*.

"If we look closely," he continued in a soft voice, "we can see glimpses of a handsome youth, a sharp mind, a loving man. Now he is none of those things. Many think he is a victim of a mysterious trauma. I don't think he is a victim at all. No. I think he finally took control of his life in the only manner he knew how."

Tina shifted her body to create a bit more separation.

"What defines insanity?" Carlitos asked. "What if he sees us better than we can see ourselves? What if his sight cuts through all the pretensions, the hypocrisy, and he observes something that by his standard is not sane? Then, what does that make us?"

"Where's Olguita?" Tina asked, impatiently.

She looked around, searching for Olga, and found her sitting on the bench across from them, holding a bag of churros and quietly observing the interaction.

Carlitos looked at Tina, aware his proximity was invasive.

"Do you mind?" she said to him.

He stood, stepped back and smiled. Olga approached, ready to go home with her churros.

That night, as Olga was getting ready for bed, Tina walked into her room and stood at the threshold, observing her. Her daughter had a beauty and charm worthy of being courted by a prince, but is life with a prince really that good? Tina knew the Márquez-Sterling family was as close to nobility as Cuba could ever have. Their ancestors were part of Cuban history, friends and relatives to Cuban artists and patriots. An engagement of this sort is what every mother would want for her daughter.

"Are you happy with him?" Tina asked her daughter.

Olga was wearing a night dress and getting into bed.

"What?"

"Are you happy?"

"Of course I'm happy. What kind of a question is that?"

"It's a perfectly good question. Think about it."

Olga didn't think about the question and Tina never brought it up again. Sixty-eight years later, while sitting in my living room in St. Petersburg, Olga confessed to not having given my father's marriage proposal any thought.

"I was a stupid little girl," my mother said. "I was of age, you know, but I certainly didn't have the maturity I see in young women these days."

"What do you mean?"

"Well, young women today are so knowledgeable about the body, sex and the desires of men. I was sheltered from it all. I had a general idea, and some basic facts of what happens in a bed, but I really didn't know much. My understanding of marriage was childlike."

"So, you're telling me that you weren't ready for marriage."

"I think it would have been better if I had waited a few more years and been a little more mature. Do you know that on my wedding night I had an accident in bed?"

"*¿Como?*" I exclaimed.

"I don't know what happened," she started to laugh.

"What do you mean by an accident?"

"You know... an accident. The kind children have."

"*Ay*, Mama! What did Papa do?"

"What could he do? Change the sheets." Her laughter came to an end. "Maybe it was all the champagne, or the nerves, but I think it was proof I was too young to get married. Back then, getting married was the goal, and I wanted to do what the other women were doing."

"Did you love Papa?"

"I thought I did, but I didn't know what love was." She paused and looked out the window, as if images of her youth were being projected on the front porch.

"Are you going to make any coffee?" she asked.

"*¿Quieres?*"

"Just a little bit. I'll have a sip from yours."

"No. I'll have mine and you'll have yours. If you only want a sip, then that's okay."

"But it's going to be a waste of a cup."

"Like ten cents worth of coffee. That's not going to break the bank."

I brewed Cuban coffee in a traditional Italian espresso maker and took the two cups outside for us to drink under the shade of the oak trees.

"Guille, I was remembering how *el Viejo Márquez*, Old Man Márquez, was terrified of me." She chuckled. "We moved into his house after we got married, because your grandfather was living alone with Manuel. And I decided to take over as the woman of the house."

"This was after his divorce?"

"Yes, he and Silvia had divorced, and he lost his housekeeper, Carmen. So, I thought I was in charge." She let out another short laugh. "I remember cleaning his house with buckets of water. I'd stand at the top of the staircase and throw water." She started to laugh. "*¡Fuaah!* An entire bucket of water down the stairs."

The expression, *"Fuaah,"* made me laugh. We picked up the expression during our years in Puerto Rico, when the locals spoke of an unexpected or forceful event.

"And your grandfather was so measured that all he said was, 'Olguita, I think that may be too much water.' But I didn't hear what he was telling me and got another bucket of water."

"Did you like the coffee?"

"Yes, it was good. A little too sweet, but still good."

"You know," I commented. "I like cleaning that way too, with buckets of water. I'll get water and just toss it over the tile floor. *¡Fuaah!* I must have learned it from you."

"Well, your grandfather didn't think it was safe. I mean, with all the wood and books and expensive furniture it must have seemed reckless to him. One night, at the dinner table, he told me I needed to read, and he went to his library to get me two books, *The Three Musketeers* and *The Count of Monte Cristo*, and I read them. Yes, I did. It was very interesting to learn about Cardinal Richelieu and the French revolution. No, no, no, no, no. My entrance into that family was a complete disruption of their life. Your uncle Manuel thought I had little birds fluttering around in my head. He would ask me to sit with him and listen to the operas."

My mother went into a rendition of the Russian opera, "Ochi Chernye," lowering her voice to baritone and standing like Pavarotti.

"I can see him now, the world could be falling apart, and your uncle wouldn't notice as long as he had an opera to play. I swear, the bigger the problems, the louder he played his music. It was his escape, until..."

I waited for her to finish, but her gaze retreated to a place where I could not go.

"Manuel is the one who named our dogs," she said while looking at the distant horizon. "He's also the one who gave his cousin, Bernardo, the nickname of Scoundrel. He was good at that, renaming people. He and your father nicknamed Fidel Castro *Bola de Churre*."

"Ball of Grime?" I began to laugh.

"I bet you didn't know Fidel always smelled."

"How do you know this? Did you ever smell him?"

"Me? No! But your father did and so did others. What do you think, Fidel just appeared one day, that he fell from the sky? He was at the university with your father. Your grandfather was his professor. It was a known fact that the man had a bad odor."

"*Bola de Churre*, that's perfect," I commented while still retaining a hint of laughter. "You know, nicknames today are considered to be mean, the kind of thing bullies do."

"Bully? The real bully was Fidel Castro. That man walked around the university with a gun on his side, and he threatened teachers who were going to give him a failing grade."

"Really?"

"Ask anyone who studied at the University of Havana. It's a known fact that Castro didn't earn his degree, at least not fully, and that he smelled terribly."

I nodded and listened to my mother begin the familiar monologue, "Castro Was the Worst." According to this lecture, everything Castro and his regime did should have been sufficient proof that a madman had taken over. As much as I agreed with her assessment of the dictator, I didn't want to hear it again. So, I stood up, signaling I wanted to go inside.

"Do you want to see an episode of *Two and a Half Men*?"

"*¡Ay, si! Ese Charlie.* He's so funny."

Thank God for comedic sitcoms.

CHAPTER 6

Manuel

October 2018
Plymouth, New Hampshire

My uncle's home in New Hampshire is surrounded by woods and wildlife. He and my Aunt Gloria routinely see bears and deer, squirrels and chipmunks, as well as a wide variety of birds while preparing sandwiches on their kitchen counter. Their little wooden home, on the side of a hill, in the town of Plymouth, had been their refuge and sanctuary for nearly sixty years. It was there that I paid them a visit fifteen months before the Coronavirus pandemic. It was late October and winter was fast approaching. I parked the rented car on their driveway and marveled at the beautiful autumn colors that speckled their town. My aunt had instructed me to knock on the backdoor, and as I approached, I saw her looking out the kitchen window. Before I could get much closer, she opened the door and greeted me with a large smile. She stood straight, still retaining a lot of energy and strength for a woman her age.

"Guillermito," she said as we hugged. "Ah, you've arrived precisely when I most need your reach. Can you place these dishes on the top shelf?"

She pointed at the built-in cabinets sitting above her kitchen counter, full of cups, dishes, accessories and seasonal decorations.

"There?" I looked at a space already crowded by other artifacts.

"Yes, yes. Just place them on top of those other ones. I was about to get a step ladder, but then you arrived. Like that. Yes. Push them back, or else I won't be able to close the cabinet."

My aunt spoke with a rate of speech worthy of an auctioneer, and both she and my uncle had a noticeable Spanish accent, never failing to roll their r's. If my mother pronounced cracker as "*Kwahker*," my aunt would have said "*Krrakerr*." Despite the accent, which marked them as foreigners, it did not stop them from succeeding as educators: she as a Spanish teacher at the local high school, and he as a history professor at Plymouth State University. Had it not been for the accent, anyone would have thought their ancestors were in the Mayflower. Yet, it was the accent that provided them the opportunity to share a heritage and history to a New England community that had a deep misunderstanding of Cuba and the Castro revolution.

"Come, your uncle just woke up from a nap. Give me your bag," she said while taking it from me. "I'll put it by the staircase for you."

I found my uncle in the sunroom hunched over some books. His glasses were perched on the tip of his nose, and an oversized sweater covered his frail torso. Our relationship had been strained by my inability to call, write or visit - a shortcoming shared with my brother. Nonetheless, when I walked in, he looked up and smiled and I was once again impressed as to how similar his appearance was to my father's.

"Hey, *Tío*, it's so good to see you," I said and bent over to kiss his cheek.

"*Ay mijito*, let me take a look at you. Come and sit." He pointed at the small sofa, which had several stacks of journal clippings and books on it. "Gloria, move these things so Guillermo can sit. I'm working on a book and this is just a mess. Gloria!" He called out again.

"Coming, coming," she said from the kitchen. "I'll be there in a minute. Guillermito, just move the stacks to the table and make yourself comfortable."

His walker was in one corner of the sunroom, and an oxygen machine fully equipped with hoses and masks was in the other. I carefully moved things around and sat on cushions that embraced me as I sunk into them. My aunt appeared with a smile and a glass of pink lemonade, and then took the stack of clippings to the dinner table.

It took less than twenty minutes to bring them up to speed with news from my side of the world. Unlike other family members, my life was pretty boring and predictable. However, it took over an hour to get a full picture of all their ailments, and the challenges my uncle was facing after suffering a massive stroke two years earlier. I recognized they were walking a geriatric tight rope, trying to balance a regiment of pills, doctor appointments, and healthy diets so as to postpone an inevitable decline that would threaten the independent lifestyle they cherished.

In order to keep my visit pleasant, we avoided all talks about politics, knowing we each were firmly entrenched in opposing parties. My propensity to vote Democrat was a disappointment to them, and they correctly assumed I suffered from Trump Derangement Syndrome. Consequently, I encouraged my uncle to retell comical anecdotes from when he was a younger man in Cuba.

"I used to follow your father around," my uncle said with a smile on his face. "I was that younger brother who wanted to be involved with everything he was doing. I thought he was cool, you know, at least to my young and impressionable eyes."

"Funny," I said with a chuckle. "Cool is not a word I would have used to describe Papa."

"Well, he wasn't cool like Fonzie in that TV show. That's a Hollywood image. Your father was cool in the sense that he was a leader, people listened to what he had to say, and he organized activities and events that I found exciting."

"Not James Dean but more Cary Grant," I offered.

"*¡Exacto!*" He slapped my knee. "Cary Grant with glasses and another fifty pounds."

"*Oye*," my aunt interjected with a chuckle. "You're being very generous, comparing your father to Cary Grant."

"Do you prefer Carl Malden, the man with the big nose?"

"From 'The Streets of San Francisco.' *Ay*, no!" She chuckled.

"The Márquez-Sterlings, thankfully, don't have big noses, but we do have big ears, which I see you inherited." My uncle pointed out with a smile. "Anyway, the point is that I looked up to your father and wanted to be included in his outings. One fall season, when he was in law school, he put together a baseball team for the university intramural games, and our mother ordered him to include me."

"You weren't in law school at the time, were you?"

"No, but that didn't matter. Each team could recruit players from other schools, or even players that weren't in school."

"Like *el tronco* Maseira," my aunt said.

I looked at them quizzically.

"*El tronco* Maseira was this big, beefy man, un *tronco*," my aunt continued. "Solid as an oak tree. He wasn't even a university student, but your father recruited him to play on the team."

"So, that's how you snuck in."

"Exactly! Thanks to my mother, Carlitos had to include me. He wasn't happy about it, so I ended up playing outfield. I didn't complain, happy to just be part of the team, but I did spend most of the time watching the grass grow."

I nodded, having experienced my share of slow-moving baseball games.

"One day, we were on our way to the field, when Fidel Castro approached us."

"Quick question, *Tío*," I interrupted. "Back then, you didn't know Fidel, right? He still hadn't become a revolutionary leader."

"Fidel was a thug!" My uncle said with disdain. "A criminal, who somehow made it into the School of Law and the only way he could meet the requirements was by forcing his classmates to do the work for him."

"He walked around with a gun strapped to his side!" Aunt Gloria said.

"But you're right. At that moment, I didn't know who he was. All I know is that when Fidel confronted us, your father started looking around, searching for an escape route."

"What did Fidel want?"

"He wanted to be on the baseball team, but your father wasn't about to have a gun toting thug on the team. He told me to stay back while he went to speak with him, and I could hear Fidel threatening him. You have to understand that as your father's little brother, I thought he was invincible. So, when I heard Fidel threaten him, I couldn't understand why Carlitos was being so careful and diplomatic. And that's when I blurted out, 'Tell this *come mierda* to get out of our way. He's going to make us late.'"

My uncle, having said this story many times before, had an actor's flair for the delivery of his lines.

"Now, I want you to picture this. Fidel Castro, with a gun in his hand, is threatening my brother, who is doing his best to save his life while also not giving in to the demands."

"Uh-huh."

"I, a skinny little tag-along, blurted out insulting words, offending the thug and making my brother's job more difficult."

"Uh-huh."

"There's a pause, and then they turn to look at me, almost in unison, and fear pierces my heart. Oh my God, what have I done?"

My aunt laughs, clearly enjoying her husband's story-telling skills.

"My eyes must have gotten this big," he said, rounding his hands to the size of a saucer.

"Did you say, 'Never mind?' " I asked while laughing.

"I should have, but I decided to act as if I was really angry. So, I got all puffed up, and stuck out my chest, completely unaware of the danger we were in."

My uncle laughed and repeated his description of the scene. I nodded and echoed his enthusiasm. My aunt laughed and stood with the intention of going to the kitchen but waited for the climactic scene.

"Then your father walked back to me, pulled me aside, and whispered in my ear: '*¡Cállate, mojón!* Don't you see this man is about to kill me? Stay here, and don't say another word, you little shit.' Your father used to call me '*mojón,*' turd, whenever I annoyed him."

My uncle slapped my knee and laughed.

"So, how did he get Fidel to back down?"

"He promised to get him on the team of Philosophy and Literature and told him the manager of that team was a good friend of his."

"And did he?"

"*¿Estás loco?* Are you out of your mind?" My aunt interjected as she walked to the kitchen. "Friends don't pass their problems to other friends."

"He gave that manager the heads-up," my uncle said with a sly laugh, "and when Fidel approached him, the manager promised to get him into the team of the School of History. And when Fidel went there, he was sent to another manager. At that point he knew he was being played." My uncle continued to laugh. "Your father managed to keep Fidel out of the games, but I almost got him killed!"

"I once heard Cristóbal say that Cuba's history might be very different if they had only accepted Fidel into the club and given him a chance to play."

"*Sí, sí.* I've heard that too. But I don't think so. That leopard showed his spots early on, and your father knew what he was doing. Fidel would have wanted to take over the team, or he would have sabotaged the game, gotten angry at the umpire, and who knows how many people he would have killed over a bad call."

"He was that volatile?"

"Yes and no. Volatile is not the word. Fidel was calculating. I'm sure there's a diagnosis that a psychiatrist could give, but I would say the word is sociopath. We saw how dangerous he was, and we weren't surprised when he led the attack on the police headquarters in Moncada."

I nodded, having studied that history lesson.

"It's surprising that the Batista regime gave Fidel clemency for that attack," I offered.

"Had they kept him in prison, and made him pay for the crime he committed, then Cuba's history would have been very different," my aunt said. I could hear the anger in her voice. She had returned from the kitchen with a pillbox in one hand and a glass of cranberry juice in the other. "Papi," she said. "It's time for you to take your pills."

She stood over him, administering his medication, which he took obediently. She then told me to wash up, because dinner would be served in a few minutes. I looked at my phone to see the time. It was barely 5 pm.

After eating an "easy to prepare and easy to digest" meal we returned to the sunroom. It was then when I tapped into my uncle's repressed memories.

"*Tío*, I've been meaning to tell you. I ran into a woman who lived in the same building as my grandmother, your mother."

He looked at me blankly, not quite sure what I was talking about.

"A woman," I clarified, "who when younger and lived in Havana, was a neighbor of my grandmother."

"Really?"

"She seemed like a fairly new arrival, maybe been in Miami for seven to ten years, and was dating my backyard neighbor."

"How was she a neighbor of my mother?" He tried to move in his chair, but only managed to shift his posture.

"She said that your mother lived in a bottom floor apartment of an older building on the outskirts of *El Vedado*."

"Belencita's apartment," he said and looked at Gloria with a knowing smile. "She moved there after Belencita died, in the early years of the revolution."

"And Belencita was...?" I asked.

"She was your grandfather's aunt. The sister of Don Manuel, your great grandfather. Your father was very close to Belencita."

I nodded and almost moved the conversation in that tangential direction, but my uncle redirected it back to his mother.

"Well, this woman..." I continued.

"And who is this woman," he interrupted. "What's her name?"

"I don't know. I'm sure she told me, but I've forgotten it. The thing is that she and a group of young women shared an apartment in that building, and they befriended her."

He nodded, waiting for me to continue.

"The woman told me that my grandmother would invite them into her apartment for coffee and pastries. She described the apartment as being fully furnished with elegant antiques, crystal figurines, beautiful art and decorative plates. She said the coffee was always served on the most elegant, porcelain china she had ever seen."

"Oh, I can believe she had never seen elegance like that," my uncle said with a chuckle. "Anything worth a dime in Cuba has either been destroyed by the ignorant brutes of the revolution or confiscated for a general's home."

"Yes. She spent some considerable time describing the fine living my grandmother had."

"*¡Imagínate!*" He slapped my knee twice. "Between Belencita's collection and my mother's fine taste, that woman you met got a glimpse of the elegance I grew up in. Many of those items had history, you know. Your grandmother collected items that belonged to historical people or founding families. Now it's all lost. The state must have taken it all when she died. Those Castro brutes don't know what they have in their possession."

I nodded and looked at him appreciatively.

"Do you know if she lived by herself, or with anyone?" My aunt asked.

"As far as I know, from what the woman said, it sure sounded like she lived alone."

"Hmm... *Sigue*, continue," he said in a way that revealed a reluctance.

"Well, she said that my grandmother regretted what she did. She regretted losing her family and connection with her two boys. It was a lament she spoke of with frequency."

"Hmm..." He said while looking blankly at the wall. "A bit late for regrets, I must say."

I sat in silence while his mind wandered through his memories.

"I tried to talk to her, you know," he said while still staring at the wall. "We were leaving Havana. Castro had militiamen on almost every street, and it was very dangerous. Every time you left your house you didn't know if you were coming back. People were killed in the street, sometimes by accident, sometimes not."

"Like Oscar Jorge," my aunt interjected. She looked at me, knowing I had no clue who she was referring to. "Oscar Jorge was a good friend who died because a *miliciano* shot him."

"In plain daylight? On the street?"

"Oh yes," my uncle said. "An unfortunate death we grieved for many years. In those early days of the revolution, if you needed to go to the store and buy milk you were placing your life at risk. It was common for a *miliciano* to all of the sudden arrest a person on suspicion alone. In the midst of that chaos, I went to see your grandmother. I had to."

He turned to me and his eyes were filling up with tears.

"I said to her, '*Mamá*, you can't stay here. It isn't safe,' but she closed the door and didn't say another word. That's my last memory of her. So, now you tell me she lived long enough to regret it. Well, what can I say? I hope she found some peace."

"Papa described my grandmother as being mentally ill."

"Yes, I think so too. We used to think it was an early menopause, hitting her hard, but now I believe she suffered from a deeper illness."

We sat in silence while his mind browsed through memories.

"She would get these fits and shout the most awful things at your grandfather. You have to understand, back then we didn't have air conditioning. The windows were always open. And when your grandmother would get her fits, the whole neighborhood could hear it. I think she used to say things for the benefit of her family, the Dominguez."

I looked at my aunt for clarification.

"They lived next door," she said to me.

"Right. I remember my father told me their house was built in your yard."

"That's right," he nodded. "Our house sat on a double lot. One of the bigger ones in *La Víbora*. Your grandmother built them a house in that yard, and it was too close. We could hear their conversations and they could hear ours."

"*Bueno*, enough. Come with me," my Aunt Gloria said. "I want to show you something."

"Where are you taking him?" my uncle asked.

"To your study in the basement."

"Oh. Then, I want to go. Help me up," he instructed and reached for my arm.

My uncle's steps were short and labored, but with the help of our hands he made it to the stairwell that led to the basement. An electric chair, installed for his disability, slowly carried his body to the bottom floor, where a room overflowing with memories, books and academic projects awaited us. A desk with an IBM typewriter sat against the wall. Black and white photos from a long-gone era were scattered through the basement, along with faded newspaper clippings and copies of his previously published books.

"Look," my aunt pulled out a photo of men posing in a baseball uniform. "This is the baseball team we told you about."

"That's my father," I pointed out to his image. "And there you are, *Tío*."

"He was so handsome, don't you think?" My aunt said.

"And over there is your brother's godfather, Cristóbal," my uncle pointed.

"He had hair!"I said. I started laughing because I always knew him as a bald man.

"*Ay mijo*, don't laugh too hard. Few are the men who don't lose their hair."

"And what's this?" I lifted a framed photo that was under several others.

"That was taken on your father's wedding day."

It was a picture of my father and uncle together. My uncle was looking straight at the camera, whereas my father was facing in a different direction. It was common for my father to not look at the camera. I'm not sure he would have done well in today's selfie culture.

"It's one of the few pictures I have of us together."

"I've heard stories about that day," I said in a whisper, lost in the image of my father.

They looked at me, waiting for me to clarify.

"My *Abuelo Manolo*. He wasn't allowed to attend his own daughter's wedding."

"No, he wasn't. The poor guy was stuck in a rivalry between Tina and his second wife."

"And then there was the drama with my grandmother Silvia," I said while putting the photo down. "It almost caused the wedding to be postponed."

My uncle looked down and kept silent. It became obvious that my visit and our prolonged conversations depleted his energies. Had it not been for my ability to lift and place him on the electric chair, he would not have ascended the stairwell. As I retreated for the night, and the temperature dropped, my tropical blood called out for warmer fabric. I found a drawer with wool socks and pulled a pair onto my feet. Unable to sleep, I slowly tiptoed to the basement, trying my hardest for the wood to not creak under my feet. There, on the table, was the photo of my uncle and father standing together. I held it, wondering if my father's inability to look at the camera was an early indicator of a future mental state. Sixty-five years later, on that October evening, I held in that photo a story that was seldom told, the genesis of my father's unraveling.

CHAPTER 7

The Alpha of the Omega

1953
Havana, Cuba

He sat straight back in a chair with his eyes closed, visualizing a sunrise over the horizon, inhaling for seven seconds and exhaling for twelve. Slowly counting, he became aware, once again, of an expansion within the timelessness of space, the Divine. A knock on the window pulled him back to reality. Two minutes later, the knock repeated. Time for the mediation to end. He lowered his window.

"It's time," Gabriel, his driver, stood on the other side. He had a pinkish glow.

"There is a time for everything, Gabriel, and a season for every purpose under Heaven."

"Yes, Doctor." He opened the door for him.

"Are you in love, Gabriel?"

"*¿Como?*"

"You're absolutely glowing. Who's the lucky girl?"

Gabriel smiled.

"Treat her right," he said while stepping out of the car. "She's good for you."

Inside the studio of CMQ, the program director was beginning the countdown. Carlos Senior went into the booth and sat in front of the microphone. The journalist looked up at him, smiled, and turned around to talk with a technician. Nearby, a musician played melodic bells to indicate the show was commencing.

"Good morning, this is CMQ, your morning news station. I am Héctor de Soto, and I am here with Dr. Carlos Márquez-Sterling to discuss the events surrounding the attack on the Moncada military headquarters in Santiago."

"*Buenos días,* Héctor," Carlos Senior said with a grave expression.

"Doctor, let's review the facts for our listeners. A few days ago, on the morning of July twenty-six, almost one hundred rebels attacked the military base and were met with the full force of our army. Nineteen rebels were caught and taken to prison on the base where they were tortured and then murdered. One of our sources is a woman who was at the scene, Haydee Santamaria. It is not clear if she was a rebel, but we are told her brother was one."

"That is correct. The news from Moncada is very disturbing."

"Yes, it is. Ms. Santamaria states she was given the eye of her brother by a soldier who claimed the satisfaction of gauging it out."

"Clearly, a sadistic act."

"As of this morning, the remaining rebels are hiding in the city of Santiago while the army conducts an extensive search for them. Doctor, is this act of brutality an isolated event, or is it part of a larger problem in the Batista government?"

"Thank you, Héctor, for granting me the opportunity to speak during this national crisis. How a government responds to wrongdoing is more important than the wrong itself," Carlos Senior spoke into the microphone. "When a government demonstrates the capacity for balanced justice, the people are able to condemn wrongful acts. But if a government responds to evil with evil, and in this case, abhorrent evil, then the initial wrong is argued to have been justified. The manner in which the Batista regime responded to the Moncada attack with sadistic torture and murder, has justified the attack itself, an act of violence that under normal circumstance would be condemned by the Cuban people."

"The national reaction against the army's brutality has been unanimous," the journalist interjected, "but one could argue these rebels forfeited their rights when they attacked the military base."

"Civil and human rights are important at all times," Carlos Senior continued, "for all people under every circumstance, but they are most needed when a person is accused of a crime and apprehended by the authorities. It is when we are in handcuffs and most vulnerable, that the power of the constitution is needed to protect us against the power of the government. General Batista has demonstrated that his totalitarian regime is incapable of respecting the basic human rights granted in our constitution."

"Reports have surfaced that many of these rebels were university students."

"It's very sad, Héctor. I fear I may know a few of those young men from the classroom. The military must be held accountable. God forbid one of our sons should get in trouble with the authorities and have their eyes gouged out."

"So, what is to be done?"

"The rebels, when captured, must be treated fairly and given a trial. That is the way civil society works, not by torturing and murdering people behind closed doors."

"Thank you, Doctor. Our segment has come to an end. You have been listening to Dr. Carlos Márquez-Sterling and I'm Héctor de Soto for CMQ. Please stay tuned as we will continue to report the news from Moncada and the city of Santiago."

Carlos Senior leaned back and looked down, despondent.

"Doctor?"

Carlos Senior looked up as if awoken.

"Do you really think some of the rebels were your students?" The journalist asked.

"Maybe, not sure."

"Like who?"

Carlos Senior shook his head. "I'm afraid you might broadcast it on the radio."

"Doctor, I hold you in the highest esteem, I hope you know I would keep your confidentiality. Whatever you tell me in confidence will remain that way."

"No, I won't risk endangering the wellbeing of a person, especially when Batista has brutes in power. I mean, gouging out eyes! Have you ever heard of anything like that before? It's practically medieval."

Carlos Senior stepped out of the studio doing his best to walk tall, despite the difficult week he was having. Two days earlier, on a Monday morning, he learned about the attack that occurred over the weekend. He approached his son, Carlitos, suspecting his network of activists might be involved. His son offered several names. Fidel was among them.

"How do you know this?" Carlos Senior asked him.

"Several weeks ago they asked me to help them in acquiring guns, ammunition, and local contacts in the region. In other words, they needed me for the logistics."

"And what did you do?"

"I told them to do their own homework and I walked away. Several days later I spoke with Abel and told him it was suicide, but Fidel had brainwashed him already."

"Can you do that, buy ammunition?"

His son looked down and didn't answer.

"What were they thinking, going against an entire military headquarters? It's lunacy."

"Illusions of grandeur."

"What was the goal?"

"Revolution."

"And how do you know these people?" Carlos Senior cross examined. "Have you lost your mind having friends of that sort?"

Carlos smacked his lips, stood in a defiant manner and walked out.

The next morning, Carlos Senior walked into the kitchen as the morning light streamed in through the window. He didn't want to believe his son was connected with rebels. The newspaper, which was on the breakfast table, had the front page story of the attack on Moncada. He looked up to find Silvia leaning against the counter and smoking a cigarette. Her robe was partially undone, exposing a shoulder and the top of her breast. Her hair was disheveled, and her eyes revealed another sleepless night.

"Another bad night?"

She didn't reply nor acknowledge his presence. He stood off to one side, weighing his options. Should he approach his wife, get closer and risk becoming the target of her foul mood, or should he step back and let her slowly fall apart?

"Carmen?" He called for the maid, who was a few steps away.

"¿Si?"

"Please take my wife to her room and either help her get ready for the day or put her back in bed."

Carmen stepped toward Silvia and reached out to fix her robe, only to be met with a threatening look. Carmen retreated.

"I can't deal with you like this." Carlos Senior said. "We've been here before and I know what follows. I'm calling the doctor."

Silvia threw her cigarette in the sink and pulled her robe back in place.

"Call the doctor," she said as she walked out of the kitchen. "Tell him to send his young intern, the one with the broad shoulders. I'd love to have his hands on me."

Carlos Senior rolled his eyes, looked at Carmen, and sat at the breakfast table to read the newspaper. Carmen placed a small glass of orange juice before him.

"I'll have your coffee ready in a minute. Eggs?"

"Yes, scrambled, if you don't mind."

The smell of coffee, the chirping of birds outside the window, and the stillness of an emerging morning, gave Carlos Senior the illusion of peace. He was immersing his consciousness into the printed words be-fore him, when a thunderous crash of furniture reverberated through the house. He ran out to the living room to find Silvia standing victori-ously over a fallen eight-foot-tall bookcase, which had crushed a reading chair, lamp and table beneath it. His son Carlitos stood paralyzed on the opposite side of the living room, staring in disbelief. Manuel rushed out of his room to look down from the top of the stairs.

"This is what I think of us," Silvia screamed at Carlos Senior while her robe slipped off her shoulder. She grabbed a book and threw it in the air. "This is what I think of our marriage." Then she threw another book indiscriminately towards the staircase. "It's what I think of you and your whole academic life."

"How in the world..." Carlos Senior stood in disbelief, surveying the destruction and amazed at the physical strength needed to overturn a bookcase affixed to the wall. From the corner of his eye he saw a book being thrown at him. He ducked, inadvertently exposing Carmen's face to the three-hundred-page volume that knocked her down.

"Grab her," Carlos Senior said to his older son.

Carlitos ran to his mother and wrapped his arms around her in a bear hug as Carlos Senior ran to the front door to call for more help.

"¡Gabriel!"

The driver was already on his way, having heard the ruckus.

"Help him," he ordered Gabriel while Carlitos wrestled his mother down.

"Carmen, are you okay?" Carlos Senior asked as he offered his hand to help her stand. She nodded and joined in the restraining of the mad-woman. Carlos Senior looked up at his younger son, who was immobi-lized at the sight of his mother fighting against six hands.

"Manuel," Carlos Senior called out to him.

His son didn't reply, incapacitated by the shock.

"Manuel!" His father's voice snapped him out of the bewilderment. "Call the doctor!"

"Which one?"

"Dr. Arellano," he said after a short moment of reflection.

As Manuel was running for the upstairs phone, the front door swung open and Bernardo Dominguez and his son, *el Canalla*, rushed in. Carlos Senior turned to face them.

"What is going on here?" Bernardo demanded as he saw his sister, half naked and fully manic, being restrained.

"He helped her," Carmen accused *el Canalla* with a pointed finger. Blood was trickling down her nose. "I saw him here yesterday, helping her undo the hardware of the bookcase."

Carlos Senior looked at his nephew, who shook his head in denial.

"I saw you," Carmen said loudly and with authority.

Silvia stopped struggling to rest her fearful eyes on her brother and nephew. Bernardo looked at his son, demanding an explanation.

"I didn't know she was going to do this," *el Canalla* offered. "I thought she was just going to move furniture around."

"*¡Mentiras!*" Carmen's accusation was full of anger. "You're a liar. I heard you talking."

El Canalla looked at Carmen, dumbfounded, not knowing how to respond.

"Bernardo," Silvia cried as she collapsed on the floor. "Look how they have me. Look how they're treating me."

Carlitos released his mother and ran toward *el Canalla*, who turned and ran out of the house. Not even the annual running of the bulls in Pamplona could match the fury of Carlitos as he ran after his cowardly cousin.

"You need to leave," Carlos Senior said as he stepped toward his brother-in-law.

"Bernardo, don't leave me here," Silvia sobbed.

"What are you going to do to her?"

"You need to leave," Carlos Senior repeated.

Bernardo looked down, turned and left, while Silvia's cries filled the living room.

The rest of the day was dedicated to cleaning the mess, repairing the bookcase, and sedating Silvia. Carlos Senior laid by her side as he watched her sleep. Calls kept coming in from different legislators and leaders, wanting to hear his opinion about the attack on Moncada, but on this day he was not available, and the messages accumulated.

Manuel came down from his studies once the bookcase was secured against the wall. He was placing the books correctly on the shelf when the sound of his mother's railing, accusing his father of withholding love, easily reached his ears. She wasn't going to lower her voice, so his remedy was to drown her out. Carlos Senior was assuring her of his love when Manuel placed the needle on the vinyl record.

"La Traviata," he whispered as his mother's voice quieted. He stood over the phonograph, waiting for the violins to strengthen. His mother's room had grown quiet, so he sat, closed his eyes and immersed himself in the opening piece of the orchestra.

The violin Prelude was ending when the rhythmic thumping began.

"Not again," Manuel complained. He stood and walked angrily to the phonograph to raise the volume, hoping the energetic opening of the first act would take him away. Halfway into the second act, Silvia's unrestrained moans ruined the performance of the tenor, Carlo Bergonzi. This only urged Manuel to raise the volume again, as high as it would go, until the orchestra filled the house with music that could obstruct the sounds of his parents reconciling.

Manuel was in the midst of shedding tears for the agonizing heroine, who was tragically submitting to her death, when the slamming of a door interrupted his dreamlike state. He looked up to see his mother, partially covered by a bed sheet, follow his father down the hall. The softer violin tones, suitable for a grieving audience, allowed the argument to be heard.

"Fine!" she yelled. "Go and make your calls. Maybe I'll find a real man who can satisfy me. Maybe I'll call Gabriel. He looks like the type of man who can finish what you can't."

"Stop it, Silvia!" Carlos Senior was wearing a robe that hadn't been fastened correctly. "¡Ya, basta! Stop with the breaking of furniture and the screaming. Stop all of it."

Silvia turned and marched toward her bedroom while her bedsheet unraveled, unaware her son was below, wide-eyed with amazement. Carlos Senior saw Manuel looking at him and realized he was partially exposed. He turned, closed his robe, and walked toward his study.

"Once again, you and Mamá managed to ruin an opera, "Manuel mumbled as the finale filled the house a minute too late.

Later that afternoon, Carlos Senior reviewed the list of accumulated messages. CMQ wanted an interview. "Of course, they did." Mixed in with the pile of messages, was one from Manolo Gutierrez, Olguita's father. He had concerns about too many wedding details. Obviously, Silvia was creating an event beyond Manolo's financial reach. This one seemed to be the easiest to deal with. He placed it near the phone.

Carmen prepared a small meal for Carlos Senior and quietly set it on the dinner table. She didn't ask if his wife would be joining. The sounds from the neighborhood slipped in through the open windows. He could hear his in-laws having dinner next door, reminding him of the error he committed years earlier when he yielded to Silvia's demand for the additional house on their lot. This error could not be avoided, since Silvia was determined to have her way. At first, he voiced his opposition. She insisted, argued and begged. Day after day, week after week, she claimed she needed her family nearby. He countered it would ruin their privacy and the property, but his points did not matter to her. One day, he came home to find workers cutting down trees and digging a hole for the foundation. She stood, arms crossed, smiling victoriously. He walked away, thinking there must be bigger problems in the world than having to worry about his inlaws.

The Dominguez family was constantly breaking the tenth commandment by coveting everything Carlos Senior acquired. They were the incarnation of envy, and Silvia fed into it. Never mind they didn't have his level of education, career, or success. They moved in as if it was their right to reside in that neighborhood and enjoy the same lifestyle. If Manuel got a new phonograph, Silvia would buy another one for Bernardo. If Carlitos got a new suit, Silvia would get a tailor to make one for her nephew. If Silvia took Olguita shopping, the next day she would take one of her many cousins too.

"This is not a charity," he once told her. "They are not people in need."

"Why can't I give my family the same luxuries I enjoy?"

"Because they haven't earned it!"

"They don't have to earn it. They're my family. I will build them a house if I want to."

Silvia could not keep the boundary asked of her. As her boys grew older, and became aware of the discrepancy, they sided with their father. Feeling outnumbered, she enlisted the help of her brother and nephew to conspire against her husband. The consequence of such deceit led to the inevitable rift in their marriage.

"Manolo?" Carlos Senior asked into the phone.

"*Sí*. Doctor, thank you for returning the call."

"Manolo, we're going to be family. Please call me Carlos. Now, you called earlier today about the wedding and certain details?"

"Yes... Carlos. I hope you don't mind, but your wife has a particular vision for the wedding and reception that doesn't quite fit with what we have in mind. She keeps asking for an event that is... grand."

"I'm sorry. Silvia gets carried away. Why don't you make a list of what you want to keep in the wedding, and the rest we can forget about. And then, send me the invoice and I'll make sure it gets paid."

There was a momentary silence.

"Manolo, are you there?"

"Yes. Yes. I think you misunderstood me. I'm not calling to ask you for money. What I'm calling about... Do you mind if I speak bluntly, Carlos?"

"Please. We don't have time for anything else."

"I'd like for the wedding to be more familial and less regal. We all want to enjoy the ceremony and its reception without feeling that we're dining with the Queen of Spain."

Carlos Senior laughed wholeheartedly into the phone. Manolo chuckled.

"Of course!" Carlos Senior said with joy. "Nothing would give me more pleasure. Please, pay no attention to Silvia. What matters is that our children are getting married. We're all delighted with Olguita. I already consider her to be the daughter I never had."

"And we really enjoy Carlitos," Manolo replied.

"So, it is agreed. The wedding ceremony and reception will be as you and Tina design. We are your guests. And if Silvia contacts you again, please let me know and I'll handle her."

Carlos Senior hung up the phone with a smile on his face. He turned to find Silvia standing at the threshold with a furious look. She silently returned to her room.

******

"She's the closest thing I have to a grandmother," Carlitos said as he walked arm in arm with Olga. "Officially, she's my grandaunt, but since I never met my father's mother, Belencita is my *abuela*."

Belencita's apartment was in the upscale neighborhood of *El Vedado*, just a few minutes away from Carlitos' home. The sidewalks were wide and lined with large trees, providing a nice shade that cooled the breeze. The engaged couple walked, holding hands and dreaming of a life together in one of the beautiful homes of that neighborhood.

"I have to confess, Carlitos, the last time we were here I wasn't sure if I should call her Belen or Belencita. So, I avoided using her name."

"Yeah, I noticed."

"You did?"

"You were too formal."

"You didn't say anything to help me."

He chuckled.

"So, what do I call her?"

"Belencita, of course, but if you prefer, ask for permission. She's almost eighty years old, and I'm sure she won't mind some familiarity with you."

"I can tell you really love her."

"I do, but more than that, the woman is fascinating. She's a human bridge to the days when Cuba was only dreaming of becoming a free republic."

"The War of Independence?"

Carlitos nodded. He released his hand from Olga's to allow a young couple, each pushing a stroller, to pass by. Olga approached the strollers with a smile and asked to peek inside them.

"Twins?" she asked.

The couple paused amicably to allow Olga to fawn over their infants. Carlitos stood to the side, enjoying her attempts to get the babies to smile. When the family continued on their walk, she looked at them longingly.

"Can you see us like that?" she asked her fiancée.

"Of course. I think it's every couple's dream."

Olga took his hand and turned in the direction they were walking. It wasn't much later when they reached the door of the matriarch's apartment.

"*¡Ola!*" The door opened wide and Sabela, Belencita's caretaker, greeted them in a thick Galician accent. "I saw you from the window, walking together. *¡Tan guapos!* Such a handsome couple!"

Inside, the walls were adorned with paintings and family photos. Belencita, a small and frail woman with gray hair styled in short curls, allowed her guests to admire the artwork, as she provided detailed explanations.

"As I'm sure Carlitos has told you," Belencita said. "Our ancestors came from Spain towards the end of the 18th century and settled in Camagüey. Have you been to Camagüey?"

"No, I haven't. Not yet."

"Carlitos, you have to take her. It's a beautiful country with rich lands full of prize-winning cattle and horses."

Carlitos nodded.

"Our family flourished in Camagüey."

"They had cattle?"

"Cattle? *No, mi niña*," she chuckled. "They were lawyers and business entrepreneurs. Although we certainly had a lot of connections with *ganaderos*, we didn't own cattle farms. It was in Camagüey where Don Manuel Márquez-Sterling, my father, was a supporter of the patriots who fought in the first war. The ten-year war."

"1868 to 1878," Olga said, showing off her knowledge of Cuban history.

Belencita nodded and continued to slowly walk to the living room.

"*Ven* Olguita.. Let's sit by the window while Sabela makes the coffee."

Olga followed her to a cluster of Louis XV armchairs that circled a small and very ornate table. Carlitos chose to sit at the sofa, silently observing the exchange, while Sabela brewed coffee in the kitchen.

"You studied Ignacio Agramonte?" Belencita asked Olga.

"Of course. It's required reading. He was such a ..."

Belencita waited for Olga to complete her sentence.

"... giant of a man. A great soldier, leader, but also an intellectual."

"Yes, very good."

Olga smiled, relieved she passed that test.

"Well, let me tell you a little story that you didn't learn in the history books."

Olga looked at Carlitos with giggly anticipation as he waved her on with a smile.

"Oh, this is perfect. I love stories."

"Did you know that my father, Carlitos' great grandfather, was a close friend of Agramonte?"

"No! Really? What was that like?"

"Well, I suspect it was like most friendships."

Sabela stepped into the living room with a silver tray and four coffee cups. She served each person and then took the final cup for herself.

"*Gracias*, Sabela. One last thing, if I could be an inconvenience," Belencita said.

"*¡Hombre!*" She replied in a thick Galician accent. "There's no inconvenience."

"Get me the silver and red box from over there," she pointed at a glass cabinet that stood against the corner and was filled with crystal figurines and porcelain crafts.

The box was carefully delivered and placed on the table between the two women. The younger one looked at it with childlike anticipation. The older one moved it aside, aware of the suspense she was creating.

"A few years before I was born, my father, Don Manuel, went bar hopping with his good friend, Ignacio Agramonte."

"Where?" Olga asked.

"Oh, this had to be in Camagüey, which back then must have been a small town. The way my father described that evening to me, Agramonte was eager to enjoy the finer pleasures available at those establishments."

"Oh my!" Olga said in shock.

"What's the matter?"

"Well, it's just that you're talking about Agramonte. Are we allowed to say such things?"

"You're so cute," Belencita laughed. "I didn't mean to imply anything improper, other than two men doing a lot of drinking, singing and dancing on that night."

"Oh, okay. That's better. I'm sorry."

"Now that we've cleared up what kind of a night it was, let me get on with the story.

At one point, late in the night, Agramonte confessed to my father that he received a premonition that he would suffer an early and untimely death."

"*¡Ay, Dios mío*! That doesn't sound good."

"I know. My father tried to talk him out of such notions, but Agramonte was convinced."

"Well, it's an easy premonition to have when you're leading a war." Belencita nodded.

"And that's when Agramonte gave his good friend a gift."

"Which good friend?"

"My father."

"Oh. What was the gift?"

"A diamond studded tie clip."

"Diamonds?"

"Yes."

"How many?"

"Five."

"Five diamonds on a tie clip? That must have been worth a fortune!"

"Especially in those days. At first my father did not want to accept the gift, but Agramonte insisted. They finally reached an accord. Should Agramonte survive the war, my father would return the gift."

"But he didn't."

"I know."

"So, what happened?"

Belencita reached over to the box. Her wrinkled hands trembled as she held it in front of Olga, offering it.

"Go ahead, open it."

Olga's eyes widened as she opened the box to reveal the diamond studded tie clip. She looked up at Belencita, who was smiling. She then turned to look at her fiancée, who also was smiling. Olga lowered the box, afraid she might drop it.

"I think you should have it."

"Me? But it's a tie clip. Shouldn't Carlitos have it and use it for his ties?"

"It would make a beautiful cross for your wedding day."

"A cross?"

"Easily done with the right jeweler."

Olga nodded, agreeing Belencita's idea sounded pretty good.

"It's been eighty years since that fateful night. My father never felt comfortable wearing it. I have only a few years left to live, and I think it would be best if you accepted it."

"*Niña*," Sabela said loudly. "Don't be afraid. Go ahead and take it. It's yours."

Olga laughed nervously, but still refused to accept the gift.

"I don't know. This is a family heirloom." Olga said to Carlitos, who sat quietly, fully enjoying the moment.

"I don't want to offend anyone," Olga continued, "but I think I should ask your father if it's okay. After all, he does wear ties, and maybe he was looking forward to this inheritance."

Belencita agreed, knowing her nephew would want Olga to have the gift.

"And how is your mother?" The matriarch asked Carlitos, who was taking out a cigarette from his shirt pocket.

He looked down and lit the cigarette. Sabela stood and placed an ashtray in front of him. Belencita waited for her nephew to reply.

"I think you know the answer to that question," he said as he exhaled smoke.

"I have an answer, but not yours."

"What can I say? Things are worse than I can describe. To give you a clue, I'm never home and Manuel plays his operas as loud as he can."

"That bad?"

"It's a torment. Bernardo and *el Canalla* are just ten feet away, scheming ways to influence her against us. In the meantime, the woman I knew as my mother... the woman I knew as my mother has become unrecognizable."

"Come here," Belencita called him.

Carlitos placed the cigarette in the ashtray and sat beside her. She took his thick, wide hand and cupped it in hers. Her frail, diminutive frame contrasted against his strength and size. No words were spoken as she leaned toward her grandnephew, who bowed, allowing her to kiss his forehead. Olga's eyes teared as she witnessed the intimate moment.

They left the apartment with peace in their heart. Olga had not seen her fiancée so serene in a long while. She reached for his hand as they walked and pulled him close. The birds chirped, a breeze cooled the back of their necks, and Carlitos knew he held the woman who would make his life right.

"Do you know what we should do?" Carlitos asked, though he didn't wait for a response. "We should go out tonight, with the group, and enjoy the best Havana has to offer."

Olga giggled and skipped like the teenage girl she was. Carlitos soaked in her genuine effervescence, a refreshing contrast to the other women in his life.

*****

When Olga stepped into the Tropicana Night Club with Carlitos and their friends, she was in a constant state of awe. The tall concrete arches lined by glass paned walls, palm trees illuminated by hidden lights, and beautiful dancers adorned in festive costumes created an illusion of divine splendor.

"Where are we sitting?" Cristóbal shouted over the brass sounds of a fourteen-member band playing rhythmic music. His wife, Marisa, was by his side.

They followed the hostess, a young woman dressed provocatively in a tight outfit, to their reserved table not far from the stage in the open-air room. Circular tables were positioned in curved patterns so the guests, all dressed in formal attire, could have an uninterrupted view of the show. Uniformed servers, carrying trays of drink and food, walked between the smoke-filled aisles, while seated spectators marveled at choreographed dancers, dressed in revealing feathered costumes, moving in sync with the seductive rhythm.

Oscar Jorge was pulling a chair for his wife, Matty, as he quietly laughed to himself.

"What?" Cristóbal asked after seeing the amusement in his face.

"I'm just thinking about what would happen if a strong breeze comes through and those feathers blow away. Would they keep on dancing?"

As the night progressed, laughter was the cup they drank from. Carlitos had the loudest guffaw, often compelling other guests to turn and see what was so funny. Eventually, a romantic song from a crooning musician pulled them to the dance floor. Carlitos knew enough dance steps to gracefully hold his fiancée. When faster paced music began, however, he quickly led her back to the table.

"Can't we dance some more?" Olga begged.

"Maybe later."

Olga looked at the dance floor as Cristóbal and Marisa maneuvered through dozens of dancing couples. Oscar Jorge was also at the table, eager to move with the intoxicating sounds.

"May I?" He asked Carlitos for permission as he extended his arm out to Olga.

"By all means," Carlitos replied.

Olga jumped out of her seat and accepted the offer. Carlitos and Matty sat at the vacated table, watching their partners dance with each other. Oscar Jorge was not only tall and athletic, but also an enviable dancer. It seemed that Olga looked at him with dazzled eyes as he spun her around and held her close in his arms. Matty tried to make conversation with Carlitos, but he smacked his lips and stood up abruptly.

"I'm going to the casino," he walked away, leaving her alone at the table.

The dance music became faint once he walked past the casino doors. Slot machine bells announced meager prizes to addicted gamblers, and dealers kept card players focused on their hand. Carlitos bought a few chips and found his way to the roulette table, where the call of a spinning wheel lit up his eyes. He studied the players around him and discreetly placed a chip on the dozen group of 13 to 24.

"That's a conservative bet," a voice behind him stated.

Carlitos turned to see a tall American man wearing a tuxedo and holding a cigarette.

"I would think a man of your position could risk a bit more," the American said.

"I'm just getting warmed up," Carlitos replied and turned to look at the fellow gamblers reaching over to place their bets.

"No more bets," the croupier called and spun the ball in the wheel.

The suspense kept thirsty players from uttering any words as the ball bounced around.

"Nineteen RED," the croupier announced and placed a reward next to Carlitos' chip.

"Congratulations, Doctor," the American said. "Cigarette?" He tipped his pack toward Carlitos, who looked at it with suspicion.

"No thanks, I have my own." Carlitos placed his winnings on black and kept his first chip on the dozen block of 13 to 24.

The American placed two chips: one on red and another on the dozen block of 1 to 12. He then turned to Carlitos and winked at him. "Let's see who's luckier."

"No more bets!" The croupier spun the wheel while Carlitos took out a cigarette and lit it.

"Fifteen BLACK," the croupier announced and tossed chips toward Carlitos.

Carlitos turned to look at the American who was smiling.

"You win some, you lose some."

"I doubt you ever lose," Carlitos replied.

"Robert Brown," the American said to Carlitos, while extending his hand to shake.

"I know who you are."

"And I know you."

"You must be enjoying the freedom Batista is giving you."

"Don't be so jealous of my relationship with the President." Brown exhaled cigarette smoke. "Afterall, we all benefit from this freedom. Go ahead, venture into other parts of the board. Let's see if your luck will hold."

Carlitos took his winnings and his first chip to place them on the third row, where the winnings are double, two to one. Brown placed his chip on the second row and winked at Carlitos once again. The croupier stopped the players from betting and spun the wheel.

"Thirty RED," the croupier called and rewarded Carlitos with his winnings.

Carlitos could not hide his satisfaction as he collected his chips and Olga came up behind him with their friends. Brown smiled at her and stepped back to make room at the table.

"*Señorita*," Brown extended his hand to her.

"Do I know you?" Olga asked. "You look familiar."

"I don't think we've had the pleasure." He shook her hand gently. "Can I get you and your friends a drink? On the house."

"*Gordo*," Cristóbal smiled at the stack of chips. "Looks like you're winning."

Cristóbal and Marisa stepped closer and nodded at Brown's offer.

"May I recommend an Alexander for the ladies?" Brown suggested.

Oscar Jorge approached the table with Matty.

"What is that?" Olga asked.

"It's very delicious. Brandy with cocoa. I think you'll like it."

"Very generous of you," Oscar Jorge said. "Are you the manager?"

"More of a silent partner," he said with a smile as he called the waitress over.

"Bring the ladies here an Alexander," Brown said to the waitress, "and the men a Rum Punch." Brown then looked at someone across the way. "I must go now. I have to tend to another guest. Please enjoy yourselves."

"Can I play?" Olga asked excitedly.

Carlos gave her a chip as he watched Brown cross the room toward a guest.

"Do you know who that is?" Cristóbal whispered to Oscar Jorge and Carlitos.

"Of course. He's mafia." Carlitos answered.

"Yes, I know the *Americano* is mafia. I'm asking about the man he's talking to."

Carlitos looked at the man Brown approached. He had a military haircut, broad shoulders and a commanding presence.

"I placed the chip on twenty-two, Carlitos." Olga exclaimed with excitement. "Marisa, place a chip on your favorite number."

"Isn't that Orlando Piedra?" Carlitos said. "Yes, baby," he turned to Olga. "Twenty-two sounds like a good bet, and place one on RED for me."

"Batista's Golden Boy," Cristóbal said. "That's why *el Americano* went to kiss his ass."

Olga placed a chip on RED seconds before the croupier called for all bets to halt.

"I heard he's the one who ordered the gruesome acts of torture on the Moncada rebels." Carlitos commented.

"Ooh!" Oscar Jorge exclaimed. "Every time I think about the gouging of eyes!"

"Twelve, RED." The croupier announced and collected the placed chips. He tossed a winning chip to Olga, who bounced with glee.

The drinks arrived and the group of friends continued to play roulette and slot machines, each with varying degrees of luck. By the end of the night, Carlitos figured they lost more often than won, easily paying for Brown's generous tray of drinks.

******

Something snapped inside Silvia when she heard Belencita had given the historic tie clip to Olga. A quiet rage grew from feelings of betrayal and futility, preventing her from sleeping that evening. She was up before the neighborhood roosters, smoking cigarettes and wandering aimlessly through the house. Her family awoke and went about their morning business without acknowledging her pain. She wanted to scream and cry, but Carlos Senior barely looked at her as he prepared for an interview at CMQ that morning.

"You may want to hear it," he said to her.

"Hear what?" she replied.

"The interview at CMQ."

"Why?"

"I'll be speaking about the raid on the Moncada military base and Batista."

"Hmm," she muttered while inhaling from her cigarette. "Do you think I care?"

"I guess not," he replied and walked out.

Carmen had the radio on while Silvia sat in the kitchen, immobile. She stared at the woman cleaning her kitchen, who raised the volume when the interview began.

"... How a government responds to wrongdoing is more important than the wrong itself." Carlos Senior's voice filled the kitchen.

"*El señor* Carlos," Carmen said. " I just love how he speaks."

Silvia didn't acknowledge the comment, not because she didn't hear it, but rather because she was contemplating a new reality. As Carmen cleaned, and the voices on the radio filled the room, Silvia realized she hated her life and despised her husband. Furthermore, this hate was the culprit of her misery. Silvia came to terms with the growing realization that she needed to leave, or else she would end up hating herself too. She slowly moved her body upstairs, removing her clothing and leaving a trail of garments for Carmen to pick up. In her bedroom, the mirror revealed an image that contrasted against the woman she thought she was. Staring back at her was a bedraggled woman who used to be beautiful, happy and loved, but was now hollow and misshapen. It was at that moment when she began to plan her exit.

In the weeks that followed she scheduled with her nephew the day and time to leave her husband. They devised a plan and coordinated the assistance she required. The day finally arrived. On a breezy October morning she joyfully executed her plan.

"Carmen," she called out repeatedly from her bedroom.

"*¿Sí, señora?*" Carmen answered as Silvia stood in front of the mirror applying layers of bright red lipstick.

"You're fired," Silvia said calmly. "Pack your things and leave. I never want to see you in this house, or anywhere near it."

Carmen stood paralyzed, open mouthed. Silvia glanced at her and smiled.

"You heard me," Silvia continued applying lipstick. "Get out."

"El *señor* Carlos said that..."

"Get out!" Silvia screamed and streaked her cheek with lipstick. She stepped toward Carmen, waving her hands and repeatedly screaming, "Get out!"

Carmen ran out of the house, only to be followed by Silvia, who was determined to slam the door behind the retreating servant.

"Bernardito?" Silvia asked into the phone.

"Yes?" replied *el Canalla*.

"It's time."

Thirty minutes later, *el Canalla* knocked at her door with two other friends. Silvia was dressed in her finest black gown and high heeled shoes. The lipstick, however, was still smeared on her cheek.

"Whatever I point to, you will take and carry to your house."

The three men nodded.

Silvia walked around the house pointing at items: the silver candlesticks, the Portuguese pottery, the El Greco painting, this chair, that chair, this lamp, that silver set, the coffee table, end table, library table, Moroccan rug, phonograph, all her clothes, several outfits her boys never wore, the silverware, dishes, and three copper pans. Silvia stood at the front door of the house, smiling with satisfaction.

"If only I could be here to see the look on their faces," she said.

"Anything else?" the men asked.

"For your payment, go to the bar and the refrigerator and take as much as you can carry. It's all yours."

The men happily raided the well-stocked home, leaving it devoid of any supplies.

Carlos Senior was leaving the University of Havana after teaching two classes when Manuel ran frantically to him.

"What's wrong?"

"I came home, and it's all gone."

"What are you talking about?"

"Everything. It's all gone. I thought we had been robbed, but then I saw Mom over at Bernardo's home. She was laughing."

Carlos Senior stood silent, unsure what his son was saying.

"It was mom. She emptied out the house."

They walked hurriedly to where Gabriel was waiting with the car. By the time they reached the house, Carlitos was standing in the living room in a state of shock.

"We've been robbed, and I can't find Mamá," Carlitos said.

"No," Manuel explained. "Mamá is the one who did this. She's next door."

The sun was setting as they slowly realized what happened. Carlitos recalled the different times when his mother, with a strange smirk, asked him silly questions.

"She's been planning this for several weeks," Carlitos said to his father and brother.

They stood still, waiting for him to continue.

"About a week ago, I was here, reading in the chair that was next to the lamp, when Mamá asked me, 'Do you like the chair you're sitting on?' And I just looked at her, not sure what she was asking. So, she asked again, 'The chair, do you like it?' And I said something like, 'Well, yes. I like it. Why do you ask?' And she just smiled and quietly said, 'Just wondering.'"

Carlos Senior and Manuel had similar recollections.

They stepped into the emptied kitchen, amazed at how thorough she had been.

"Call Carmen," Carlos Senior said to Manuel. Find out what she knows. Maybe she was here when it occurred.

The sounds of opera music being played on a phonograph came in through the open window.

"No!" Manuel protested and ran to the library. They followed him, alarmed. "She took my phonograph and several records from my opera collection." He was running his fingers through the records. "I'm missing about... about... a third. How could she?"

The three men walked into the kitchen, slowly seething. Carlitos was smacking his lips. Manuel kept asking the same question, "How could she?"

The voices of Bernardo and Silvia floated in through the open window. Carlos Senior and his sons leaned in toward the window, aware they were listening to something meant to be overheard.

"Lower that music," Bernardo ordered his sister. "How can you stand that opera? It doesn't even have a beat."

"I know. Imagine having it played every day, sometimes at full volume, and you have to pretend you enjoy it," Silvia replied.

Manuel looked at his father with injured eyes.

"I'm so glad to be out of that house. They didn't care for me. I was another piece of artwork, a perfect hostess for Carlos to use in his fancy dinners."

"Really? You seemed to enjoy that fancy life."

The sound of a vinyl record getting scratched by the needle interrupted their dialogue. Manuel jumped instinctively, wanting to see if there was any damage to his record.

"Enough of that," *el Canalla* said. "I have here another record I found. *Oigan esto*. Nat King Cole."

Once again, the needle of the phonograph made a scratching sound as it was roughly placed on the vinyl record. The melodic voice of Nat King Cole singing "Pretend."

"That's your record," Manuel said to Carlitos, who was smacking his lips.

They leaned in toward the window and looked across the way to see Silvia and several others seated in a living room cluttered with their belongings.

"Well, I do have to admit that being married to that man had its benefits," Silvia said while somebody lit her a cigarette. "I did get to buy all this, and I'll end up with the house too. You'll see. By the time I'm finished with him, Carlos will be sleeping on his office couch." Silvia laughed. "And I think I'll start dating a few men. I know a few *Batistianos*, Batista supporters, who have money."

"I don't know, Silvia. Carlos Márquez-Sterling is well connected."

"That's all he is. Believe me, if it weren't for his connections, he couldn't even be a court stenographer."

Several people laughed, including the Scoundrel, who had a very distinct laugh. Silvia was delivering a monologue to an audience that egged her on. She paused to inhale from a cigarette. Its smoke filtered through the kitchen window.

"The man can't even satisfy me," she continued. "We can be doing it all day and I'll be left just as hungry as when we started."

"You don't say," Bernardo's wife said, clearly wanting to hear more.

"Oh yes! I can barely wait for the divorce so I can find myself a real man, someone who knows what to do in bed. Maybe Bernardito can introduce me to a few of his friends."

Laughter resonated through that home. Carlitos and Manuel could not look up, ashamed of what they were hearing.

"How much money do you think I'll get for that silver coffee set?" *el Canalla* asked.

Carlitos turned toward his father indignantly.

"Belencita gave us that coffee set," Carlos Senior said to his son.

"You may want to keep it," Silvia replied. "Consider it one of my wedding gifts to you."

"His wedding gift?" Carlitos asked with surprise and looked at his father, who seemed to be just as surprised.

"Your bride should have the best of everything, so take your pick."

"I can barely wait," the Scoundrel said, his voice laced with glee. "for my cousin to find out that my wedding will be larger and grander than his."

"And on the very next day," Bernardo, his father, commented.

"*¡Que carajo!* He's getting married a day after you?" Manuel asked his brother.

"I can't listen to any more of this," Carlos Senior said to his sons while pacing the floor.

"Me neither," Manuel said. "I'm going to my room and covering my ears."

Carlitos stood still, fuming with anger. The sounds of laughter continued to flow in through the window.

"*Vamos*, get away from that window," Manuel said.

"Let's go over there and bust them up," Carlitos said quietly.

Carlos Senior stopped pacing as he considered the proposal.

"Let's end this," Carlitos said with clenched fists, "and give them what they deserve."

They stood silent as Carlitos smacked his lips and declared, "Tonight it ends."

"Agreed," his father replied. "Let's end this now."

Carlitos, invigorated with a new purpose, went to the back of the house while his father reached into the bookcase, knocking the books down.

"What are you talking about?" Manuel asked fearfully.

"It has to be here," Carlos Senior said as he searched behind the books.

"What?"

"My gun."

Carlitos returned to the living room with two wooden bats.

"Let's go beat the shit out of them," he said and gave one bat to Manuel.

Carlos Senior found the gun behind a book, checked to see if it was loaded and tucked it into his belt. Manuel stood with the bat in his hand, petrified.

"You can't be serious!" Manuel protested while awkwardly holding the bat.

Carlos Senior took the bat from Manuel and nodded at his older son. They marched out the front door, turned left, and, after twenty deliberate steps, were standing at the front door of Bernardo's residence. Manuel sheepishly followed. The sound of Nat King Cole singing could be heard through the door, as well as Silvia's laughter.

Carlitos was about to turn the doorknob when his father stopped him.

"This is our house," he said. "Not theirs. We paid for every inch. Remember that."

"Wait! Think about what you're going to do," Manuel implored.

Carlitos and his father stepped back and in unison kicked the door open.

They rushed in like maddened rioters, swinging their bats, breaking everything in view. Carlitos, with the force of a vengeful baseball player, smashed pottery, vases, glass tables and even the phonograph playing his Nat King Cole album. Manuel followed, unsure of what to do. He saw his mother scream in horror as her husband splintered the furniture.

Bernardo attacked Carlos Senior who managed to respond with a swing of the bat across the man's torso, knocking him down. The Scoundrel ran to defend his father. In the struggle the bat was thrown through the window, smashing it. That's when Carlos Senior took out his gun and began firing. He fired at every member of that family as they ducked and ran for cover.

Carlitos, who had just broken through several glass ornaments, threw his bat down and began to struggle with his father for the gun. This gave *el Canalla* and Bernardo the opportunity to charge at them together. Manuel was horrified at the spectacle before him: His mother screaming for help, his father exchanging punches with Bernardo, and his brother wrestling their cousin while yelling insults. Although in a state of shock and paralyzed by fear, Manuel managed to make eye contact with his mother. She did not ask for help. Instead, she hid behind the sofa as another shot was fired that ricocheted through the house.

Minutes later, the police arrived to break up the fight. Silvia screamed accusations that echoed through the neighborhood. Bernardo and his son had to be taken to the hospital, while Carlitos and his father stood in the front yard before police officers. The moon was nearly full, hiding behind clouds. Their rage ebbed and the reality of what transpired began to sink in. Manuel was nowhere to be found. The young police officer kept asking questions, but Carlitos kept his eye on a distant figure, hiding in the shadows.

"You will have to go to the station with me," the officer said.

Carlitos did not respond. He kept looking at the distant figure as the moonlight began to shine through the clouds.

"I need you to get inside the vehicle," the officer repeated.

Carlitos nodded and did as told. He moved to the far door, making room for his father, but also to better see the person who moved behind the shadow. It wasn't until the police car drove away that *el Caballero de París* stepped out into the light. His unruly hair and black coat glistened under the moonlight. He waved at Carlitos, who stared blankly out the window.

******

"Today is the anniversary of the debacle," my mother said in a matter-of-fact tone of voice. I looked at her, unsure of what she meant.

"It was on a day like today, October first, just weeks before I was to get married."

"Oh, you're referring to the day when Papa and *Abuelo* went to kick their cousin's ass?"

"Such a proper man, *tan medido*, and always was in control of every word. I couldn't believe *el Viejo Márquez* tried to kill his wife."

We were sitting under the shade of my oak trees in St. Petersburg, as my mother waded through her memories.

"I had to go with your father to see the damage with my own eyes. To think that *el Viejo Márquez* would shoot a gun! No, no, no, no, no."

"Where were they, the Dominguez family?"

"What do you mean?"

"When you went to see the house and the damage, were they in the house?"

"No. They all left. Well, now that I think about it, Bernardo's wife was there. Yes, because she and your father got into an argument."

I sat silent, trying to imagine the scene.

"You're not going to trim those branches, are you?"

"No mom, I'm not. I like my tree the way it is."

"*Bueno*, one day it'll be too late, those branches will fall on your roof and you'll remember me. But you can feel good about keeping them, because they look pretty."

"So, where did they go?"

"Who?"

"The Dominguez family. My grandmother. What happened to their house?"

"It was sold as part of the divorce settlement. I remember the people who moved in, a nice Jewish family who had a daughter Manolín's age. I tried to get Manolín to go out with her, but he wasn't interested. You know, there were a lot of Jewish people in Cuba who came after the war. My good friend Franny escaped from Nazi Germany and was in a ship that the U.S. turned around. *Los Americanos* wouldn't let them in. Can you believe that?"

"Yes, I know," I answered. "There was a lot of anti-Semitism in that time."

"Luckily, the ship came to Cuba."

"Mom, that's nice, but circle back to my grandmother. Tell me, after the fight, did she and my father ever talk again? Did they try to reconcile?"

"*Ay* Guille, you're asking me things I don't really remember. I wasn't paying attention. The wedding was five weeks away, and your father wanted me to postpone the ceremony, but I was determined to get married. My own father told me I shouldn't go through with it. He thought it was a mistake, so did other people in the family, but nobody could convince me."

"Hmm... how sad. So, on the day of your wedding, was she there?"

"Silvia? No. She didn't come. That week of the wedding, I was waiting at the bus stop with the wedding dress in my hand, and I saw her drive by. Gabriel, the driver, was pulling over to give me a ride, and I saw her wave him on, telling him to leave me there. I was dumbfounded. Can you imagine that?"

"Who was the *madrina* in the wedding?"

"Lolita, your father's aunt."

"*Abuelo's* sister?"

"Yes. She was married to a really nice man. I can't remember his name now."

"And your father, who should have been the *padrino*, wasn't at the wedding either. So, who walked you down the aisle?"

"*El Viejo Márquez* walked me in. Yes, we were... what's that word?"

"Dysfunctional?"

"Yes, that's it." My mother laughed. "Dysfunctional." She laughed again but stifled it when I didn't join her. "You know, that word didn't exist back then. Nobody classified anything as dysfunctional. But if there ever was a dysfunctional wedding it certainly was mine, and it was partly my fault. I should have postponed the wedding and given the family a chance to make amends. Maybe my father would have been able to walk me down the aisle, but the invitations had gone out and everything was ready."

"It must have been difficult for Papa."

"What?"

"The wedding, Mama. We're talking about the wedding," I replied impatiently.

"*Ay, mijo.* Don't get like that. Yes, you're right. It was hard on your father. He was in a daze. Weeks later, when we were looking at the wedding photos, I noticed that he never looked at the camera. Everybody in the photo is looking at the camera except your father. And I asked him why he was always looking away. Do you know what he told me?"

"No."

"He was looking for his mother. He thought he had seen her in the crowd."

"Could she have been there?"

"Of course not. That woman was so stubborn. I never understood her. *Ay*, Guille, my heart broke at that moment because I realized I should have listened to him."

We kept silent the rest of that afternoon. The realization of my father's state of mind on his wedding day weighed heavy on us. It took an episode of "Two and a Half Men" to lift us from our mood. Several days later, over breakfast, my mother continued the conversation.

"Your grandmother Silvia wasn't well, you know," she said while biting into a buttered piece of Cuban bread.

"I've been told," I replied from the other end of the dining table.

"And you know, those illnesses are hereditary."

"Are you saying I'm a bit crazy?" I joked.

"No, *mijo.* Stop playing around. I'm saying I think your father suffered from it too."

"Well, Papa definitely had issues. He was a different sort of man, who became bitter, but I don't know if that qualifies him as mentally ill."

"I think the night of the fight was the start of many of his problems. It was also the end of..." She trailed off as she sipped her coffee. "... the end of a relationship with his mother. Maybe they both suffered from something. Who knows."

She paused the conversation while she chewed.

"I always think about how his second wife, Mariana, also lost her mind," she said while spreading Apricot jam on the bread. "You know, there's too much coincidence there. It makes me wonder what kind of karma... Is that the word, karma?"

"Yes, karma is the word."

"So, yes. I wonder what kind of karma your father carried."

"Look at you!" I said jokingly. "The devout Catholic using words like 'karma.' I'm going to tell the priest you've been venturing into Eastern philosophy."

"*Ay*, Guille," she chuckled. "*Deja eso.* I've read about karma. I've heard people talk about it. Why not? Don't you think it's possible?"

"Oh, I think it's very possible. I'm just surprised you think so too."

"So, how does karma work? Does it explain why some people suffer injustice? I'm thinking of the people who died at no fault of their own. Is that karma?"

"Mom, according to what I've read, karma is ..."

"Like my good friend Oscar Jorge," she interrupted. "He was killed in the early days of the revolution. A young *miliciano* shot him by mistake. Oscar Jorge died there on the spot. *Ay*, Guille, that was the worst. I thought I was going to die of a broken heart. He was such a good man, so handsome and funny, and his wife had just given birth to their son. Is it karma, what happened to him?"

"I can't say for sure. What I understand about karma is that the militia man who killed your friend developed bad karma at that moment."

"But he didn't mean to kill him. That's what was strange. It was an accident."

"Yeah," I said, shaking my head. "But somebody died because he chose to carry a gun on that day. That death could have been avoided had he not been walking with a loaded rifle. It's as if I were to walk around with an open can of paint, and then call the paint drippings an accident. Do you know what I mean?"

My mother looked at me, truly interested in what I was saying. She had spent a lifetime trying to make sense of her friend's death.

"If I join the militia and I carry a rifle," I continued, "I have to as-sume that at one point or another I will use that weapon to end some-body's life. It's a different karma from the person who decides to be a nurse and carries a stethoscope. That *miliciano* probably spent the rest of his life making up for his bad choice, and according to Eastern theol-ogy, in the next life too."

My mother looked down. I could see the grief, decades old, swelling in her eyes.

"What about..." My mother spoke slowly as she discerned which words to use. "Is there karma for an entire nation, for an island like Cuba? Could it be what we have been living through, as Cubans, is bad karma at a bigger scale?"

"That's one hell of a question, Mama, one hell of a question. It sure would explain a lot of things." We sat in silence for a minute, and then in an effort to pull her out of the sadness she fell into I asked, "How about an episode of 'Two and Half Men?' "

"No, I don't think so. I think I just want to sit here."

I walked to my room to respect the need for silence. We both needed to contemplate questions that have no answer.

CHAPTER 8

Dreamers

1 956
Havana, Cuba

It was a breezy, summer afternoon. A tropical storm was brewing in the Caribbean and the palm trees yielded to its winds. Carlos Senior came down the stairs of his home, wearing a white linen suit, his hair perfectly slicked back, and his face glistening from a splash of cologne. Downstairs were his two sons and his daughter-in-law, debating which name was better suited for the brand new puppy that graced their home.

"He looks like a fuzzy elf," Olga said while holding the 12 week-old puppy in her arms. "I think we should name him Jolly."

"Jolly? That's silly," Carlitos responded with a chuckle. "Imagine yourself calling out for the dog. Are you really going to yell 'Jolly' out in the street for everyone to hear?"

The puppy, as if comprehending the conversation, raised his head and, in an effort to assert some authority, angrily yipped at Carlitos. Laughter was the immediate reaction, and the puppy, not content with being laughed at, yipped again at the amused trio.

"Finally, some laughter in this house," Carlos Senior said with a smile as he joined the merriment. "I had my reservations about the dog, but I must admit, *Gordo*, it was a good idea."

His son nodded, gracefully accepting the compliment.

"Do you want to hold him?" Olga asked and presented the puppy to the elder statesman.

"No, no, no, no, no. I don't need a splash of puppy urine on my white suite."

"You're looking rather dashing," Manuel commented. "Where are you going?"

"I have a date."

"Oooh," the group exclaimed in unison.

"And how did this come about?" Carlitos asked as he stood to fix his father's collar.

"It was Belencita's idea. She's been telling me to get out there and meet the many artistic socialites of Havana. Well, it just so happens that I heard about these sisters..."

"Sisters?" Olga teased him.

"... one of them is an artist and journalist, and the other is recently widowed."

"So, who are these sisters?" Olga asked again in a playful tone.

"Olguita, por favor. I happen to know the family, Hernández-Catá."

"Please don't tell me they're young enough to be my sisters," Manuel expressed.

"Young? Well, they're younger than me, but not like you. I think the older one, Sara, you may have seen. She's had a few interviews published on Vanidades."

"I like that magazine," Olguita commented.

"And the younger one," Carlos Senior continued, "Uva, was recently widowed and has three daughters."

"Sounds promising, but I need to hear more." Manuel encouraged with curiosity.

"That's it. There's nothing more to say."

"And which of the two sisters are you meeting tonight?" Olga teased. "You must have one in mind, or else you wouldn't be wearing a linen suit."

"Olguita, please. There's no need to be indiscreet."

"Papá," Manuel rose to Olga's defense. "Her question is perfectly valid, and your evasiveness is only raising suspicions."

The group waited in silence.

"Papá, get on with it. Who's your date with, the journalist artist?" Manuel asked.

"It's with the younger sister, Uva."

"The one who was widowed?" Carlitos clarified.

"Well, you look very handsome," Olga stood with the puppy still in her hands. "I'm sure you'll win her over the moment you step into the room."

"*Ay*, at my age, it's no longer about first impressions, but a good linen suit never hurts." Carlos Senior chuckled and looked at the dog, who was emitting grumbling sounds. "Did I hear correctly, you want to name him Jolly?"

Olga placed the puppy on the floor, and it began to chew Manuel's shoe with ferocity.

"Grumpy might be a better name," Manuel suggested and moved the pup aside.

"*Bueno, bueno,*" Carlos Senior said and left the room.

******

Uva was a tall, fashionable and intelligent woman. Her sister, Sara, possessed similar features and she splashed on color with ease. They invited him to dine with several friends, and to Carlos Senior's surprise, the conversations around the table did not involve politics, as if it were the house rule.

"Yes, we told the other guests they were forbidden to talk politics," Uva confessed as she strolled by his side. They were walking alongside each other, without touching, under the trees of the Miramar neighborhood.

"I see," he replied. "And did I pass the test?"

"What test are you referring to?"

"The test to see if I can talk about something other than politics."

"Oh, that test."

"Yes, that test."

"Well, I am very pleased to inform you that you passed a variety of tests, all with glowing marks, but you may have to make amends with Sara."

"How so?"

"Well, you did praise Alejo Carpentier's 'Pasos Perdidos' without acknowledging that the novel is overflowing with *machismo*."

"Hmm..."

"Maybe you should read it again?"

"No, I don't think I need to. Now that you mention it, I can see what she is referring to."

"And I think you insinuated that he is a communist."

"Who, Carpentier? I only insinuated that the man is a communist, because I didn't want to talk about politics, but make no mistake. The man is a communist."

"Oh, I agree. Just be ready to defend yourself. You're able to see how the man is a communist, but somehow you didn't see that he's *un machista?*"

"Are you saying I have a blind spot?"

"My sister might say that."

"And what do you say?"

"I think your vision is just fine," Uva said and reached for his hand.

They walked hand in hand to the house, where the group of friends welcomed them with raised wine glasses to celebrate the beginning of a courtship. From that day forth, Carlos Senior and Uva spoke every night on the phone and saw each other with frequency. He quickly fell in love with her three daughters, and found himself getting rather protective of them. It was several months later, while sitting by her side and gazing at the moon, that he revealed his deepest longing and innermost worry.

"I think by now you know who I am," he said while tenderly caressing her hand.

"Right now, at this moment, you're the most wonderful man,"

"Right now, I'm a man with a hundred worries pulling at me."

"I've known that about you. It's not too hard to see."

"Between the law firm and the university, I have enough work to keep a dozen people busy. Actually, my accountant would say that I produce work to keep seventeen people fully employed and they all need to get paid."

"But isn't that good? You're a successful lawyer and professor."

"Yes, you're right, but it keeps me too busy. I don't have time for you and more importantly, I don't have time to think about what I should be doing?"

"We see each other enough, don't you think?"

"We do, but what I'm trying to say is that my preoccupations consume every minute and every thought I have. It's not healthy. I need time, on a daily basis, to sit and think and figure out what I'm going to do."

"You need to think? About what, me?"

"No, not you, but yes, you along with everything else that is happening in my life. Don't you see? The country's slowly falling apart. Batista is not stepping down, and I don't know how to force him down. A leader is needed and I should step forward with a solution. I can see a future for Cuba, full of promise, for this island to be a shining example in the world. It's a dream, I know, but I think it can happen. And it's that possibility that has me... obsessed."

Uva listened and kept silent.

"Cuba's in Limbo at the moment. Staying busy with land disputes, listening to quarreling corporations and teaching economic theory is not what I should be doing. This here, with us, is very good," he said while caressing her hand. "I'm happy. I like being by your side, but somehow, it's not enough. It can't be. Do you know what I mean?"

"Uh-huh," she nodded affirmatively.

"What do you think?"

"I think you need to ask me to marry you, that's what I think."

Carlos Senior looked at her and smiled.

"Will you marry me?"

"Only if you promise to become the leader you dream of."

******

While Carlos Senior and Uva dreamt of a life together, Fidel Castro and Ernesto (Che) Guevara dreamt of a revolution that would change the world. It was at a dinner gathering in Mexico City, safe from the persecutions of Batista's army, where Fidel and Ernesto met for the first time.

"Fidel, I want you to meet an interesting fellow," Raul, his brother, said while leading a handsome man to their table.

"*Bienvenido*, come and join us." Fidel stood and smiled.

"Ernesto," el Che introduced himself and shook Fidel's hand.

"Come, have a seat. Have you eaten? Can we offer you a drink?"

"*Gracias*. Yes, I already ate at home, thanks to Hilda, my wife."

"Ah, you're from Argentina. I love how you Argentinians speak, calling each other '*boludo*' and '*che.*' It's very amusing."

Ernesto laughed while Raul sat next to him.

"*Bueno*," Ernesto replied, "you don't want to be called '*boludo.*' We reserve that title for a man whose stubbornness surpasses his intellect."

"Yes, of course. Raul, tell me, where did you meet this Argentinian?"

"I was at that little café we like, *La Habana*," Raul said, "when I heard a woman talking about Marx and Lenin. It caught me by surprise, that this woman, Peruvian by the way, was so well versed in political theory. So, I had to meet her."

"He's talking about my Hilda," Ernesto interrupted.

"So, there I was, talking political theory with this small, Indian looking woman, when along came this handsome doctor."

"You're a doctor?" Fidel asked.

"*Si, si.* That's how I met Hilda."

"She was your patient?"

"No, we were both in Guatemala during the coup d'état against President Arbenz."

"Oh, you were there?"

"*Si, si, si.* When I was in Panama, I had read about the president and his land reforms. I wanted to see with my own two eyes how the American fruit company was going to give land back to the people. It was two years ago, on Christmas Eve, that I arrived in Guatemala. *Che,* I tell you it was life changing. I've traveled through most of South and Central America. I've seen all sorts of living conditions, but Guatemala..."

El Che shook his head with despondence, "...what is happening in Guatemala really is an injustice. It was there in that small country where I dreamt of a new world."

"A dreamer! I love it!" Fidel exclaimed. "Raul, get this man a drink. So, what was your wife, a Peruvian, doing in Guatemala?"

"Hilda was working with the Labor Party, instructing the indigenous people how to get organized for better working conditions and I was there as a doctor, giving the people medical exams. Serving the people who work the land is... humbling. *Che,* you probably know, but I'll say it anyway, because not everybody knows what is so obvious."

"What?" Raul asked from the bar as he squeezed lime juice into three drinks.

"The majority of Guatemala is indigenous, descendants of the Mayans, but most of the land, if not all, is owned by families of Spanish and European descent. Guatemala fought for its independence one hundred-twenty years ago, and they thought they won, but those fucking Spaniards didn't leave. They stuck around to continue their slavery and exploitation with the United Fruit Company."

Raul placed a tall rum drink in front of Ernesto and another in front of Fidel.

"A toast," Raul said, raising his glass. "to our new friend, Ernesto."

"No, I can't be part of that *brindis,*" Ernesto said. "It's too vain. Please, let's toast to something more worthy."

"Do you hear that, Raul?" Fidel stood up. "Such humility! Well, then, let's toast to the dream of a free Guatemala and a free Cuba."

"That I can raise my glass to," Ernesto said and stood up.

The three men joined their glasses and drank with enthusiasm. Raul then placed his arm around their new Argentinian friend, "Tell us more about your adventures and encounters. Tonight is a good night for storytelling."

"*Che, por favor,*" Ernesto complained. "I'm not a storyteller."

"That's right," Fidel said loudly and pounded the table. "He's a dreamer! But even dreamers must have plans to make their dreams come true."

"To dreams and to plans," Raul raised his glass again and the three men drank once more.

"So, what's the plan?" Fidel sat down and asked. "How can you free Guatemala from American exploitation?"

"Guatemala tried to do it through the democratic process," Ernesto said. "They had legitimate elections and Arbenz won, but the American president, Eisenhower, could not allow Guatemala to determine its own destiny. He denied the Guatemalans the same right his country fought for. So, he ordered the CIA to orchestrate an attack on President Arbenz."

Ernesto took a third and final drink from his glass while Raul and Fidel listened attentively. The Argentinian wiped the moisture off his lips, looked up at the wooden rafters of the ceiling, and continued his monologue while focusing his eyes on a distant sight.

"I have to ask myself 'why?' Why is the profit of a fruit company more important than the freedom of the Guatemalan people? Because Guatemala is the new plantation of the United States. You see, those North Americans didn't really abolish slavery. They just moved it further south. *Che,* there's a new empire ruling over our lands, it's the American empire, and the only way to gain our freedom is through revolution. Forget trying to elect our way out of this mess. Revolution and bloodshed is the only way."

More exiled Cubans joined their gathering, men who had been imprisoned with Fidel and fought by his side. Eventually plates of food were served, women were invited to sit with them, and more drinks were poured. The air was thick with laughter and celebration, reminding the merry gathering that life was worth living. As the hours passed, the rebel men adjourned for the night, some accompanied by a woman, others by a bottle, but for Fidel and Ernesto an intellectual dialogue needed to occur. A conversation was started that had not yet reached completion, and they found themselves alone, seated under the star-filled sky strategizing a dream for revolution. By sunrise, a new alliance had been formed.

"*Compañeros*," Fidel called his rebel friends to gather around him. "We came to Mexico to save our lives, but instead we found a new friend with new ideas." He placed his hand on Ernesto's shoulder and brought him closer. "We now have a doctor. We'll return to our beloved island, all eighty of us, to fight for her freedom with a new comrade in arms, *el Che!*"

******

The afternoon sun was setting and the sound of children playing, women preparing dinner, and neighbors playing dominoes reverberated through Manolo's neighborhood, *El Rosario*. He passed through the doors of his home but his right foot got caught on the threshold. His body came forward while his right leg stayed behind. In a natural act of self-preservation, he repositioned his left leg to keep himself from falling.

"Are you drunk?" Jenny asked him.

"No. I don't know what happened. I'm just so tired I can't even walk right."

"Look at you! Have a seat and rest. Do you want a drink?"

"Not now. I think I'll just sit here for a little."

"Papá," his two daughters ran out to greet him as he sat on the sofa.

"*Ay,* here are my two princesses."

"Do you know what the baby did today?" His younger daughter asked.

"He went to the store to buy some milk?"

"No, don't be silly. He's a baby."

"Then, he threw his *tete* at you and it hit you on the face."

"No!" The two girls exclaimed in unison and laughed.

"Tell me, what did the baby do today?"

"He rolled over. Look, come," the older one said.

"*Niñas,* leave your father alone," Jenny lightly guided the girls toward their room. "He's tired and you both need to clean up this mess you made."

"Can we play with the baby?" the girls asked.

"No. The baby needs to sleep. Leave him alone."

Jenny came back with a smile and looked at her husband. "I think I want a drink before dinner. Are you sure you don't want one?"

"Well, if you're going to have one, go ahead and serve me one too."

Jenny poured golden rum into two glasses and then added a squirt of lime into each glass. She sat next to Manolo and placed her hand on his thigh.

"*Salud,*" she raised her glass as he tilted his and clinked it with hers.

They sipped the rum drink together and looked at each other.

"I think I like this little tradition we're creating," Jenny commented with a smile.

"As long as we keep it to one drink, I'm alright."

"*Si, si, si.* One drink, that's all I want." She leaned over and kissed Manolo. "And a kiss from my blue eyed lover."

They sipped and kissed again.

"I had to work at the engraving table today," Manolo said with a defeated tone.

"No! Why?"

"Paquito didn't show up and we have to finish the Pan American brochures."

"How are your hands?" She reached for them.

"I was lucky and escaped any burn or cut. It's my back that's killing me, and the heat got to me. I don't know why Pedrito won't buy an air conditioning unit."

"Because he's a cheap bastard, that's why!" Jenny stood up with indignation. "I swear, Manolo, you should quit already!"

"And do what? This is our business and this is how the work gets done. You don't hear the baker complaining about getting burned by the oven, or the fisherman crying when he has to pull a net full of fish. Engraving is hard work, but it's what we do."

"No. This is what you do. I don't see any other Gutierrez working the engraving table. Pedrito didn't jump in to help you, right? No. He stayed in the office, counting money, right? That's your problem, Manolo, you let people walk all over you."

"*Bueno, bueno*, let's not ruin a perfectly good moment. Come back and sit with me. Let's change the subject. Tell me about your day."

Jenny returned to sit next to Manolo. She was going to take another sip from her drink when the cries of an infant filled the house.

"Mami," the girls called out in unison. "The baby is crying."

She looked at Manolo, placed her drink on the table and walked to the baby's room.

Later that night, as the children slept and the moonlight cut through their bedroom window, Manolo fought the desire to sleep, so he might bring his young wife to a heightened moment of ecstasy. Although the call to drowse was strong, he knew this effort would keep her mood from turning against him. When he collapsed beside her, sweating and out of breath, her breathing was equally stressed.

"Oh my God, you never fail," she said. "How you know what I want and when I want it, is just... simply amazing."

"My love, I make it my business to know everything you need."

They were staring at the ceiling when he reached for her hand and squeezed. She squeezed back and looked out the window to see the lights of a plane silently traversing the star-filled sky.

"When are you going to take me somewhere?" She asked.

"What do you mean, we went to *Varadero* last month."

"No, I mean somewhere far, on a plane. I've never been on a plane. It must be so nice to see the world while flying in the clouds. But I don't want to go to New York. I don't want to see any part of the United States, or hear any of those Americans speaking English. I can't stand the sound of it. Take me instead to Mexico City. I want to see a bull-fight."

Manolo remained silent.

"You know, I heard on the radio that Fidel Castro went to Mexico. He's raising money for a revolution that would restore our country. I read his manifesto, 'History will Absolve Me.' I gave it to you. Did you read it?"

Manolo didn't answer.

"Honey, did you read it?" She pulled at his hand.

"What?"

"Fidel's manifesto, did you read it? It's on the living room table."

"Oh, yeah. I read it."

"I think he's so smart, the way he describes the origin of our problems. Did you know it all began with Estrada Palma? That's how far the corruption goes, although I think it goes further back, to the Spaniards. *Esos cabrones*, the way they plundered our land and killed the natives. Somebody should make them pay for what they did. That's another place I don't want to visit, Spain. Why go there and see how the queen and the Catholic Church got rich from all the gold they ripped out of our lands? Although I would visit *las Islas Canarias*. That's where my grandfather was born, and it would be nice to see it. Don't you think?"

Manolo responded with a quiet snore.

Jenny stood and walked to the window. The cool evening breeze caressed her naked body. Away on the horizon, lightning flashed, momentarily illuminating the gathering storm clouds. She turned and looked at her husband, laying naked on the bed.

"*Vamos*, wake up," she said while laying beside him. "Let's do it again."

He opened his eyes to see Jenny attempting to rouse him.

Sleep was not going to be his companion, at least not yet.

CHAPTER 9

Dodge the Bullet

March 1957
    Havana, Cuba

The two dogs sat at the top of the driveway, scanning the street for stray cats. *Blanquita y Negrita*, were the unclaimed offspring of Carlitos' wire haired Fox Terriers. Named for their color, white and black, these sisters were never given a home. Consequently, they lived on the street, but always within proximity of Olga, who they recognized as master. In a display of uncanny brilliance, the dogs moved from home to home with Olga. When *el Viejo Márquez* remarried and moved into the home of his new wife, Carlitos and Olga moved a few blocks away to a small apartment. One morning, to her surprise, a dead rat lay at her front door, a love offering from the furry duo, who sat at a short distance. A year later, when Olga and Carlos moved in with Tina, several miles away, the dogs managed to track her down. Within a few weeks of the move, they were at the top of the hill, scanning the street for stray cats. Often, the dogs served as companions to Carlitos, sitting near him as he worked on engines in the carport.

In the years after the fight that ended his relationship with his mother, Carlitos became obsessed with rebuilding engines. He sat for hours in the garage, recalibrating valves and cleaning pistons with grease-stained hands. Tina looked at her garage and winced. Oil drippings, screws, bolts, engine parts and tools littered the once perfectly clean space. She worried about the neighbors and what they thought, but more importantly, she worried about her son-in-law, who wasn't working and wasted his time on a car that, by her estimate, would never run. To make matters worse, he encouraged the murdering dogs to chase after every cat.

"*¡Destruye!* " He commanded the pair, who sped off to terrorize a cat. Every once in a while they would manage to catch an unsuspecting feline and chase it up a tree.

The carport became Carlitos' unofficial office. There he met with other young men to whisper about matters that Tina found troubling. Her suspicions peaked one afternoon when she overheard Carlitos and three visiting young men discuss an insurrection. She opened the door of the kitchen and stepped into the carport with a tray of coffee cups. Carlitos was leaning against his car, speaking to the three men who huddled around him.

"Tell *Manzanita*..." Carlitos said in a volume he considered to be a whisper but was loud enough to be heard several feet away. "...that he'll need to paralyze the city during the attack."

"*¿Café?*" Tina said as she approached them.

The young men looked appreciatively at her.

"*Gracias, señora,*" they said while reaching for their cups.

"Are you here to help Carlitos clean this carport?"

They laughed, thinking she was joking. Carlitos turned, accepted a cup of coffee, and thanked her indifferently. He then smacked his lips, annoyed at her presence.

Tina examined the visitors, who didn't seem to be much older than her son, Manolín.

"Are you students at the university?" she asked.

"Yes, ma'am. I'm studying law," said the first.

Tina looked at the next one.

"Engineering," he said.

She looked at the third, waiting for him to claim a degree.

"I'm not a student yet," he said. "I'll be applying for admission this summer."

"Uh-huh," she nodded. "Carlitos graduated five years ago. Are you here to be mentored by him, or are you planning something else?"

They looked at her prosecuting eyes and grew nervous. Carlitos turned to her, placed his empty cup on her tray and thanked her. The young men followed his lead.

"Don't be using my carport to plan things that will land you in jail," Tina said through clenched teeth. "You should be ashamed, each of you. You're all too young to be having these conversations. Go home and focus on your studies and not on schemes that will get you killed."

The young men looked at Carlitos for direction.

"Go and wait for me by the car," he instructed.

They slowly stepped back, as if afraid to turn their backs on Tina, and waited for Carlitos on the sidewalk.

"Do me a favor," Carlitos said. He spoke in a deliberately slow, tempered voice. "Don't insert yourself in my conversations, and don't be telling my friends what to do."

"Really? This is my house and my carport," Tina said, her voice rising in anger. "I'll do as I please."

Carlitos walked away from her while she stood with one hand on her hip. The young men huddled around him for a few more minutes, speaking inaudibly. Tina went inside and vigilantly watched them from the kitchen window.

Carlitos turned the attention of his visitors toward the dogs, as he commanded them.

"*¡Destruye!*"

The dogs ran toward a tree, looking for a cat, and then off through the neighborhood. Carlitos and the three young men laughed as the dogs returned from their unsuccessful hunt and awaited further instructions. Carlitos was still laughing when he entered the house and saw Tina standing in the kitchen, staring angrily at him.

"I hate it when you command the dogs to chase a cat."

"*Ay, coño,*" he mumbled to himself.

"And I hate how you've turned the carport into a junkyard."

Carlitos smacked his lips and walked away.

"And I really don't like it when you encourage young men to do stupid things against the government. I heard you. I heard you talk about an attack."

"You didn't hear anything," he spun around and pointed his finger at her. Tina stepped back, surprised by the anger in his voice. "Whatever you think you heard, is not your business, and don't be telling anyone about it."

"Really? So, who's *Manzanita*?" she asked defiantly.

Carlitos was standing still, meeting Tina's stare, when Olga walked in.

"What's happening?" she asked nervously.

"Your mother is stepping out of bounds," Carlitos replied and returned to the carport.

"And he is leaving grease stains everywhere," Tina said while tossing a cleaning rag at Olga. "Clean that doorknob and the countertop too."

Olga lowered her purse and turned her attention toward the grease stains.

"What in the world is happening to your husband?"

"I don't know, Mima. I don't know, but it's getting bad. The other day we went to visit *el Viejo Márquez* at his new home, and Carlitos couldn't stop making snide comments about his stepmother and stepsisters."

"*¿Como?*" Tina said in an outraged tone.

Olga paused, surprised at her mother's reaction, and stood tall in front of her.

"You're a fine one to judge," Olga replied. "You're full of snide comments about Papá and his new family."

"Don't compare the two. Your father left me for that woman."

"And you will hold that against him for how long? For how long do Manolín and I have to sneak around to see our father and half-sisters?"

Olga tossed the cleaning rag back at her mother and retreated to her room.

"Who's *Manzanita*?" Tina asked loud enough for Olga to hear.

"Who?" Olga stepped back into view.

"*Manzanita*. Do any of your friends have that nickname?"

"I don't know that name," Olga said with a genuine look of confusion. "Why?"

Tina turned around, deciding to keep silent and focus on dinner.

José Antonio Echeverría, widely known as *Manzanita* was a twenty-four-year-old architecture student and president of the F.E.U., credited with creating the Revolutionary Directory, an organization to channel the rebellious energies of students and alumni. Echeverría was a handsome man, with robust cheeks that glowed like freshly polished apples, hence his nickname. He was intelligent, articulate and well-liked. Like most students, his extracurricular activities aimed to tarnish the dictator's reputation in hopes of restoring the island's democratic process. This was too large an endeavor for one man, so *Manzanita* often sought the advice of a F.E.U. alumni, Carlitos.

"Will you join the Revolutionary Directory?" Manzanita asked Carlitos earlier that year. "We need your leadership."

"You don't want me," Carlitos answered rather abruptly. "I'm too high profile and my name will attract unwanted attention. Ask any Garcia or Fernandez."

Manzanita leaned back and looked down, obviously disappointed by his reply.

"Listen," Carlitos reached out, "ultimately, you want to run both the F.E.U. and the Directory."

"I was thinking of Fidel, but..."

"*¿Estás loco?*" Carlitos protested loudly.

"I know. I know, but he has soldiers and we need as many as we can get."

"If you get him involved, you'll regret it. Leave *Bola de Churre* in the Sierra, where he can be a distraction. You're here in the city, changing the course of history."

"Alright, but where will I find more soldiers?"

"Don't worry. It won't be difficult to recruit more men. Focus on planning the attack. Where will you be?"

"What do you mean? I'll be at the front."

"That's a mistake."

"I can't stay home like a coward!"

"Do you want to die like Martí?"

"No, but I don't want to be hiding either."

"I'm not suggesting you hide, quite the opposite. You need to be in a position of leadership, but not in the line of fire where you'll get killed."

"Many people will get killed."

They stood in silence. The gravity of those words gave them pause.

"Have you ever shot a gun?" Carlitos asked.

"Of course, I've shot a gun."

"At a man?"

Manzanita didn't reply.

"I didn't think so."

"Have you?"

"No, which is why I'm not pretending to be the kind of man who can. You're like me. We're men of thoughts and words, and we'll be more valuable to the cause after the attack. Cuba needs to be reconstructed. The people don't know who to follow or what is good for them. They need us, they need you, to lead the island back to democracy."

"So, what do you suggest I do?"

"Go to the radio station and talk to the people during the attack."

"At CMQ?"

"Exactly. Explain to them what is happening. Let it be your voice that calls out for freedom. Think about the effect this will have. The people need to understand the importance of what we're doing and you need to say the words that will mobilize them. You can inspire them to be part of this movement."

Manzanita left that day with a lot to consider, preferring the role of leadership and inspiration over the strong possibility of getting shot down. The weeks passed and more men volunteered to join the attack. One of their new recruits was part of the security team for the palace, an asset who provided a complete diagram of the building's layout. This made the decision easy, the attack on the dictator's life would be at the Presidential Palace.

It was March thirteenth when Carlitos sat in Tina's living room, chewing his fingernails and listening to the news broadcasted on CMQ. She stood in front of him with a purse in hand.

"Carlitos, lower that volume a little," Tina said.

His mind was going over the details of the plan, but subconsciously he heard her request and lowered the volume.

"Mario is in town, over at my sister's house. Olguita and I are going to visit."

Carlitos shifted his weight in the chair.

"Can you give us a ride?"

"I'm sorry. What did you say?"

"Does that car work? I heard you start the engine yesterday."

"The engine runs, but the transmission is off gear."

"Oh well, I guess we'll continue to take the bus, even though there is a car sitting there." Tina's annoyance was evident in her voice. "When are you going to get it running?"

"Are you ready to leave?" Olga asked from the hallway.

"*Si, mija.* Grab your purse and let's get going. The bus is about to pass."

"Where are you going?" Carlitos asked as if hearing her for the first time.

"To see Mario," Tina said loudly. "Are you not listening?"

"Mario who?"

"My brother. You met him when we went to Güira."

"Right. The guy with the knife. Sorry, but you can't go."

Tina looked at him, as if being challenged, and waited for him to clarify.

"It's not safe today. As a matter of fact, call your family and tell them to stay home. It's not safe to be out in the city."

"*¿De que tú hablas?*" Olga returned to the living room with a purse in hand. "What are you talking about?"

"It's not safe. Call Mario and tell him to stay indoors."

"Is this the attack I heard you talk about?" Tina asked, suspiciously.

Carlitos didn't reply.

She put her purse down and with a nod, instructed Olga to do the same.

"There's going to be an attack?" Olga asked.

"Sometime this afternoon," he said while biting his fingernail.

"How do you know this?" Olga asked.

"I just do."

"What kind of attack? Another bomb?" Tina asked while Olga leaned forward, eager to hear the reply.

"It's a coordinated attack on Batista. It'll be over by nightfall."

"*¡Ay, Dios mío!* An attack on Batista, this can't be good."

"Where's Manolín?" Tina asked. "Is he working today?"

"I think so," Olga said with a tone of uncertainty. "Or he might be with his friends."

Tina ran over to the phone that sat by the lamp. She dialed nervously, mumbling curses at the rotary phone.

"Who're you calling?"

"*El taller.*"

The time required for the call to connect seemed like an eternity as Olga stood hovering over Tina.

"I get a busy signal," Tina complained and slammed the phone down.

"I think you must have misdialed. Let me try," Olga said as Carlitos began to pace.

She dialed the numbers very carefully, making sure the rotary movement was taken to full completion, only to hear a busy signal once again.

"I'm calling Papi's house. He might be there," Olga said.

"Really?" Tina asked, surprised.

"Yes, we go there every once in a while," Olga said as she dialed. "What do you mean you go there?"

"Does it matter now?" Olga screamed at her. "We go there. He's our father."

Tina looked down, knowing this was not the time to argue.

"That's busy too," Olga said confused. "Could something be wrong with the phones?"

"It's a possibility," Carlitos said. "Phone lines might be cut."

The women looked at him in shock.

"It keeps the police from knowing what's happening."

"I have to find him," Tina said loudly and reached for her purse.

"Where are you going?" Carlitos asked and put his hand on her purse.

"I have to find him."

"If he's at work in Old Havana, he's safe as long as he stays there, but the roads through that part of the city will be dangerous."

"I don't care." Tina replied.

"I do."

Tina was surprised by his statement.

"Stay here. I'll go."

She examined his eyes for honesty.

"I'll find him. I promise," Carlitos said without wavering.

"Bring him home," she said with a cry in her voice. "Bring him home to me!"

Carlitos stepped out to the carport and walked toward a toolbox that was on the floor. Tina looked at him, perplexed.

"I thought you said the car didn't run."

"It doesn't," he said while taking tools out of the box and pulling out a wad of bills that rested at the bottom.

"Just in case," he lifted a roll of *pesos* before tucking it into his pocket.

"Where did you get all that money?" Olga asked.

"At the races. I won big," he said, half smiling.

"*¡Ay, Dios mío santo!*" Olga exclaimed once again.

Tina turned to Olga with clenched teeth.

"Why would Manolín go to his father's house, when I specifically have forbidden it."

Carlitos heard Tina's question as he walked toward the bus stop.

"Jesus! That woman can't let it rest," he commented to himself.

Carlitos took a bus to *El Paseo del Prado* and then hopped onto a trolley for Old Havana. Traffic was flowing nicely, which indicated the attack on the Presidential Palace had not yet occurred. He got off at *Calle Sol*, one block from Fotograbados Gutierrez, and a few blocks from the port. The sound of rhythmic music and men arguing flowed from a bar behind the bus stop. Two women, dressed provocatively, were standing on the corner.

"*Oye guapo*, don't walk away. We won't bite you," one of them called. He didn't bother to look at them as he crossed the street. They responded to his rejection with mocking laughter that could be heard as he entered the building. He found Manolo in the front office, talking with Angelito and Pedrito. They turned to Carlitos and ceased their conversation, surprised to see him.

"What's wrong?" Manolo asked, alarmed.

"Is Manolín here?"

"Why? What happened?"

"Is he working today, here?"

"Yes, he was. He left already. What's happening?"

"I need to find him and take him home. Does your phone work?"

"No. The lines went dead a couple of hours ago," Pedrito offered.

"Do you have a radio?"

Angelito pointed toward his desk, where a radio sat on the shelf behind it.

"Put on CMQ," Carlitos ordered.

Angelito quickly stepped toward the radio and turned it on.

"Nothing," Angelito said, turning the knob to find the station. "They must be off the air."

"It's begun," Carlitos said to himself but loud enough to be heard.

"What's begun?" Manolo grabbed Carlitos' arm. "What's happening, and why are you looking for Manolín?"

"There's trouble in the city today. All of you should stay indoors until it passes. Listen to CMQ. Keep it on. An announcement will be made."

"Trouble? What kind of trouble?" Angelito asked.

"An attack on Batista," Carlitos turned to Manolo. "Where can I find Manolín?"

Manolo looked up, searching his mind for a possible answer.

"I promised Tina I would bring him home," he explained.

"He left about an hour ago," Manolo said quietly. "I think I know where he might be. Did you bring a car?"

"No. I came by trolley."

"Lend me your car," Manolo said to Pedrito, who shook his head and pretended to not know. Manolo then looked at Angelito, who immediately tossed his keys at him.

Manolo glanced at Pedrito, who began making excuses as to why he didn't have car keys with him. Carlitos quickly walked out with Manolo following closely.

"He has a friend who works in the *bar de putas* across the street," Manolo said.

As they crossed the street, one of the women standing outside called out, "*¡Oye, gordito!* Tell me what you like. I'll be gentle with you."

Carlitos and Manolo ignored her, and they opened the doors only to be greeted by a plume of cigarette smoke. They paused at the threshold, waiting for their eyes to adjust to the darkness. A bartender stood in the center with several men sitting around his counter. Scantily dressed women stood against the wall, waiting to be chosen by paying customers. A group of men played billiards while others sat at nearby tables, flirting with the women.

"There he is," Manolo said, "*Malanga.*"

"Who?"

"The kid. That's the name he goes by," he said with a shrug and walked toward the billiard tables. Carlitos remained at the door, not wanting to interact with the customers or vendors of the establishment. He watched Manolo stumble through the darkness, politely refusing multiple waves of advances, and reaching a young man who had a woman on his lap.

"Are you going to enter?" A bouncer asked Carlitos.

"No, I don't think so. I'm just waiting for my friend."

"Then I need you to wait outside."

Carlitos looked at Manolo, who was apologizing to the man he approached.

"Do you know a young man, *un muchacho*, called *Malanga*?"

"What do you want with him?"

"We need to ask him a question." Carlitos pulled out a bill and offered it to the bouncer.

"He restocks the bar and sells accessories to the women," the bouncer replied while discreetly taking the bill.

"That wasn't him," Manolo returned looking slightly frustrated.

"Accessories?"

"Yes, accessories," the bouncer repeated.

"Can you take us to him," Carlitos asked and pulled out another bill.

"No, but I can bring him to you."

"Perfect, we'll be here, waiting."

"Like I said, you can't stand here."

Carlitos took one step in and another to the side. "This better?"

The bouncer left, becoming a silhouette in a room full of shadows. As they waited, several women emerged from the penumbra to tempt them with proposals. Manolo politely refused each time while Carlitos remained silent. Several minutes later the bouncer returned with *Malanga*, who led them outside, requiring, once again, to pause at the threshold and adjust to the bright day.

Carlitos looked at the baby faced minor with dark, almond shaped eyes.

"We're looking for Manolín," Manolo said. "Do you know where he might be?"

"You're his father, no?"

"*Si, niño.* You've been in my house."

"Yes, I have," *Malanga* said and looked away. "Manolín's not here."

"We know. I need to find him. It's urgent."

The teenage boy shuffled, clearly looking uncomfortable.

"He's got a woman he spends most days with, but I don't know where she is."

"Do you know who would?" Carlitos asked.

"Not really."

Manolo looked around, fidgeting. Sweat beads were building up on his forehead.

"Listen," Carlitos said to the youth. "We don't have time to go on a hunt all over the city." He took out a folded peso and tucked in the youth's shirt pocket. "Give us a good lead. I promise you it's for his good."

"You're Olguita's husband," *Malanga* acknowledged Carlitos.

"I am. You work here?" Carlitos asked.

"I do. A few hours a week. It gives me access to the women, so I can sell accessories."

"Accessories?"

"For their hair," he nodded. "I also sell jewelry, cream, and lubricant for..."

"I get the picture."

"*Niño*, where's Manolín?" Manolo asked again.

"He's probably at the bar on Refugio street," the youth looked down. "He likes one of the whores there. Andrea."

"What do you mean he likes a whore?" Manolo was shocked.

"Yeah, he's become her regular."

"*Vamos*," Carlitos said to Manolo. "I know that street. It's a few blocks from the palace."

As Manolo sped through the streets of Old Havana, the sounds of gunfire startled them. Police cars raced toward the palace with sirens on, and the voice of *Manzanita* could be heard from every radio, "*Pueblo de Cuba*, People of Cuba, the dictator Fulgencio Batista has finally been brought to justice. The echoes of the gunshots that ended the life of this bloody tyrant are still reverberating in the Presidential Palace."

Carlitos and Manolo reached Refugio street, only to find traffic wasn't moving.

"Let me out," Carlitos told Manolo. "I'll find him. You turn around. Go to the Malecón and make sure the car doesn't get blocked in. I'll find you there."

"Wait for me at the corner of *Malecón* and *Angeles*."

Carlitos nodded, knowing that it was a major intersection. He walked on the cobblestone street, filled by a line of cars that were unable to move in any direction. The drivers were standing outside their cars, trying to decipher what was happening. The sound of gunfire created a panic, and people began running from the tumult. Carlitos saw Manolín as he approached the bar. He was standing at the entrance with his shirt undone and a woman by his side.

"What's happening?" the woman asked.

"I don't know," Manolín said, bewildered by the panic in the street. "Manolín!" Carlitos called out.

"What are you doing here?"

"I've come to get you."

"What's going on?"

"Batista is dead. We need to leave. It isn't safe," Carlitos said. Manolín looked at the woman and then back at Carlitos, unsure of what to do.

"Come now. We need to leave."

"*Dale*, " she said and then pulled Manolín closer to her for a kiss.

Manolín's kiss lasted too long for Carlitos, who lost his patience.

"*¡Vamos, coño!*" He pulled at his brother-in-law, only to see the woman pulling back.

"He owes me," she said.

Manolín looked at Carlitos apologetically.

"Really?"

Carlitos reached into his pocket, placed several bills on the table, and led the reluctant youth down the rapidly emptying cobblestone street. They walked hurriedly with several hundred pedestrians who instinctively knew Old Havana was not safe. As they approached the *Malecón*, the sound of increased traffic, sirens, distant gunfire and crashing sea waves fueled their agitated steps. They reached the intersection at *Angeles* but Manolo was not there, forcing them to wait while sea waves furiously crashed behind them.

"You have a cigarette?" Carlitos asked Manolín as ocean spray wet the back of his shirt.

The youth held out a pack for Carlitos to help himself.

"Why are you at a whore house?" Carlitos attempted to light the cigarette, but the wind kept blowing out the flame.

"Here," Manolín leaned in, shielded the cigarette from the wind, and expertly lit it.

"Don't you know you can pick up a nasty bug in a place like that?"

"You're kidding, right?"

A car sped past them honking furiously. Manolín stuck his chest out and challenged the car. "*¡Come mierda!*" he yelled at the driver.

"Relax," Carlitos said, pulling him back. "Listen, whore houses are no place for a nice young man like yourself. They're nothing but trouble and the women are not worth it."

"*Oye*, did you not see the woman I was with? She's definitely worth it."

"Did you not see the ten other men she was with before you arrived?"

"It's not like that."

"No? What's it like?"

"You wouldn't understand."

"To her, you're just another paying customer."

"You don't need to lecture me. I know what she does for a living."

An ocean wave crashed over the sea wall. Carlitos inspected his cigarette and deemed it dry enough to keep on smoking.

"Does your mother know you're doing this?"

"*¿Estás loco?*"

"Listen, I don't want to tell your mother where I found you, but I can't look away either. You're like my little brother."

Manolín stood still, trying to be respectful, but still revealing an attitude.

"Get yourself a nice girl," Carlitos said. "There's plenty of girls in the neighborhood that you can take for a walk in the park, or to the movies. It's what you should be doing."

Manolín looked away, not appreciating the lecture. A policeman in a cruiser drove slowly by, patrolling for rebels. He looked at the stranded pair but kept driving.

"By the way, I'm glad someone knew where you were, otherwise, we never would have found you."

"I can take care of myself."

"I'm sure you can, but you're still a minor and I'm taking you home to your mother. Understood?"

Manolo arrived and pulled in next to them. They were getting inside the vehicle when the police cruiser stopped, and the officer ordered them to exit.

"Stand over here and show me your identification."

The men quickly obeyed and stood on the sidewalk, side by side.

"We're just going home, officer," Manolo offered.

"Identification," the policeman barked.

Manolo and Carlitos reached for their wallets. Manolín, however, stood with his hands by his side.

"Identification," the policeman ordered again.

"I don't have it with me," Manolín said.

"He's my son, officer," Manolo explained in a raised voice so as to be heard over the moving traffic.

"What are you doing in this part of the city?" The officer asked while he examined his identification card.

"We work in *Calle Sol* and were diverted by the trouble."

The police officer stood in front of Carlitos, reading his identification card.

"Márquez-Sterling, the politician?"

"That would be my father."

"Your father, huh? So, what are you?"

"I'm Márquez-Sterling, the good friend."

A car drove perilously close to them. The policeman looked at that car with menacing eyes but decided to stay with the three suspects before him.

"I have friends in the government," Carlitos continued, "and I can tell them what a good job you're doing."

"What? You think I need you to vouch for me?"

"No, of course not, officer..."

"Montañez. Go ahead, write it down. Who are you going to complain to?"

Carlitos remained silent.

"Batista is dead!" A young man heckled at the policeman from his car. The officer turned around, ready to get into a fight.

"*¡Maricón!*" The officer yelled at the moving car.

The young man's laughter faded with the moving traffic and the officer returned his attention to Carlitos and Manolo.

"You haven't answered my question." His annoyance was palpable. "What are you doing in this part of town? And don't tell me you were avoiding the trouble."

"We work at Fotograbados Gutierrez on *Calle Sol*. We were diverted by ..."

"We were at a *bar de putas*," Carlitos interrupted. "A whore house, on Refugio street," "This young man was there, and when the trouble began, I went to take him home."

"Really?" Montañez smiled at Manolín. "Was this your first?"

Manolín looked down and another wave crashed over the seawall, spraying all of them.

"Go ahead and smell him. He reeks of whore."

The policeman got within an inch of Manolín's neck and sniffed.

"Yeah, I recognize that stench," the policeman said. "What's her name?"

"Excuse me?" Manolín asked, confused.

"The whore. Did you get her name?"

"Andrea."

"Would that be Andrea *la mulata*, or Andrea *la culona?*"

Manolín looked down, not knowing how to answer. Carlitos reached into his pocket and took out the wad of bills.

"Maybe you can let us take this young man home to his mother."

Montañez looked at the money, turned toward the street, and in one motion swept his hand over the entire bundle.

"*Niño*, I hope you had a good time," the policeman said to Manolín. "She just cost you a whole lot more than she's worth." He turned to Manolo, who was unable to hide his nervousness. "Take San Lazaro street out of here, and don't turn around."

Manolo nodded, but could not bring himself to thank the police officer, who marked his dominance by tapping the baton on the hood of the car. The trio drove away in silence, trying to reconcile anger with relief, anxiety with gratitude. With every passing minute, the sounds of chaos grew fainter, and the resonating rhythm of suburban life grew closer. When they parked in front of Tina's house, the normalcy of Olga waving from the front porch seemed bizarre.

******

It was with much pageantry on the first Friday of 1957 that Santeria priests proudly entered the Presidential Palace. The dictator, Fulgencio Batista, had gathered them to listen to their predictions on the economy and his own wellbeing. This was an honored moment for those priests, for no other president or high-class Cuban would ever admit believing in Santeria. After several rhythmic dances, accompanied by drums and singing, the Santeria priests, dressed in white and reeking of gardenia perfume, kneeled before Batista to reveal the sign for the new year: *Òdí Ìká.*

The priest stepped back and looked at the sign with a grave face.

"What is it?" Batista asked with concern.

"It is a warning. This year the king will be attacked by his enemies."

A priest, who sat at a distance, stood to make himself known. He stepped forward with much reverence and kneeled before Batista.

"What is it you want to say?" Batista asked.

"I have a different sign, but equally concerning," said the priest. "*Obbara Meyi:* The king must search for exits in places known to him."

Batista smiled while the priests held on to their graven faces.

"Thank you," he said. "You have given me the warning and the solution. Today is a good day. Let the celebrations continue."

The drums played while the servants led the priests to the dining hall, and Batista fearlessly welcomed the new year.

Three months later, as the students of the Revolutionary Directory fought their way into the palace, Batista sequestered himself in his office on the second floor. The students moved forward, grenades in hand, firing guns, confident the severed phone lines isolated the tyrant from all communications. Having been warned by the Santeria priests, Batista used a shortwave radio to give orders to the military and police. Their rapid response not only surprised the students but also kept the reinforcing wave of rebels from assisting.

On the other side of the city, CMQ Radiocentro was preparing for the release of a new Elvis Presley song. Young men and women were waiting anxiously in the courtyard for free posters of the American rock star, when two cars with armed students came to a screeching halt at the front of the building. The fans of the hip-thrusting celebrity scattered as José Antonio Echeverría and four other students marched toward the front door and ordered the porter to let them in. Wherever the rebel leader went, he assured the frightened people nobody was going to get hurt. "Don't worry. You're not in danger. We are revolutionaries."

Once inside the control booth, Echeverría interrupted the unsuspecting newscasters and ordered Hector de Soto, at gunpoint, to read a statement.

"*Radio Reloj* reporting, the Presidential Palace has been attacked. A group of unidentified civilians have stormed the Presidential Palace using rifles and machine guns. The attackers, taking advantage of the surprise, have managed to break into the interior of the Presidential Palace, where President Batista is residing."

Echeverría then ordered the usual ringing of bells, as was customary between news segments, and ordered the other newscaster to read the next statement.

"*Radio Reloj* reporting.... President Batista is dead," he read from the script. "A group of assailants have managed to reach the third floor of the Presidential Palace, where Batista resided. Taking into account the seriousness of the events recorded, the president of the University Student Federation, José Antonio Echeverría, will address the Cuban people."

Manzanita, while sweating profusely, took the microphone and delivered the following speech: "*Pueblo de Cuba*, People of Cuba, the dictator Fulgencio Batista has finally been brought to justice. The echoes of the gunshots that ended the life of this bloody tyrant are still reverberating in the Presidential Palace. People of Cuba, the dictator Fulgencio Batista has received what he deserves. Now, it's your turn to participate! People - take to the streets to support the triumph of the revolution with your presence. Worker - immediately quit your job and join the revolutionary strike! Soldier, sailor and policeman - join the fight with your brothers, the common enemy has already been liquidated! People, join us and help liberate Cuba!"

Unbeknownst to him, the broadcast was interrupted halfway through his speech. The people never heard his call to arms. Echeverría and his companions left the radio station without injuring anyone.

They were on route to reunite with other rebels when they encountered a patrolling police cruiser. Echeverría didn't reach his destination, nor did he ever learn the outcome of the attack. He was gunned down in the street, never having fired his gun.

While Echeverría lay dead on a sidewalk, the few remaining rebels at the Presidential Palace managed to reach the door to Batista's office. Most of their fellow rebels had been killed, and the fate of the mission rested on them. Knowing Batista was inside, they launched a grenade that blew open the door and killed the guards on the other side. The rebels ran in before the smoke cleared, only to find an empty office. The dictator had disappeared. Behind them, army soldiers and police officers were advancing. Tanks were being deployed and a city-wide lockdown was beginning. The rebels retreated only to be caught as they fled.

Years later, historians learned the Presidential Palace had a secret door that opened to a secret passageway leading to the residential wing of the palace's third floor. The Santeria priests danced on that day, claiming victory for saving the life of their most influential advocate. In the days that followed, every person listed on the Revolutionary Directory was incarcerated, and business leaders from all Havana came to the palace to pay homage to Batista.

******

The sound of metal clanging woke every member of the house. Carlos Senior and his second wife, Uva, sat up in bed, startled and unaware of who could be pounding the door. At the threshold of their room stood three frightened girls, Uva's daughters. Carlos Senior was about to tell them everything was under control, to go back to bed, when the loud banging resumed.

He put on a robe, slipped his feet into a pair of moccasins, and rushed out of the bedroom door as the banging continued to resonate through the house. Uva also donned a robe, slipped on her house shoes and followed him. Her daughters were close behind.

"Stay here," he said and turned to descend the stairs.

Uva and her daughters looked at each other and silently decided to disregard his order. Agustín, the butler, and Piedad, the housekeeper, stood in the living room, each in their evening robes, wide eyed and waiting instructions.

"Piedad," Uva said, "bring the girls a blanket or robe. I don't want *el Sereno* to shine on them. The moon is bright tonight."

Piedad ran to an inner room as Agustín walked with Carlos Senior toward the backdoor, and the loud banging. They opened the door, stood at the edge of the small, moonlit courtyard, to adjust their eyes. The sound of metal banging on metal got louder as Carlos Senior and Agustín approached the wrought iron gate, covered by a plate glass door that barricaded three police officers from entering. Carlos Senior opened the glass door while keeping the iron gate closed and locked. He looked at his watch and with a silent look demanded the men explain themselves.

"Doctor Carlos Márquez-Sterling?" The officer asked, with one hand grasping the gate and with the other a gun, presumably used to make the offensive sound.

"Yes?"

Uva and her daughters, wrapped up in robes and blankets, approached from behind. The moon was almost full and no clouds roamed the sky. Yet, the men stood in the shadow of the night, hiding their faces from those they awoke.

"We need you to get dressed and come with us."

"On whose orders?" Carlos Senior asked.

"As you know, there has been an attack on the Presidential Palace, and we need you to come with us. It won't take long."

Uva placed her hand on Carlos' shoulder.

"Do you have an arrest warrant?"

"No. Doctor, you are not under arrest. We need to ask a few questions at the station. We'll make sure you're back here, with your wife and daughters, by sunrise."

Uva's teenage daughter, Uvita, stepped forward to get a better look at the men. They instinctively stepped back to hide their façade under the shade of a lush vine.

"This is not an appropriate hour to be going anywhere," Carlos Senior calmly replied. "At this hour, your intentions are highly questionable. In the morning, I will speak with Batista himself and answer any questions. Now, if you don't mind, we wish to return to our rooms."

"I understand," the police officer said. "Do you mind if I go inside and use your phone? I need to call my *coronel*."

Carlos Senior grew suspicious. "Do you mean, *Coronel* Orlando Piedra?"

The police officer did not reply, staring stoically at Carlos Senior.

Carlos Senior shook his head. "This door will not open for you, or for any of your men. If you want to make a phone call, there is a pay phone around the corner."

The officer turned to look at his men, and was about to shrug his shoulders, when Manuel walked up to the door.

"What's happening?" Manuel asked.

One of the men, who was hiding in the shadows, grabbed Manuel by the arm and pushed him against the gate. Manuel, with his back pressed against the gate, looked at the aggressor and asked once again what was happening. The men did not answer.

"He's my son," Carlos Senior said while a collective gasp broke the silence behind him.

"Open the gate, Doctor," the officer demanded.

He stood behind the gate, considering his next move.

"We need you to open the gate and come with us."

"I've already given you my answer. Call your colonel and figure out your next move. This gate is not opening."

The officer hesitated, looked at Manuel, and then turned to locate the pay phone.

"Keep him here. I'll be right back."

Manuel felt a sharp pain shoot through his arm as his captor, who was trained in the art of torture, dug his thumb into the artery that fed Manuel's arm. The young man's fingers darkened from pink to blue and his hand trembled involuntarily. He caught sight of the sadistic smile of his oppressor and realized he still held a sliver of power: suppress the expression of pain and withhold satisfaction. It was an act of immeasurable strength to silently bear the needle-like sensations of asphyxiating fingers.

Carlos Senior knew his only move was to keep the gate closed. If Orlando Piedra was behind this, the gate was his only protection from the unspeakable crimes the colonel was known for. The image of gouged eyes and severed body parts kept him resolute. Yet, his son stood at the mercy of a fictitious phone call. In an act of compassion, Uvita, his teenage stepsister, reached between the bars to touch Manuel's shoulder, hoping the meager placement of her finger could transfer the strength and courage he required to survive the next few moments.

"Let him go," the officer said as he returned. "My captain has ordered us to move on."

The vice-like grip released Manuel, allowing the obstructed blood to rush back to his darkened hand.

"*Gracias, Virgen María*," Uva exclaimed as Manuel collapsed and held his arm. The men walked away, chuckling, but Carlos Senior stood still behind the gate, suspicious of their departure. He turned and raised his hand to silence the celebrative sounds of his stepdaughters.

"Manuel, go see if they've left."

His son stood paralyzed, disbelieving the directive.

"Before I open this gate, we need to make sure they're gone."

Manuel, still nursing his bruised arm, tiptoed to the edge of the property and peeked around the hedge to see the three police officers entering a car. Behind them was another car full of silhouetted figures. Holding his breath, he turned and sprinted toward the open gate. He collapsed in his father's arms as Agustín locked the gate behind him.

"They were here to kill you, Papa." Manuel said with a quivering voice. "There was a car full of hoodlums and they were here to kill you."

"I know," Carlos Senior calmly said while crossing the courtyard. "I could smell their thirst for blood. Piedad," he called to the maid. "Please make a cup of tea for my son. He is going to need it to calm his nerves."

"I need one too," Uva exclaimed.

"Me too," Uvita joined in, along with her sisters.

Gratitude and relief swept over Carlos Senior as Uva tenderly held his hand, and the girls listened to Manuel narrate the details of his torturing captor. Eventually, they each returned to their bed unaware the terrorizing officers were roaming Havana, seeking for another victim. The headline in the morning newspaper announced the brutal death of Dr. Pelayo Cuervo, a political colleague of Carlos Senior, dragged out of his home in the middle of the night and killed for his public critique of Batista, even though he had nothing to do with the attack on the palace. The somber reality of what they escaped burned like a bullet grazing their side.

******

"The line was grotesque," Manolín said.

He was sipping Johnny Walker Black from his home in Miami, retelling how he and Pedrito went to bow before the praise-thirsty tyrant two days after the attack.

"I went with Pedrito because everyone else had to work." He took out a cigarette while involuntarily expressing disappointment. "We hated Batista but had to do business with the government. Our absence would have been noted."

He stood and indicated he wanted to smoke that cigarette. We crossed the living room and walked to the balcony, overlooking a two-acre backyard lined with shade trees on both sides of a pond. The two-story house with a Mediterranean oasis for a yard, in an upscale Miami neighborhood, was his reward after building a photoengraving empire in Puerto Rico. It was his thriving business that provided employment for the whole family. More importantly, he provided what our single mother couldn't: a role model of a hardworking man, who laughed often, usually at the expense of his index finger, which he dared us to pull.

As a young father, barely making enough money to support my family, I frequently visited his home, because, quite frankly, I loved the man. My love for him made it easy to overlook his deeply flawed worldview, which in today's culture would have gotten him canceled a thousand times. It was in his home where I, and many others, laughed with frequency, joked in extremely improper ways, and subconsciously paid homage to the man who built a prosperous life for us all. He blended genius with ambition and infused it with testosterone to embody a confidence that made his presence the only one that mattered. If Brad Pitt were to stand beside him, Manolín's swagger would make the celebrity seem like an insecure, pimple-faced teenager.

"Close the door," he asked while pulling an ashtray closer to him.

Closing doors behind us was very important, especially in his home. It most likely had to do with the cost of air conditioning, but I also suspect it was a habit developed over years of not wanting conversations to be heard in other rooms.

"So, how could Batista force you to be there?" I said while closing the door. "What if you were busy, or not in town?"

"It's not Batista that forced us. It was his network. They were taking names. If we hadn't gone, there would have been some form of retribution. The line of men waiting to kiss Batista's ass extended for blocks. Regardless of what we thought, we had to express gratitude for his escape from the failed attempt on his life."

He took another sip of whiskey, and then with a sigh expressed a sentiment I had heard too often, "The history of Cuba would have been so different if the attack had succeeded."

"What about Papa, did he have to stand in line too?"

"Your father? He wasn't even working at the time. No. He was obsessing over car engines, wanting to build the perfect race car."

"I've been told," I said with a bit of indifference, having heard multiple complaints from my grandmother about the mess in her carport.

My uncle began to chuckle as he looked toward the horizon. A memory had resurfaced, and I leaned forward to indicate my curiosity.

"Your father once took me on a ride," my uncle said in between snorts. "It was an Italian car, a convertible, and he put a bigger engine in it, for racing. We went speeding up and down the streets. And then..." My uncle paused to laugh while I eagerly awaited for the punchline.

"...the car blew up."

"What do you mean it blew up?"

"The hood went up in the air and landed behind us. Car parts went flying out. He lost control and crashed the car against a tree." His laughter increased and his midsection shook with force. "Your father got so angry he started smashing the car while smoke was coming out of the engine, and cursing like I had never heard before."

My uncle re-enacted my father's temper tantrum as his body bent over in laughter. It took a while for me to join him, since I didn't think the story was funny. Yet, I was inevitably infected by his belly-jiggling guffaws as he repeated the curse words my father had angrily screamed.

"What happened to the car?" I asked once we were breathing normally.

"He left it there," and he began to laugh again.

"*¿De qué se ríen?*" asked Marta, his fourth wife, as she joined us out on the balcony, wanting to know why we were laughing so hard. She was about twenty years younger than him, only slightly older than me and loved a good story. As expected, we spent several minutes watching her chortle and chuckle.

"Your father was good to me," my uncle said. "He gave me guidance at a time when I needed it, but he was a very different sort of man." He paused for a moment, and sighed. "Dogs loved him. Wherever he went, if there was a dog anywhere, it would come up to him. He had these two dogs..." he paused again. "I can't remember their names."

"*Blanquita y Negrita*," I said.

My uncle raised his eyebrows in surprise at my correct response.

"¿*Blanquita y Negrita?*" Marta asked. "Were they white and black?"

"Yes, isn't it obvious?" he replied with annoyance.

"I just think it borders on... inappropriate."

"And how is that different from anything else in this house?" I asked jokingly.

"Yeah," she laughed. "You're right."

"What's wrong with *Blanquita y Negrita*?" My uncle asked defensively.

"Well, imagine if you had to call *Negrita* in public," Marta explained. "A black person could get offended."

"It's the name of the dog. There's nothing offensive about that."

"Not to us," she continued, "but to others maybe."

"Well, that's their problem. Not mine."

"I've heard," I interrupted in an effort to move the conversation along, "that the dogs followed Mama when she moved from neighborhood to neighborhood."

"Who?" Marta asked.

"The dogs, *Blanquita* y *Negrita.*"

"Yeah," he began to smile, "right."

"What?"

"Those dogs didn't follow her. I picked them up and drove them. Your mother was so gullible. How could a dog find her clear across town?"

"Did you ever tell her?"

"No," he chuckled. "Maybe I should and watch her reaction all over again."

I laughed, this time fully appreciating the joke, but he only smiled.

"Yeah, those dogs loved your father. Always sat with him..." his mind wandered off. "Before you leave today, I need you to get those yard tools over there and move them out of the way, if you don't mind. I almost ran over them yesterday."

"Who left them there?" I looked at the section of the yard he was pointing to.

"Not sure, but, if you don't mind, I'd appreciate it."

We sat in silence for a few minutes and I heard him humming. I looked at him, recognizing the Afro-Cuban tune and we exchanged a smile. Infused with a burst of energy, he stood and started singing, "*Songo le dio a Borondongo.*"

"*Borondongo le dio a Bernabe,*" I joined in and Marta started to laugh.

"*Bernarbe le metio muchilanga, le hecho burundanga, le hichan los pies. Molina...*"

We held that final vowel in the air and then sat back down, laughing at ourselves.

"*Ay, coño,*" he said. "I haven't sung that in years."

"How do you know that song?" Marta asked me.

"He's the one that taught it to me."

She looked at him and he nodded proudly.

"Yeah, Guillermo was always strange that way," he said and chuckled.

"*Tío,*" I said with curiosity. "You don't really talk too much about your past in Cuba. As a matter of fact, I think today is the most you've shared."

He nodded in agreement as he put out his cigarette in the ashtray.

"What for?" he finally said. "The past is gone. I have too much to think about with what's happening today. Marta," he turned to his wife, "bring me another drink, if you could be so kind. This time, add a little less water."

Marta returned to the living room to prepare him a drink, closing the door behind her.

"Why are you so interested in Cuba all of a sudden?"

"It's not all of a sudden. I have these conversations with other family members, and I just realized that you don't really talk about Cuba. But hey, that's all right."

"But hey," he mocked me.

"But hey," he said again. "You want to know why I don't talk about Cuba? Because it doesn't matter anymore. The only thing that matters is work and the money you bring to the house. You'll see. How old are your kids now?"

"Eight, seven and..."

"Just wait," he interrupted. "Just wait till they get older, start to drive and go to college. You better hope your non-profit job will cover those expenses, because brother, you'll see then how much money matters." He paused to playfully rotate the cigarette box in his hand. "I still don't understand how you work at a non-profit. What is wrong with making a profit? Your generation thinks money grows on trees, or something."

I must have annoyed him. His sharp response and use of the word "brother" indicated a turn in his mood. Like other family members in his generation, my *Tío* Manolín would roll his r's and say, "brrodderr." If he used it in conversation, it meant he was getting ready for a heated argument. Heated arguments were how we communicated, with little regard to how it affected the others in the room. Everyone accepted it and we just moved on. That is, of course, until the next heated argument.

"All those people on the radio talking about Cuba," he said while keeping his eyes on a distant horizon. "Fidel, and the embargo, they're all *hablando mierda*. They act so high and mighty, saying how the Americans need to intervene. It's easy to be angry now, but where were they when the *milicianos* came to shut down our business? You see them, pounding their fists, but when we were being chased out, they hid in fear, and many were even part of the mob!"

I sat quietly, regretting I raised the subject.

"No, no, no, no, no. When I left Cuba, I left all that behind." He looked at me straight in the eyes and clenched his teeth. "Life is too short to be looking back."

He rolled his thumb and index finger together and repeated his favorite words, "*La billilla.* Money is what matters."

"Hmm...," I challenged him with a smile. "I'm surprised you didn't say a romantic life with a woman is all that matters."

"That too. There's nothing like a well-shaped woman in your bed, but again, if you're unable to provide, eventually she'll leave you for another."

"Then maybe she wasn't the right woman."

"Most likely not, but few are the men who find the right woman. You hold on to Maria, because she obviously sees something in you that is hidden to all of us."

"It's that Gutierrez charm," I stood and rotated my hips. My uncle laughed.

Marta came out with a drink in her hand and caught me rotating my hips.

"Hey, hey, hey!" she complained. "What's with the moves?"

We laughed and it triggered a whole new set of inappropriate jokes. I departed that day in the same manner I did for countless years, laughing. Now that he's passed away, I think, "Who was he fooling? It wasn't the money that mattered. It was the laughter."

CHAPTER 10

Cristóbal

July 2019
    San Juan, Puerto Rico

Cristóbal and Marisa moved to Puerto Rico shortly after they fled the Castro Revolution along with thousands of exiled Cubans. It was there where they nurtured an extensive community of friends and family, of which I was fortunate enough to have been part of. My mother asked Cristóbal to be my brother's baptismal godfather, and over the years his godfather role included me too. I visited *Padrino* and *Madrina* during a time of political turmoil in Puerto Rico when every Islander was anxiously awaiting the governor to resign. At the time, they were both in their eighties, living in a house engineered to withstand the forces of a major hurricane, and decorated with an art collection gathered over six decades.

I was greeted at the door by my godfather with a welcoming smile. He stood tall and slender, with the help of a cane, and called out my childhood name, "Memo." It transported me to younger days when my full name was only said as a precursor to a reprimand.

"*Coño, Padrino*," I replied while kissing his cheek and lightly hugging him.

"*Madrina*, have you been drinking from the fountain of youth," I said jokingly after kissing her cheek and giving her a slightly stronger hug. Our eyes rested on each other, as we appreciated the moment, long overdue.

"You look great," she said and squeezed my arm.

"I now have an AARP card," I said jokingly.

They looked at me quizzically. I forgot they were not as bilingual as the Miami branch of the family. We walked in slowly. My godfather's neurological condition forced him to take very small steps. His slow pace allowed me to admire the artwork and décor as we proceeded slowly through the house. I was particularly drawn to a long bookcase holding their books and family photographs.

"*Mira*," my godmother said to me, lifting a photograph of my beautiful mother when she was in her early thirties. In the photograph, my brother and I were clinging tightly to her dress.

On a neighboring shelf sat a photograph of their deceased son, Carlos, known to us as Charlie. He died in his forties, years after an accidental dive in shallow waters that turned him into a quadriplegic.

"*Mira*, Charlie," I commented as I lifted the framed photograph. "Always with a smile."

"That was taken on his boat off the coast of Fajardo." A moment of silence passed and then she returned the photo to its place. "He must have been thirty there," she sighed, and we continued towards the living room.

My godfather had already taken his seat in front of the television set, which was displaying silent images of the island-wide protests over the vulgar and offensive comments made by their governor, Ricardo Roselló.

"Look at that," my godfather pointed at the video on the television screen, showing millions of people marching peacefully toward the island's capitol. "I have never been prouder of the Puerto Rican people than I am today. They're doing something extraordinary."

The handheld signs matched the collective chant, "Ricky. *¡Renuncia!*"

"It's amazing," I replied as I sat on a chair next to his recliner. "Do you think the governor will resign, or will he be stubborn and hold on?"

"He has no choice. All the mayors and officials are with the people. Hold on. *Mami*, raise the volume. Let's see what this man has to say."

My godmother took control of the remote, and we heard a political commentator noting the historical moment. It became obvious he wasn't going to say anything new, which led her to mute the program once again.

"Think about how quickly the Puerto Rican people formed a united voice to repudiate unacceptable behavior," my godfather said.

"I read the article. Roselló made numerous sexist, racist and homophobic remarks."

"Numerous is an understatement. It's over eight hundred pages of offensive slurs. The real Ricardo Roselló, the man hiding behind the hypocritical smile, is a pig."

"And how did these text messages and emails get out?" I asked.

"Good journalism, as always."

"So, is there no ethics clause in the constitution that would give grounds for his dismissal? How can an elected official stay in power after using such language?"

"Unfortunately, there is none. A vulgar man can be elected into the highest office. The people decide if they accept the vulgarities, usually at the polls, today on the streets."

"What I find interesting is that Roselló doesn't seem to have any supporters. If this were to happen in the mainland, counter protestors would show up to stir problems."

"He has supporters, but nobody can deny he said those things." My godfather smiled victoriously at the bird's eye view of the streets in Old San Juan filled by a sea of people.

"If only we had been able to do the same in Cuba," my godmother remarked.

Marisa, my godmother, survived a meningitis infection in her early seventies that left her thought process impaired. A decade later she was fully aware of this disability and often apologized for not being able to retain information. Consequently, she wore a pleasant and silent smile while I visited. Yet, every so often, to remind us she was listening and still present, she would join the conversation with brief comments and insight.

"Which point in Cuban history are you referring to, *Madrina*?" I asked, wanting to elicit her participation.

"Well," she paused. "At many points. It's the spirit of the protest I am referring to."

I nodded.

"She's talking about the non-violent demand for change and actually achieving it. Am I right?" Cristóbal said and reached for her hand.

"Yes," she said with a pleasant smile. "Cuba's history is riddled with violence, as if we knew no other way to get rid of corrupt politicians. This," she said, pointing at the television screen. "This is a real inspiration."

"*Padrino*, you were active with the university's student union, right?"

"The F.E.U., *Federación Estudiantil Universitaria*."

"So, I read something disappointing. The F.E.U. was responsible for the failed attack on the Presidential Palace in 1957."

"Yes, it was. Why do you say disappointing?"

"Because they were university students with access to new ideas, like non-violence, which was already known back then. Don't you think university students should have attempted a non-violent protest like this one?"

He readjusted himself in his seat, giving me time to prepare myself for an impromptu lesson in Cuban history, a subject he loved to lecture on.

"They did. The students were always engaged in some form of protest. I don't want to condone violence, but it's not that simple. I knew some of the students in the attack, because the university was a close-knit community, and I had started working there as professor, but let me explain something..."

"I didn't know you taught," I interrupted.

"It was short lived, almost three years, and then Castro came, and it all fell apart."

"What did you teach?"

"Whatever the senior professors didn't feel like teaching, but let's return to the attack on the Presidential Palace. There were many efforts to remove Batista through peaceful means, and they all failed. What you need to understand is that the Batista phenomenon can be traced to the presidency of Grau San Martin. He was a vindictive and corrupt man who caused much damage to democracy as an institution. By the time Batista came into power, the people had given up hope. To further muddy the waters, the Cuban economy was booming, Fidel and his rebels were in the Sierra Maestra, and the politicians were in constant disagreement. This type of chaos only benefited Batista, who allowed for the sham election to take place in 1958, knowing the political parties couldn't agree on anything, including something as basic as the electoral process."

I nodded, silently connecting the dots between then and now.

"The F.E.U. historically took on the mantle of challenging social injustices," my godfather continued. "They organized protests, but none were as effective as what we're seeing here in Puerto Rico. Why? Because the Cuban people no longer believed change could happen through peaceful means. Do you see the difference? Here, in Puerto Rico, the people believe they can force a governor to resign. The Cuban people of 1957 had no hope, so they resorted to a frustrated act of violence."

"I understand your point, but wasn't there a higher expectation of the students, the emerging intellectual class? I know they wanted to end the dictatorship. I'm just surprised they stooped to the level of rebels, like in the Moncada raid."

"Let me make one thing clear. The attack on the Presidential Palace was almost successful. Had they accomplished what they set out to do, Cuba's history would have been very different. Instead of Fidel Castro coming down from the Sierra Maestra we would have had José Antonio Echeverría, restoring the constitution that your grandfather so arduously defended."

"*Manzanita*," my godmother said with a pleasant smile.

I turned to her for an explanation, but she remained silent.

"Ah yes, *Manzanita,*" my godfather clarified with a smile. "That 'little apple' was one hell of a guy, and very well liked."

"I get it, *Padrino*. If only this had occurred, or if only that had happened. It's the same analysis I've been hearing my whole life, a series of 'ifs.' I'm just throwing another 'if' at you. What if, instead of students going on a suicide mission against an entire army, they would have promoted non-violent demonstrations, like the kind we're seeing here on TV."

"You're looking at the event sixty years later. You live in a country where peaceful protests are protected by the constitution. Let me tell you a story about a law student who everyone called *Bicicleta*."

"Because he got around on a bicycle?"

"I imagine so, although I never saw him on one. Like most nicknames, he probably earned his as a child and it stuck, because even his family members called him *Bicicleta*."

My godfather began to laugh as he recalled the memories.

"The man behaved as if it were perfectly normal to be called by that nickname. I remember him walking and the other students saying, 'Here comes *Bicicleta.*'"

We continued to laugh, reflecting on the cultural trait of that generation to rename people.

"So, *Bicicleta* was not only a good law student but also an organizer. He met with field laborers and helped them negotiate better working conditions. He often led student marches in front of the capitol and could be seen arguing policy with many leaders. In other words, *Bicicleta* was a pain in the ass of the Batista regime."

I smiled, happy to hear about the work of an activist.

"One day, a car exploded in front of the police station. Nobody was hurt, and this was one more bomb in a series of many others that were exploding on a weekly basis."

"Don't tell me they blamed *Bicicleta* for it?"

My godfather smiled and raised his finger to slow down my racing mind.

"The police chief at that time, a large, fat man by the name of Salas-Cañizares, was a cruel and sadistic man. He and a group of police officers marched into the university, arrested *Bicicleta*, and charged him with the bomb."

"What happened to him?"

"*Bicicleta* was never heard from again. He disappeared. Our best guess is that he died while in custody and his body was discarded."

"What do you mean? What about his family? Wasn't there a court to oversee this?"

"Normally, that would have been the case, but in those days the Batista regime was doing whatever the hell it pleased and animals like Salas-Cañizares were not being held accountable. Violence seemed to be the only way to retaliate, especially when *Bicicleta* and the memory of his injustice was so fresh. You ask why the students did not lead a peaceful protest, and my answer is *Bicicleta.*"

"I understand, but two wrongs don't make a right," I shook my head in disagreement.

"I'm not saying you should agree," he said energetically. "Acceptance and agreement are two different things, but this is the closest explanation I can give you."

The conversation was animated, but eventually it lost to our hunger. My godfather eagerly insisted we go out for lunch. I drove them to an Argentinian restaurant they recommended. There, we spoke about his impressive donation of Cuban music to Florida International University in Miami, a collection he developed and cataloged for over fifty years. My godfather, like most historians, was full of anecdotes. Unlike the members of the Miami diaspora, he did not politicize Cuban music.

He spoke with appreciation for the art, regardless if the artist was from Castro's Cuba or the exiled community in Miami.

"*Ay, Padrino*," I said with a smile. "It's refreshing to hear you talk in that manner."

"What do you mean?"

"*Bueno*, you don't seem to have the emotional baggage. You have the same memories as every exiled Cuban, but you describe the past with joy, despite having lost so much."

He looked at me while chewing a portion of his meal and with a nod indicated he wanted me to continue.

"Maybe it's just a matter of personality, but I don't hear any resentment when you talk about Cuba and the rise of Castro. Do you know what I mean? You talk about Cuba the way you talk about Charlie."

"Hmm... interesting. Well, you know I'm not a religious man, but what I'm about to say is the closest I'll ever get to anything religious."

I placed my fork down and leaned forward in an effort to hear his soft voice.

"I had that resentment you speak of. It was there, deep in my heart. I didn't want to leave Cuba. None of us wanted to start over in a foreign land, but the problem wasn't just Castro, it was the thousands of people behind him. You bet I was angry, especially those first few years in Miami. Those were hard years. Miami was a small country town, full of small-minded people who didn't want us Cubans around."

"Did you experience racism?"

"We all did! The Americans didn't know how to coexist with us, and we were arriving by the hundreds every day, but that's not your question."

"What's my question?"

"Your question is how I'm able to speak about the past, about Cuba, without resentment."

"That's right. Sorry, continue."

"The music," he said after taking a sip of wine.

"Your music collection?" I asked, recalling childhood memories of his study, the walls lined by shelves full of vinyl records.

"Yes. I immersed myself in music, and that healed me from that dark resentment you talk about. It was my therapy."

He paused again. His voice was losing strength.

"Music became the mirror for me to reflect on why our Cuban society collapsed. I saw too many people trying to pick up those crumbs to re-bake the cake, but time has proven there was nothing to return to. So, in the face of such loss one has to ask, what's left?"

He paused and I remained silent, thinking he was being rhetorical.

"Tell me, what do you think is left?"

"Your innermost being. Your heart and soul."

"Exactly. You see, we were run out of Cuba, but that persecution was not about me, Cristóbal Díaz Ayala. It was about them. It's very sad, if you think about it, but once I came to terms with it, I found it easier to build a life for me and my family, and eventually forgive."

"And even forgive the ones who pushed us out," my godmother interrupted, "when we saw them years later walking on the streets of Miami."

Cristóbal turned to her and raised his eyebrows.

"Remember Joaquin?" she asked.

I waited for more details.

"Joaquin," my godfather explained, "was a close associate of my uncle, and he worked in the newspaper, *El País*, which my family owned. Well, I don't want to go into details, but Joaquin became a *Fidelista* and he led the dismantling of the newspaper. It was a betrayal like we never imagined. Years later we bumped into Joaquin in Miami."

"What did you do?"

"We were surprised by the encounter and stood there, looking at each other in silence."

"And?"

"And nothing. He lowered his head and stepped aside. We decided to keep on walking."

"Wow! I'm not sure I would have done the same."

"It goes back to your original observation, about not having resentment. Do I feel the loss? You bet I do, but I can't allow the loss to disfigure who I am."

"And you got all that from a song?" I said jokingly. "Let's play that music, because more people need to hear it."

When the meal ended, I redirected the conversation to my childhood and his influence on me. I thanked them for taking an interest in the raising of my brother and me.

"Well, you and your brother were good companions for Charlie," he said. "I didn't mind including you in our outings. Besides, I owed it to your father to help guide you."

The server came to the table to ask if we wanted anything else.

"¿Un café?" My godfather asked.

I nodded and he asked her for three espressos.

The coffee arrived a few minutes later and we immediately reached for our cups.

"Papa mentioned several times how you were the friend he could rely on," I said. "If he called, he knew you would show."

He nodded and waited for me to say more.

"If I'm not mistaken, you were the one that helped him get out of the psychiatric hospital after his nervous breakdown."

He leaned back and opened his eyes wide, surprised I mentioned the event.

"Yes, I did do that," he said and paused to retrieve that memory. "I had forgotten about it." He took another sip from his espresso, finishing it, and placed the cup down very slowly.

"I imagine it must have been difficult," I said.

"The act itself was easy. What was difficult was watching your father in that condition." My godfather shook his head. "We all have a season in our lives when everything seems to go wrong, inexplicably, through no fault of our own. We search for a reason, only to realize there is none. It's just life. *Así es la vida*."

He looked down and his face saddened, as if a hidden grief surfaced. We sat in silence for a minute, as he journeyed through his memories.

"He called me when Charlie died, your father." He looked up at me and I saw his eyes were moist with tears. "I was inconsolable, and he knew that. So, we traded proverbs."

"Proverbs, really? Like what?"

"I'm not exactly sure. It's been too long, but I think your father quoted Juan Luis Vives."

"Death is," my godmother began to recite, "the soul's lack of tools through which life can be prolonged."

"Yes," he smiled at her. "The soul's lack of tools... So, I replied, I think, with a proverb from Baltasar Gracián."

My godfather looked at his wife, waiting for her to recite once again.

"For the young, death is a ruinous shipwreck, but for the old it is docking at port."

"Very good *Madrina*!" I exclaimed.

"*Ay mijo*," she blushed. "That's how we use to study, memorizing poems and proverbs."

I asked them to recite other proverbs, a challenge my godmother enjoyed. My godfather tried to contribute a few, but his voice became inaudible. I took it as our cue to ask for the check and end my visit. As I left their home, backing up from the driveway, I paused to watch them wave goodbye. Two people who lived through more loss than I could ever comprehend and were nurturing members of the village that raised me, stood at the threshold of their home wishing me well. Predictably, I was overcome by a blend of conflicting feelings, and I realized I had no proverb to describe them.

CHAPTER 11

Guantanamera

April 1957
    Havana

Carlitos was in Tina's carport, assembling a carburetor, when two university students approached him. One was tall and chunky, the other short and slim. Both were disheveled. The dogs trotted up to them with wagging tails.

"Doctor," the short one said. "I didn't know you're a mechanic."

"*Ay mijo*, it's just a hobby," Carlitos replied while standing to greet them. "How's it going for you?"

"Well, you know. We're both hiding because our names are on the directory."

Carlitos shook his head.

"It's only a matter of time before they catch up with us," the tall one said.

"Then what are you still doing here? Shouldn't you both be hiding in the eastern part of the island?"

"Yeah, I'll be going to Camaguey with my wife's family," the short one said while looking at the carburetor. "What's wrong with it?"

"The choke valve is getting stuck." Carlitos picked it up and turned it around in his hand. "What about you," he asked the tall one. "What are you going to do?"

"I'll be leaving for Miami. I heard there's work there."

"Miami? *¡No jodas, chico!* Are you kidding? Why would you go there?"

"It's only for a short while, until things calm down."

"Doctor," the short student interjected. "We need a favor."

Carlitos remained silent, waiting to hear their request.

"We have a little gift for Batista, but we have nowhere to store it. Can we leave it with you for a few days?"

Carlitos smacked his lips, anticipating the nature of the gift.

"How long?"

"A day or two."

"More like three," said the tall one.

"Let's take a look at it," Carlitos nodded.

The men walked with him to their car and opened the trunk. Inside, under a blanket, sat a homemade bomb about the size of a shoebox.

"Where's the detonation device?" Carlitos asked while inspecting it from a distance.

"It's on the backseat."

"It's perfectly safe, you know," the short student said.

Carlitos shot him a look of incredulity.

"What are you going to do with it?"

"We're going to get Batista, that *hijo de puta*."

"And how are you going to do that? What's your plan?"

The students looked at each other, as if deciding how much to say.

"All we need is for you to hold on to it for a few days," the tall student said. "With all the raids the police are doing, we can't keep it with us."

"Will you help us?"

"Bring it over," Carlitos said as he turned around. "But keep the detonator."

The short student held the bomb as if it were a wet dog and followed him to the carport. *Negrita* sniffed the air behind them, trying to determine if the content of the box was edible. Carlitos opened the trunk of the car, cleared a space, and pointed to where the package was to rest. They placed it down carefully and Carlitos tossed a dirty shirt over it.

"If you're not here in three days - Thursday - I'll toss it in the bay."

"Fair enough," the tall student said.

Tina watched them leave from her kitchen window, wondering who they were and what the nature of their visit was.

"Olga," she called out.

"*Sí?*"

"Call your husband. Dinner is almost ready. Tell him to wash up."

At the dinner table, when the meal was over, Tina observed her son-in-law and determined he was suffering from melancholy. She knew it was a condition, since her ex-husband would have bouts of melancholy after the headaches receded.

"Carlitos, *mijito*," she said in a soft tone. "I know the death of your friend, *Manzanita*, has really affected you. It was a horrible way to die."

Carlitos leaned back and looked at her.

"I've seen the flowers and candles people have left on the sidewalk where he died," she continued. "He really was loved by many."

"Did you know the police are breaking up all those flowers?" Olga commented. "They don't want anyone grieving his death. They call him a traitor."

"The traitor is the one living in the palace," Carlitos said and looked down.

"So, I know you're upset and sad," Tina continued. "I know you don't want to work for your father and pretend everything will be alright, but have a little bit of faith, and you'll see that everything will work out for the better."

"You don't get it, do you?" Carlitos replied in a soft voice while still looking down. Olga leaned in to hear him. "We've lost the one opportunity to regain control of the government. The right man with the right vision to restore our country has been shot down." He looked up at Tina with a pained expression. "How can you say that everything will be alright? Don't you see what's happening? If anyone is suspected of being anti-Batista, they're thrown in jail. Fidel is building an army and it won't be long before he brings it to the city."

"But you can't stay like this," Tina implored, "sitting on the floor, getting your hands greasy. You're a Márquez-Sterling, not a cheap mechanic. Your grandfather, Don Manuel, wouldn't want to see you like this."

Carlitos' eyes began to fill with tears.

"You know we love you." Tina reached over and placed her hand on his. "This will always be your home, but you can't continue like this."

Carlitos nodded while looking at his plate.

"You have a law degree, a philosophy and history degree. I'm missing one, no?"

"Literature," Olga contributed.

Carlitos looked at his beloved and smiled.

"And literature," Tina continued. "Of course, literature. My point is that you spent so many years working for these degrees, don't you think there's something you can do. Talk to your friend, Cristóbal. His family owns the newspaper. Maybe you can work there. Talk to your friend, Oscar Jorge. He's very smart. I'm sure he has ideas of what you can do. I know you don't like working with your father, especially after he remarried, but it's not a bad option. A lot of people have far worse."

Carlitos nodded while Olga looked on quietly.

"You are loved by many. I've seen it." Tina reached over and placed her other hand on his. "You have more friends than I will ever have, and more options for a career than I can imagine. You're a Márquez-Sterling. Don't waste your time by sitting in the carport."

Carlitos was not used to Tina talking to him with tenderness. He felt the palm of her hand on his own and a single tear ran down his cheek. He lifted her hand and kissed it, repeatedly. Olga, moved by the long awaited moment, also began to shed tears.

In the morning, Carlitos was full of energy. He sang as he showered. He joked with his mother-in-law, and he patted Olga on the rear before walking out the front door. She giggled as she watched him depart and turned around to see her mother give her a knowing look. Olga blushed and giggled some more.

"Olga," Tina said while looking at the carport.

"*Sí?*"

"Would you help me organize the carport? I think it would look so much better if we could get Carlitos' tools and car parts in some kind of order."

"I don't know," Olga bit her lip, "he doesn't want me touching his engine things."

"Well, I think he has a new purpose. Don't you see it? He's bound to come back with news that he's working at *El País*, or at the law firm with *el Viejo Márquez*. Besides, I'm only talking about organizing the area. He can still work on the car if he wants."

One personality trait the mother and daughter shared was their need for order. The thought of turning the visible chaos in the carport into a structured system brought glee to their heart. The labeling of paper bags, the storing of screws inside little boxes, the throwing away of needless items, as well as the sweeping and wiping, made them downright giddy. Within a couple of hours, the two women stood back to admire the transformation of the carport from a disorderly, greasy mess, into a space that made sense in their order-hungry mind.

******

It is said Havana was planned and designed by drunken poets lost in love. The grid of Old Havana is slanted and often interrupted by smaller dead-end streets, which tend to have a plaza for the locals to congregate. Many of the streets are named after historical figures, like Ignacio Agramonte and Jose Martí, while other streets are named after saints, like San Lazaro and San Nicolas. Every once in a while, you come across a street named after a sentiment or a human condition, moving you to ponder metaphors. There were no repeating patterns, causing residents who lived in the newer neighborhoods, where the grid made sense, to get lost. For Carlitos, however, it was home.

He was at the *Plaza del Cristo*, which housed a 17th century church in dire need of restoration, when he saw *el Caballero de París* walking toward him. His black coat faded into gray, and his voice echoed against the buildings as he recited a well known poem by Jose Martí.

I am a truthful man from where the palm tree grows
And my dying wish is to release my soulful verses.

"Oh, c'mon now," Carlitos complained. "We learned that one in grade school." Carlos could see the mud stained hair of the madman, as he neared and continued to recite.

I grow a white rose in July and January
for the sincere friend who offers his forthright hand...

"You're bleeding," Carlitos realized it was blood, not mud, on his hair. He stepped closer to inspect, but *el Caballero* moved back defensively. Carlitos retreated and the homeless poet continued his recital with an extended hand for dramatic effect.

...and for the one whose cruelty tears my life-giving heart
thistles and nettles I won't grow - I grow the white rose.

"Martí wrote my poem," *el Caballero* said. "It's as if he knew my soul."

"Yours and mine. Why are you bleeding?"

"Why shouldn't I bleed? When a man stops bleeding, he stops living."

"Did someone hit you? Were you harassed by the police?"

El Caballero laughed.

"What?"

"I fell off a tree yesterday," he said and continued to laugh.

"A tree? Are you a monkey?"

"I had to see the sunset. Didn't you see the colors in the sky?"

"No."

"*Oye hombre*, it was glorious. Rays of orange for angels to dance on."

"Let's go get some coffee."

"*No, gracias*. I already had my cup. A group of tourists made me rich last night. Every time an American cruise ship comes to port, I win the lottery."

"Is that why you have *Guantanamera* in your head?"

"*¿Como?* No, a tourist wouldn't evoke such poetry. It's you. I saw you from a distance, sitting in front of this chapel and I thought, 'there sits *el hombre sincero*. If Rodin were alive, I'd ask him to make a statue of you. You are a truly genuine man. "

Carlitos laughed as the madman continued his way with a slight skip in his step. He stood, recalling the poem in its entirety and made his way to *Calle Amargura*. By the time he reached his father's law firm, he was humming *Guantanamera* and no longer worried about the country falling apart.

"*Y que, Gordo?*" Carlos Senior greeted his son with the term of endearment reserved for family and an inner circle of friends. It was his attempt to reconcile from the harsh words spoken a few nights ago.

"What's your favorite Jose Martí poem?" Carlitos asked his father as he sat in front of his desk. "But you can't quote his *Versos Sencillos*. It's too easy."

"Why?"

"C'mon. Play along. I bet you secretly yearn for 'The Guatemalan Girl' with her little white shoes." Carlitos chuckled.

"Please," Carlos Senior protested and sat in front of his son. "That sappy love poem?"

They chuckled together before Carlitos asked again.

"Well, like everyone else," Carlos Senior answered, "I happen to like 'I Grow a White Rose,' but if I were to put that one aside, as you asked, I'd have to go with 'I Dream Awake.' And you, what's yours?"

"Thank you for asking, because it leads to the point I want to make, but before I go there, I'll answer your question."

Carlitos paused and looked at his father, who seemed to be losing patience.

"It used to be 'I Searched for You,' but now I like 'Inside of Me.' "

"The impeded lion?"

"Exactly. Ask me why?"

"Just say what's on your mind."

"I find myself pacing. In my head, I can't stop pacing. I'm angry at many things. I'm even angry at you."

Carlos Senior observed his son silently.

"But really, I'm angry at myself," he continued. "That scene I made in your new home, in front of your new family, was uncalled for. They're not to blame for that day and how things went down with Mamá."

"That day?"

"You know. The day when..."

"I know what day you're talking about," Carlos Senior interrupted. "You can't simply blame it all on one day, can you?"

"Well, it was a pretty bad day. You did go in with a gun, shooting at everyone."

"And I guess I should thank you for wrestling the gun away from me."

"No. What I'm trying to say..."

"What are you trying to say? That you're sorry? Are you trying to apologize for being an ass to my new wife and her daughters?"

Carlitos smacked his lips.

"It's not me you have to apologize to. They're the ones who have to hear it. That is, if you can bring that impeded lion in your heart to stop pacing and offer an appropriate apology. Does it bother you I moved into her home? Does that upset your sense of order?"

Carlitos stood and began pacing, angrily.

"I didn't come here to apologize!"

"Then why are you here?" Carlos Senior raised his voice.

Carlitos smacked his lips and kept on pacing.

"Do you know your name is on the list?" Carlos Senior said in a stern voice.

Carlitos stopped and looked at his father, who stared back angrily.

"That's right. Osvaldo alerted me to it. But don't worry. I took care of it."

"*Coño*, Papá..." Carlitos said softly.

"*¿Coño, Papá?*" Carlos Senior repeated in a mocking voice. "Is that all you can say? *¿Coño Papá?* Thank God, not everybody in Batista's regime is an *hijo de puta*. Thankfully, a decent man saw your name and told us about it. These are treacherous times. You need to choose your friends wisely. In the meantime, I need you to apologize. Not because you owe it to me, but because it's the right thing to do, and those girls deserve to be treated as if they're your sisters."

Carlitos left his father's law firm with his head hung low, and his back hunched over. The buildings on *Calle Amargura* were old, but nicely maintained. It was one of the few streets that led to the capitol building. Locals joked that the bitter work of governing was responsible for its name. Among the waves of pedestrians, Carlitos passed a man selling lottery tickets, a woman tossing a bucket of dirty water onto the cobblestone street, a group of teenage boys laughing at some mischief, and three nuns each with a small shopping bag. He reached the end of the street, in front of the capitol, and paused to contemplate the historic steps from where his father announced the ratification of the island's constitution. He was a child at that time, filled with pride that he stood next to the man who made it all possible. A dream was born in his young mind during that historic moment: to follow in his father's footsteps and one day stand on those steps as a servant of the people.

Carlitos walked away unsure if that dream would come true. He took a trolley to *El Vedado*, his childhood neighborhood, and got off one block away from where his mother was renting. Her voice floated with the wind, faint at first, but stronger with every step. She was standing at her front door, talking with his cousin, *el Canalla*, who was ending his visit and spinning car keys in his hand. Carlitos watched as the Scoundrel said farewell to his mother and they kissed lightly on the cheek.

Silvia saw her son standing at a distance.

"Bernardito," she said. "Get that stray dog out of here, before he bites a child."

The Scoundrel turned to look and began laughing when he saw Carlitos.

"*Sácalo*, get him out of here," Silvia ordered before retreating back inside and slamming the door shut. She, too, was laughing.

Her words echoed in his head as he rode the bus back to *Víbora Park*. The bus passed Tina's house before stopping one block away. Carlitos saw the clean carport from his bus seat and his mouth dropped. He jumped out and ran towards the house in disbelief. *Blanquita y Negrita* ran out to meet him as he stood in front of the carport, unsure of what he was seeing.

"Doesn't it look good?" Olga said smiling, as she came out to greet her husband.

Carlitos didn't reply and stared in shock at a perfectly clean and organized carport. Engine parts had been moved against the far wall. A line of labeled paper bags and boxes rested on the shelf. His tools were presumably inside the toolboxes, which sat in line on the next shelf.

"Come, let me show you what we did."

He was speechless as Olga described the work accomplished.

"I placed all your screws and bolts in these bags," she said, clearly proud of herself. "And look, we even cleaned the car. It was full of rags and grease stains."

He shot Olga an alarmed look.

"What?" she asked as he ran to the trunk, opened it and saw the bomb, uncovered.

"I don't know what that is," she pointed at the shoebox bomb. "I had to move it closer to the edge to make room for this toolbox, which I think you wanted here."

Carlitos looked at her wide eyed.

"Your tools are all inside the toolboxes. And every little thing on the floor I labeled. I figured out your system," she said proudly. "I realized you were placing things in certain areas on purpose. So, I wrote it all down for you."

He followed her and shockingly viewed the bags she pointed at.

"Carlitos," Tina called out from the kitchen door. "Are you going to eat lunch?"

He turned to see his mother-in-law smiling at him.

"It looks much better, doesn't it?" Tina said. "C'mon in. I have lunch ready."

Carlitos took a labeled bag and lowered himself to the floor, defeated. *Blanquita* licked his hands as he started to cry.

"What's the matter?" Olga said. "Did I do it wrong?"

He ripped the bag and the screws spilled onto his lap.

"Why are you crying?"

"What's the matter?" Tina asked. "Is he not hungry?"

"I don't know," Olga kneeled next to him. *"¿Qué te pasa, mi vida?* I swear I can tell you where every little screw was. Look, these were next to this tire. You see? I wrote it on the bag."

"Leave me alone! Stop touching me!" he barked at her and tossed the ripped bag aside.

"But…"

"I said, leave me alone!" he screamed with such ferocity that Olga jumped back.

"Ven," Tina said to Olga. "Come inside and leave him alone."

Carlitos sat on the floor, next to the car, crying while the two dogs licked his arm.

"But I don't understand," Olga said. "It's all here. He doesn't have to get upset. I don't know why he's crying."

"Just leave him alone," Tina pulled at her daughter and looked at Carlitos with worried eyes. "He doesn't want to hear our explanations right now."

The earth sank below him, covering him with darkness. Within seconds he was unable to move, and the only way his lungs could exhale was to release a wail from deep within his being. Olga went to hold him, but Tina pulled her back.

"Get inside," she ordered as she pushed Olga into the house.

"But... but... but..."

"You can't help him now," Tina closed the door behind her.

They stood with their backs against the door as the sound of his anguish filled their ears. The reverberations of tormented pain, escaping after years of incarceration in an unyielding heart, sounded almost inhuman, until his rage found an outlet. Carlitos became a human demolition machine, destroying shelves and slamming objects against the floor. The minutes passed and the demolition continued, sparking curiosity in Tina, who slowly opened the door to look. Her eyes opened wide at the sight of shelves and their contents being thrown on the floor. The shock of seeing her carport littered with spilled paint, fragmented wood, and overturned boxes kept her attention long enough for Carlitos to make eye contact with her.

"You didn't even know my grandfather!" He screamed with fury. "You can't begin to imagine how he would think, because you don't know how I think!"

"*Ay coño*," Tina said as she slammed the door shut and leaned up against it. "Get me *el Viejo Márquez* on the phone."

The door shook behind Tina, as if a bull were trying to break it down. Olga stood wide eyed, paralyzed.

"Call *el Viejo Márquez* now!"

She ran to the phone and cried for help as her husband slammed every useful item in the carport against the clean floor. Tina whispered prayers to the Virgin Mary as Olga walked back and forth, rubbing her hands. The minutes were endless, but eventually Carlitos ran out of items to break and his rage subsided. The explosive sounds of his destructive fury yielded to silence, and the far-off sound of thunder announced an approaching storm.

When the police officers arrived, sheets of rain and the wagging tails of dogs welcomed them. Instinctively, the officers ran under the protective roof of the carport unaware that Carlitos was kneeled beside the car, splattered in paint, trying to unscrew the odometer from under the dashboard. The four officers were inspecting the debris-strewn space when he straightened up and looked at them.

"Carlos Márquez-Sterling?" A policeman asked, unsure if he was standing in front of the right person.

"Yes," he answered with trepidation.

"You? Your Carlos Márquez-Sterling?"

He nodded affirmatively.

"We need you to come with us."

Carlitos stood, looked at the trunk of the car nervously and then at the men.

"Now?"

"Yes, now."

Olga opened the kitchen door and peered out to see her husband being handcuffed.

"Call Papá," he said to her. "Tell him what's happening. He'll know what to do."

She stood, tearfully biting the collar of her blouse, as he repeated instructions from the police car. Curious neighbors looked from a distance as he was driven away, and Olga found herself stepping into puddles of blue paint. Carlos Senior, wet from the rain, walked up to the edge of the carport, having witnessed the arrest from a distance.

"It's as if a bomb went off in here," Tina said to him.

"Or a tornado," Olga whispered.

"If I didn't see this with my own eyes..." Carlos Senior began to comment when Olga ran up to him, sobbing. He had no option but to embrace her.

"I'll take care of this," he said while caressing the back of her head. "It'll be okay."

******

Carlitos sat in the back of the police car, certain he was being taken for questioning by the military. Instead, they parked in front of a psychiatric clinic. He was led inside, uncuffed and instructed to undress under the supervision of male and female nurses. Minutes later, flimsy blue pajamas became his uniform, and sterile rooms void of throwable objects his residence. Carlitos watched his neighbors walk around in a daze, babbling incoherent thoughts and yelling obscenities. The orderlies, dressed in white, behaved like adolescent boys who resented their assignment while entertaining themselves at the expense of the patients.

He was studying his new environment, looking for any weakness in its system, when an Afro-Cuban janitor slowly passed by, sweeping the floor.

"Oye, *hermano*. I need some help," Carlitos whispered discreetly. "I can get you a hundred *pesos* if you give me access to a phone."

"How are you going to do that?" the janitor asked amusingly.

"I need to get some help. Believe me. Just one phone call. You have nothing to lose and a lot of money to gain."

"Two hundred."

Carlitos agreed, and a nearby office with a phone was made available. The janitor stood at the door and watched him sit by the phone in silence.

"Go ahead. Make your phone call. What are you waiting for?"

"I'm thinking."

"About what?"

"About who to call."

"Man, get out of here," the janitor walked up to Carlitos. "You're wasting my time."

"No. Wait." Carlitos picked up the receiver. "I'll make it now."

His fingers trembled as he placed them inside the numerical spaces, slowly taking each rotation of the dial to full completion.

"Cristóbal?" he spoke into the phone. "I need your help. I'm in a difficult situation."

Later that night, under a downpour of rain, Cristóbal knocked on the back door of the hospital where he met the janitor and paid him an exorbitant amount of money in exchange for a few minutes of conversation with Carlitos. He was led inside to a waiting room, where he saw his friend wearing a restraining jacket.

"*Gordo*, what's going on?" Cristóbal asked in shock. "Why is he like this?" he asked the janitor and the male nurse who stood next to Carlitos.

"It's just a precaution," the nurse said, "to make sure he won't hurt anyone."

"Take this off him," Cristóbal commanded angrily.

The nurse turned and looked at the janitor, unsure if he should obey. Cristóbal flashed a bill to the nurse. With the jacket removed, Cristóbal paid the nurse and the janitor for additional privacy. The men stepped to the other side of the door, still within listening range, forcing Carlitos to whisper.

"*Gordo*, what's happening?"

"I don't know. My name is on Batista's list, but instead of being taken to prison, I've been brought here."

A metallic door slammed nearby and they both jumped, startled. A nearby orderly argued with a patient, who giggled with derangement.

"It doesn't make sense. Why would they bring you here?" Cristóbal said, still in shock at their surroundings.

"This must be a new interrogation method for the military," Carlitos said, lowering his voice even further. "There's probably too many journalists at police headquarters. Here, I can be interrogated, and no one will know. I'm in more danger here than in *La Cabaña*."

"Does your father know?"

"I don't know. I need you to talk with him, but first I need you to go to Tina's house."

Cristóbal leaned in to listen, as Carlitos' voice became almost inaudible.

"In the carport there's a car I'm working on. In the trunk of that car there's a package, like a shoebox. You have to get rid of it."

"Okay."

"Carefully. Do you understand what I'm saying to you?"

"Carefully, because..."

Carlitos checked behind him to see who was there, and then leaned in closer.

"It's a bomb."

"¡*Coño!*" Cristóbal replied a bit too loudly, forcing Carlitos to pull him in and whisper in his ear. "You have to get rid of it. If they find it, Tina and Olga will be jailed."

The janitor and the nurse stepped into view, announcing their time was over.

"I'm on it."

The nurse placed his hand on Carlitos' shoulder, triggering an immediate twitch.

"Come back and tell me what Papá is going to do," he said as he was being led away.

Cristóbal stood at the glass door, watching his friend being escorted away. The sound of other patients, clamoring for attention, filled the room. Outside, the moon was hidden by rain clouds that had emptied themselves over Havana. The celebrative sounds of crickets and frogs accompanied Cristóbal as he drove to Tina's house. There he found the house fully lit, with Olga and Manolín cleaning the carport beside a pair of servants, who Tina supervised. Cristóbal approached her, not sure how to broach the subject. Tina looked at him with her hands on her hips, silently demanding he explain his presence.

"*Buenas noches*. Olguita," he called out politely.

Olga looked at her mother and then walked toward Cristóbal, who was unsure as to why such a cleaning endeavor was taking place at that hour of the night.

"I've come from visiting Carlitos. Do you know what's happening?"

Olga looked down and began walking toward the sidewalk. Cristóbal followed.

"We had a little incident here."

"What kind of incident?"

"Well, I still don't understand, but Carlitos had a nervous collapse, and he..."

"Destroyed the place?"

"Yes. Those servants there," she pointed at the two women dressed in servant uniforms. "They're from *el Viejo Márquez*."

"So, he knows?"

"I had to call him. I didn't know how to handle it. He got some policemen to take him away. I think they've taken him to *Mazorra*."

"No, he's not at the asylum," he said, wincing at the thought. "He's at the smaller one, the clinic. Olguita, I have to get to the trunk of that car."

"Are you here for what those men wanted?"

"What men? Were they military or police?"

"No. I think they're university students... They came and left very quietly. I saw them through the window. By the time I came out they were gone. It was only later that I realized they came for the box that was in the trunk."

"Have you told your mother, or anyone about it?"

"No. Mima is in a terrible mood. I think it's best if I don't say anything."

"That's right. Don't mention it to anyone. It's very important you don't say anything. And if the police come and ask you about it, what will you say?"

"I don't know what they're talking about."

Cristóbal looked up to see Tina's prying eyes, trying to decipher their conversation.

"Are you going to see him?" Olga asked.

Cristóbal nodded.

"Please tell him... tell him...." Olga began to cry and Cristóbal wrapped his arms around her. "I don't know what happened. He just..."

He held her for several minutes, and then drove back to the psychiatric hospital. The rain clouds had cleared, and the moon was shining over the city.

"I can't let you in," the janitor said. "Everyone is asleep, including your friend."

"Can you get a note to him?"

The janitor didn't respond.

"Wait here. Give me a minute."

Cristóbal ran back to the car, wrote a note and grabbed some money. He handed it to the janitor along with the folded paper.

"Here, a little something for your trouble."

Carlitos never received the note. For the next week, the janitor continued to serve as a paid messenger who delivered all notes to the attending physician. During that time, Carlitos was given the standard battery of exams. It was after passing the tests with scores the doctor had never seen, that Carlitos called the attending physician a cretin unable to diagnose a late term abortion. The offensive language justified the doctor's order for a precautionary application of electroshock treatment, which was administered twice that week.

"I suggest you keep him here for another thirty days," the doctor told Olga. "It would give me the time needed to make a better diagnosis."

"You mean, you still don't know why he had a nervous collapse?"

"Olguita, these things take time," Tina reassured her daughter.

"Well, he exhibits behavior typical of geniuses." The doctor lowered his glasses.

"Genius?" Tina exclaimed.

"Yes," the doctor looked up at Tina. "Many geniuses suffer from depression and have related personality disorders. Often this is due to an inability to relate to everyday life. If you allow me to observe and test him for another thirty days, I'll be able to offer a more detailed diagnosis and treatment."

"Whatever you think is best, doctor." Tina said, trying to reassure her daughter.

"Can I see him?" Olga asked.

"Certainly. At this moment he's in the activity room with other patients."

Tina and Olga followed the doctor to a one-way mirror that rendered a view to the activity room, and the patients in it. Some were in pairs, others sat alone, rocking themselves incessantly. A few patients were in the midst of an imaginary world, conversing with non-existent companions. Carlitos sat at a table away from the others, skim reading a book.

"As you can see, they're perfectly safe, each interacting according to their ability."

"I want to take him home," Olga replied.

The doctor and Tina turned to face her. She looked at both of them, squarely in the eyes and, with resolve, said, "Get the paperwork ready. I'm taking him home."

The next day Carlitos was released from the psychiatric clinic, and it was not his birth family waiting outside, but rather the one he married into. They greeted him at the doors with the same attitude one greets a friend who is returning from a long trip, with the exception that no one asked about his time away. They smiled and escorted the patient to Manolo's cream-colored car, as if they were going to take a Sunday drive with the top down. Manolo, who served as driver, attempted to hug his son-in-law, only to be rejected by his crossed arms. To make matters even more awkward, Tina had to sit in the front seat next to the man she had not forgiven. She turned on the radio and raised the volume, hoping the music could fill the space where resentment resides. The melodious voice of Beny Moré came on with the love song *"Cómo Fue,"* asking how it was that he once fell in love. Tina reached to change the station, but Manolo moved her hand from the dial, motioning at the reunited couple in the backseat.

They drove by *el Malecón* to watch the waves crash against the seawall. Lovers walked on the promenade, holding each other tight. Families watched their children scream in glee every time a wave spilled onto the walkway. Olga rested her head on Carlitos' shoulder, and sang along with the ballad as the wind swept her hair. For a moment, Carlitos forgot where he spent the previous week. He closed his eyes, allowing himself to relax under the warmth of Olga's soft embrace, and remembered, along with the euphonious voice in the radio, how it was he once fell in love. When he opened his eyes, expecting to see an idyllic world, *el Caballero de París* was before him, sitting on the seawall, oblivious to the surrounding activity. His matted hair and mud stained beard shimmered with droplets of sea water, reflecting the midday sun. A peaceful glow emanated from the madman, one psychiatric medications could never instill.

The image of *el Caballero* was still with him when they pulled into Tina's garage. It was clean and empty, lacking any trace that a car, and its parts, was once there. Carlitos stepped out of Manolo's car, looked around, and, without a word, entered the house.

******

I didn't know he was being taken to a psychiatric clinic," my mother explained. "How was I to know *el Viejo Márquez* would make that decision? I mean, I think they, his family, should have come and sat with him. Belencita had such a good effect on your father, but nobody wanted her to know he had a breakdown."

She was standing in front of the stove, heating chicken noodle soup I bought at the supermarket. Her hands trembled as she held the long wooden spoon used to stir the soup.

"I always enjoy a good soup," she said.

"So, he never found out you were the one who called for help?"

"He must have. I don't know who told him, but he confronted us at your brother's wedding. Don't you remember? He came to our table and in front of everyone, started yelling insults at your grandmother."

I nodded, sadly remembering the night when my father flew into a rage over events that occurred decades earlier.

"Guille, help me here. This is too heavy."

I lifted the saucepan and poured the boiling soup into a bowl.

"And get me a piece of that Cuban bread, *un pedacito*," she said as she sat at the dinner table. "It's probably hard by now, but the soup will soften it."

We sat in silence while she ate her dinner. I was at the other end of the table with my laptop, surfing the internet. Eventually she looked up at me, as if noticing me for the first time.

"*Ay*, Guille, you scared me. You're so quiet, I forgot you were here."

"I've been here all along. You saw me sit and open my laptop."

"I know. I know. I just... I guess I slipped into another world and forgot you were there. Aren't you going to eat?"

"No, Mama. It's not even five o'clock yet."

"I've been meaning to tell you that there's a ghost in this house."

"Really?" I chuckled.

"*Si, señor*. You have a ghost in the house. I saw her last night."

"You did?" My interest peaked. My mother had a history with ghosts and experienced multiple sightings of them in her life.

"She's tall, with very long legs and short black hair. I've never seen her before, but she stood next to my bed. I think she was keeping watch over me."

"A guardian angel?"

"Could be. I didn't think she was an angel, but she could be."

"Did she say anything?"

"No. She just stood there, with her hands like this." My mother folded her hands. "I reached over to turn on the lamp, and she vanished, but first she nodded her head at me. Like this." My mother nodded with a serious look. "I think she was trying to tell me something."

"Interesting," I commented and turned my attention to the Covid-19 website for Florida. "Did you know that two hundred seventy-two people died yesterday from Covid?"

"In the nation?"

"No. That's just in the state of Florida."

"Don't tell me those things now. I'm eating."

"Sorry."

"Two hundred and what?"

"Seventy-two."

"*¡Ay, Dios mio!* I never would have imagined this. Had you told me a few years ago there would be a worldwide disease, killing thousands of people a day, I wouldn't have believed you."

"And they say it's going to get worse in the winter."

"You know, your grandparents lived through the Spanish flu of 1918. They learned to clean the back of their throat with hydrogen peroxide. *Muchacho*, I'd come home from school and the first thing I had to do was gargle with hydrogen peroxide and then Mima would swab the back of my throat with Methylene Blue, *Azul de Metileno*. It's probably something we should be doing now. Do you know if the pharmacy sells it?"

"Not sure," I said, not really wanting to agree.

"And *el Viejo Márquez*, he would wash his hands up to ten and twelve times a day. He was such a clean man. Meticulous. In his closet every shirt was perfectly starched. And his drawers! If you opened any drawer you would find every item folded, the socks rolled up like little apples. No, no, no, no, no. The man was disciplined in everything he did."

My mother stopped talking momentarily to dip her bread in the soup and chew, but then with a mouthful of bread said, "He too would see ghosts. Plain as day. *Si, señor*."

"He told you this?"

"Of course, he told me. He would get visits from the ghost of Don Manuel."

"Which one, his father or grandfather?"

"I'm not sure, now that you ask. I assumed he was talking about his father."

"And what did he tell him?"

"About what?"

"The ghost. What did he have to say that was so important?"

"Oh, I don't know."

"Didn't you just say he told you about it?"

"Yes, but he never said what they talked about. He actually laughed. Thought it was comical that his father's ghost was paying him visits."

I searched in my memories to recall images of my grandfather, and I pictured him using laughter to dismiss an unworthy topic.

"Besides," my mother went on. "What he and the ghost of Don Manuel spoke about was none of my business. If Don Manuel wanted me to know, he would have paid me a visit."

"Instead, you get angels with folded hands." I said and closed my laptop.

"I do," she agreed and then cleaned her bowl with the last piece of bread, wiping it clean of any broth.

"I think she's trying to tell me something, the angel."

"Maybe she's telling you to fold your hands and stop touching your face, like Dr. Fauci."

I laughed at my own joke. She didn't join in, partially because she was trying to swallow a huge chunk of bread, but also because visiting angels were not to be laughed at.

"No," she said after swallowing. "I think she's telling me I'm right."

"About what?"

"That the world is going to end, and I need to be ready. I keep telling you, but you don't want to believe me. You think I'm crazy. I know you do."

"No, Mama. I don't think you're crazy. It's just that there's nothing for me to do. What am I going to do, run around and tell everyone the world is ending?"

"Well, I know what I know, and the angel is telling me I'm right. That's why she nodded her head. Think about it. Why else is there a pandemic? Why else do we have a crazy man for a president? We're living in the end times. You don't want to face it and you laugh at me, I know."

"Mama, I'm not laughing."

"It's okay. I know what you think. But take a look at all that's happening, *el chino gordo* in Korea sending rockets into the sea. It's only a matter of time before one of those rockets makes it to our shores. And there's men doing terrible things, coming into our homes to do things you don't want me to talk about, but it's happening. I know it is. I keep telling you it's not safe, that your daughter is in danger, but you won't listen to me."

I looked at my mother and realized, once again, there was a world of fear living in her. In that frail, bent and wrinkled body of hers, an entire universe of conspiracy theories and doomsday scenarios flourished. There was nothing I could do about it. No amount of reasoning would convince her otherwise. So, I did the only thing I could, offer her more food.

"Do you want a little bit of *guayaba con queso*?"

"*Ay, sí*," she answered enthusiastically, "and a small cup of Cuban coffee. *Un buchito*, just a small sip."

I gladly percolated coffee and served dessert. If the world is coming to an end, it can wait for the small pleasures in life.

CHAPTER 12

El Viejo Márquez

1987 (or so)
Miami, Florida

My grandfather, Carlos Márquez-Sterling Senior, was not much of a hugger. Whenever I paid him a visit, I greeted him with a kiss and a hug that he awkwardly accepted. He was happy to see me, of that I'm sure, but he was not openly affectionate about it. For him, a pat on the shoulders and a big smile was sufficient. If I insisted on expressing more, he would chuckle and say, *"Bueno, bueno,"* and then lead me to the living room where we could sit and have a meaningful conversation, usually about Cuban history or my ancestors.

He and his second wife, Uva, left New York City shortly after he turned eighty and moved to the home of her daughter, Uvita, in Miami. With his change of residence, we could finally begin to visit the famous patriarch who was a giant in Cuban history. When I moved to Miami in the mid 1980's, I became a regular at that house, mostly to visit my cousin, Uvi, who was also my fiancé's best friend.

"Hola, Abuelo." He met me at the door wearing a long sleeve, button-down shirt and a striped tie. He wore his pants above the waistline, the way old men usually do, and tucked his shirt perfectly into his pants. Although he was in his late eighties, my *Abuelo* dressed as if he still taught at the university. Not once did I see him wear shorts or a T-shirt. I'm not sure he even owned any. I greeted him with a kiss on the cheek. He chuckled and said, *"Bueno, bueno."*

Uva, who, for all practical purposes, was my grandmother, greeted me in the living room. "*Hola, Guillermito. ¡Tan guapo!* Look at your hair." She touched the back of my hair, which I was determined to grow. She stood tall but had become thin and frail. Uva was a good twelve years younger than my grandfather. She was a proud woman from a family of intellectuals, and always dressed as if she had a luncheon to attend, even though most of her days were spent indoors. Every memory I have of her is with large earrings, jewelry, high heel shoes, and hair fashioned in a beehive. Everyone agreed she and my grandfather were a handsome couple.

"Uvitica is not here, you know," she said as I stepped forward.

Uvitica, my cousin, suffered the same fate as the men in my family named Carlos. She was the third generation of women named Uva, forcing the placement of a double diminutive to distinguish her from previous generations. Luckily, we called her by a cute variation, Uvi.

"Yes, I know," I said while giving her a light kiss on the cheek. "I came to sit with *Abuelo* for a little while."

"*¡Ay, que lindo!* I love how you like to spend time with your grandfather."

We quickly made our way toward the sofa, where my grandfather preferred to sit. As I followed, I couldn't help but look at the artwork decorating the living room. The size and beauty of the paintings were impossible to ignore.

"*¿Qué cuentas?* Guillermo, what do you say?" This rhetorical question was his common greeting. I smiled as I sat next to him so I could speak directly into his good ear.

"How are your studies?" Uva asked, while sitting across from us.

"*¿Como?*" He tilted his good ear toward her.

She repeated the question loudly and then smiled at me.

"His hearing aids aren't working very well," she explained. "We have an appointment with the specialist. Hopefully he'll get some better ones."

"I've gotten deaf," he chuckled. "Most of the time I don't mind." He pointed at Uva. "Drives her crazy," he laughed some more. "Anyway, that was a good question. How are your studies? Will you be applying to medical school soon?"

"I'm switching majors, *Abuelo*. I don't want to study medicine anymore."

He listened patiently as I told him my plans to pursue a degree in literature.

"Weren't you almost done with your pre-med requirements?" Uva asked. "Medicine is such a beautiful career, and it would have been so good to have a doctor in the family."

"Yes, I know. It almost feels like wasted time, but I'm much happier now."

"Well, there's no such thing as wasted time," my grandfather said. "Especially if you are earnest about your studies. All that science just makes you better rounded. But the question you have to answer is, why are you changing course?"

"Well, I was always eager to finish my physics homework so I could write a poem that was floating around in my head."

"A poem?" he asked.

"*Si, Abuelo*," I said louder. "I have poetry swimming in my head."

"And you didn't like your physics homework?"

"No, not really."

"Well, I can't blame you. I wouldn't like it much either," he chuckled.

My grandfather lightly slapped my knee, to assure me he knew what I meant.

"A professor said in one of his lectures that we had to follow our bliss. I thought about it and realized all that science and calculus is not my bliss," I said. "Poetry and literature are. So, here I am, with a new focus."

"I've seen some of your poems," Uva said. "They're very nice."

I nodded and smiled. "Nice" was about the best compliment I was going to receive.

"Well, you'll figure it out," he said and slapped my knee again. "The Márquez-Sterlings are men of letters. I think you're making the right choice."

I continued to talk about the university when suddenly he interrupted my narrative.

"You're named after my father, Guillermo Guiral, who also wrote poetry. His poems were never published, but that's not the point. He had a poetic spirit, like you. And I have to say, you hold a certain similarity to him. So, I'm not surprised you have poems floating around in your head." He chuckled some more. "My father died very young in the War of Independence, while my mother, Maria Dolores, was in Spain dying from tuberculosis. They died within days of each other. Isn't that curious?"

"It must have been terrible for you," I interjected.

He leaned in and turned his ear toward me.

"It must have been terrible to be orphaned so young," I yelled into his ear.

"Well, I don't really remember much about that," he said halfheartedly. "I was too young. My uncle, Don Manuel, took me in and adopted me. He gave me the choice at age eighteen to change my name to Márquez-Sterling. He had done so much for me, and he was, after all, the only father I knew. It was the correct thing to do. So, I inverted the names, putting Guiral at the end, instead of the other way around."

I had to think about what he was saying, and it must have shown. So, he spelled it out for me. "Carlos Márquez-Sterling y Guiral."

"I have to return some calls, Guillermito," Uva said, "but stay here with your grandfather and continue your visit. If you need anything, help yourself. *Estas en tu casa.*"

I remained seated while she left, and my grandfather turned to a book he had under the lamp next to him.

"I'm reading this book about Theodore Roosevelt. It's in English so I'm going through it very slowly," he chuckled as he picked it up. "My English is not the best, *pero yo me defiendo.* I'm enjoying the author's focus." He turned the book around in his hand. "Don Manuel met Roosevelt. He actually interviewed him after McKinley was assassinated. Don Manuel was not impressed with him... found him to be uncultured and rather racist."

"Don Manuel should have played chess with him, don't you think?"

"¿*Como*?"

"Don't you think he should have played a game of chess with him?"

"Because he was a master chess player?"

I nodded.

"No, no, no, no, no. Don Manuel would have swept the board clean." He chuckled intermittently while narrating. "That only would have created an adversary and Cuba needed the Americans. The republic was too young and it was in danger of falling apart. Years later, Don Manuel returned to Washington as ambassador, this time to abolish the Platt Amendment. I guess he could have played chess at that time, but he chose to not strain the relationship. I don't play chess very well," he softly laughed. "I don't have the patience."

He looked at me and patted my knee affectionately.

"He was a great man, Don Manuel," he continued as he returned the book to its place. "He traveled the world, and I was fortunate enough to tag along everywhere he went." He chuckled some more. "I didn't know it then, but that was quite an education I received. It gave me a wider understanding of life. When Don Manuel was ambassador in Peru, he took me to see the ruins. I created quite a stir, running up and down all those ruins," he chuckled again.

"*Abuelo*, you should write about your life, a biography. It sounds so interesting."

"I've thought about it. I even have a few notes I compiled a few years ago, but I think a lot of people would be upset if I wrote a true biography. I'd have to say a lot of unpleasant things about a lot of people and about what happened in Cuba. I'm not sure people want to hear it. Sometimes it's better to leave the past alone."

"What do you mean?" I raised my voice in strong disagreement. "The past holds the lessons we need for today and tomorrow. The true history of what happened is priceless, not only for us Cubans in Miami but also for those still on the island."

"*Ay*, Guillermo," he sighed. "History is being re-written. Castro has his version, full of lies, and the commentators here in Miami have theirs, full of blind spots. The truth of the matter is that we created the monster named Castro, and nobody wants to hear that."

"But don't you think people need to know."

"*El hombre Cubano* doesn't want to know." His tone revealed anger and I witnessed a gradual transformation of his demeanor to an intensity I had not seen before.

"The Cuban man is not interested in learning about the past, nor is he interested in the political ideals of democracy. For years I lectured, spoke on many news programs, and talked to as many people as I could about the danger Batista was posing to our democracy and to our constitution, which I worked so hard to ratify. Did they listen? Did they give a damn? The only thing that mattered to them was the economy and the money they were making. All those *Batistianos* who kept Batista in power, the ones who traded one dictator for another, where are they now? Where?" He slapped my knee forcefully. "They're here, *hablando mierda*, refusing to acknowledge they were the ones who created the conditions for revolution. And here we are, living in exile. All these men, who I happen to know were part of the problem, are on the radio, revising history and blaming communism. *¡No jodas, chico!* Fidel is not a communist. He's a son of a bitch, *un hijo de puta*. That's what he is."

His eyes were blazing with anger as he looked directly into mine.

"If the Cuban man had to choose between democracy and a big dick, he would choose the big dick." He slapped my knee again, and this time it hurt.

"Carlos!" Uva stepped out of the kitchen and protested loudly. "*¡Por favor!*"

He turned to her but didn't acknowledge her complaint. I sat still, shocked at the analogy. Never before had my grandfather cursed like that.

"They didn't listen to me then, why would they be interested now? No, no, no, no, no. It's better I don't write anything. I'd have to say a lot of unpleasant things."

"*Pero Abuelo...*"

"The mistake people make is to blame the one man," my grandfather interrupted. "It's not about Fidel. It's about the many people who supported him when he was in the Sierra Maestra. These are the people who jeopardized democracy: business leaders, journalists and celebrities who disregarded the electoral process. I traveled the island, telling them revolution was not the answer. My warnings fell on deaf ears. Now, those people say they were misled, that Castro lied to them, but they know I know." He looked down and repeated, "They know I know."

I tried not to subdue my grandfather's anger, but my eyes must have widened because he chuckled momentarily.

"I get very upset when I talk about these things, Guillermo. People don't understand how delicate democracy is, especially in Latin America. It doesn't take much to crush it. A well written constitution is a beautiful thing, but it's only as strong as the people who are willing to protect it. I don't think Cuba will ever be able to enjoy the fruits of a hard fought constitution. It makes me very sad to think about it. Very sad."

My grandfather paused, and it seemed to me his eyes were momentarily filled with tears, but like a good academic statesman, he did not allow the tears to linger.

"We're about to cross the line of no return," he continued. "If Castro is still in power by the end of this decade, he'll be there until the day he dies. You want me to write a book, but I can't. I just can't."

"I understand, *Abuelo*. I can see..."

"*Y total*, in the end," he interrupted again. "I don't think it would matter. The educational bar has been lowered. The average Cuban now, coming out of the island, is illiterate when it comes to democracy and its ideals. Fidel has created two generations of political illiterates who don't have a clue how civil society should look like. A third generation is about to be born into that mess, and what are they going to know? Forget about that! *¡Olvídate de eso!* The Cuba I knew is long gone. Long gone. I lost hope for any sort of restoration a long time ago."

"*Pero Abuelo*," I said forcefully so as not to be interrupted. "Would you consider writing about certain moments that were critical in your life and part of history."

"Like what?"

"Like, despite the chaos and opposing factions, you managed to successfully lead the writing and ratification of the constitution in 1940."

"I already wrote about that, and so have others. It's in my book, *La Historia de Cuba*."

"Ok. Then, how about you write about your conversation with El Che Guevara when you were imprisoned at *La Cabaña*."

"El Che? Well, yes," his face relaxed a bit. "That was interesting. El Che wanted to kill me with a firing squad. I thought I was a dead man, for sure. They were killing so many people in those days. I was in *La Cabaña*, which was a prison built by the Spaniards. So, you can imagine how terrible it was. Simply terrible. Water seeped in and the whole place was full of rats. I remember thinking that at any moment I was going to be taken to the firing squad when all of a sudden El Che walked in to speak with me."

"What was he like?"

"What was he like?" he tipped his ear toward me.

"Yes," I said louder.

"*Un barbudo apestoso*. A smelly bearded man, who only had disdain for democracy. He was smart... much smarter than Fidel, I'm sure. He acknowledged that if I had won the election, the revolution would have ended. You see, I offered Fidel amnesty. It was part of my campaign. I told him to come down from the mountains and become part of the political process. I vowed my administration would serve as a transitional government, restoring the constitution and its institutions. And then, two years later, we would have another election with Fidel on the ballot, but he had to stop that revolutionary nonsense. So, you see, it would have been a huge inconvenience to the revolution if I had won, which I did."

He looked down at his hands and then back at me. The disappointment of the "what if" was evident in his downcast guise. Uva returned and sat on the chair opposite us.

"El Che was a communist, for sure, and a murderer too. Batista handed Cuba over to him on a silver platter. They practically gave those *barbudos* the keys to the front door, and the rest is history. *Oye*, Guillermo, I'm almost ninety years old." He chuckled. "Ninety. Do you know what that is? I'm lucky I can sit on this sofa and read a biography. I no longer have the energy required to write one. It's hard work, and it would be too upsetting to relive it all."

My grandfather looked down again and became quiet.

"Guillermito, how is your mother?" Uva asked. "She likes it there in Puerto Rico, no?"

"Yes, she does. She and her husband have a nice apartment in Luquillo."

"Please tell her we send our love."

"I will. My father is also doing well. You know, he moved back to Illinois."

Uva nodded, politely, and then looked at her husband, whose gaze was blank.

"Your grandfather has become rather emotional in this conversation. I think he needs to take a nap. So, if you don't mind, I'm going to take him to our room. Thanks for visiting. He really does enjoy your visits a lot."

"Yes, of course." I stood.

I tried to kiss and hug my grandfather, who chuckled at my attempt. He patted my shoulder and, while smiling at my long hair said, *"Bueno, bueno."*

As I walked away, I remember thinking it had been nearly thirty years since my grandfather had to flee the country he loved so much. Thirty years since he entered a new land whose citizens didn't know the difference between Cuba and Mexico. For how many nights, in those thirty years, did my grandfather toss and turn in his sleep, replaying the events of 1958 that led to the triumphal entry of Fidel Castro? In those thirty years, how many times did he have to explain to ignorant people that el Che Guevara was a terrorist and should not be idolized? It became obvious on that day, as I returned to my frivolous life, one where having long hair was important, that I could never fathom the depth of my grandfather's grief. How could I fully know the pain of losing one's country? I'm not sure I ever will, and I pray that I don't ever have to.

CHAPTER 13

Desperate Measures

January 1958
    Havana

Angelito, Olga's uncle, was a photography aficionado who owned multiple cameras and had cabinet drawers full of lenses and parts needed to reassemble any camera. When *Fotograbados Gutierrez* moved to a new location on Calle Sol, he personally designed and built the darkroom. It was primarily for the work of the business, but also for the enjoyment of his hobby, one he shared with Carlitos. The two men were not friends, nor did they spend much time together, but often at family gatherings they sat together to compare cameras and talk about the nuances of their pastime. On December 31, 1957, Carlitos kept a sharp look out for his fellow shutterbug, while attending a New Year's Eve gathering at Pedrito's home.

Carlitos, wearing a white, perfectly starched guayabera that Olga bought for him and a Leica M3 camera on his shoulder, stood alone on the porch overlooking the backyard. Behind him, at the threshold of the living room, was a small group of wives all in wool dresses to ward off the winter winds that historically blew on that day. He turned around to see teenage children, cousins to each other, running around a ninety-pound pig that was being roasted on a fire pit. Manolín, also in a white guayabera, was on the lawn holding hands with his latest girlfriend, Teresita, a nice young woman from his neighborhood.

Carlitos aimed his camera at the young couple and took several pictures of them snuggling into each other.

"Carlitos," Angelito called out.

He turned around to see the happy-go-lucky uncle in a white guayabera, with a camera bag strapped to his shoulder, walk enthusiastically toward him.

"*¿Qué cuentas?* Angelito, what do you say?"

"Look what I bought for Christmas," he said, while pulling a protective case from his bag. "Here, hold this." He handed the bag to Carlitos and opened the case with fanfare. "Straight from Chicago, a Minolta SR-2."

Angelito held the camera for Carlitos to admire.

"*Coño*," he elongated the last "o" to appropriately show praise.

"It's Japanese," he said, slowly handing the camera to Carlitos, cradling the base in his hand as if it were a baby's head.

"Japanese?" Carlitos looked through the viewfinder and then glanced over at Angelito with surprise.

"You see that? They placed an additional mirror that lets me see exactly what I'm photographing," he said. "And check this out!

Angelito took the camera back, rotated the lens to remove it and inserted another.

"*¿Como?*" Carlitos asked. "Where are the screws?"

"That's just it. No screws. You can change lenses in seconds."

Carlitos took the camera, removed the lens and then inserted it again. He then lifted it to his eye and looked through the viewfinder. He focused on a group of young women gathered around a six-month old boy and her mother. Olga was waiting her turn to hold the child.

"Very nice, but does it take a good picture?"

"Just as good as your Leica. Maybe better. Go ahead, take a photo."

Carlitos zoomed in on Olga, whose face was blushing when the child was handed to her. Manolo came into view, wearing a white guayabera. He approached the circle of women and placed his hand around the proud mother. Carlitos realized Olga was holding her half-brother. He snapped a photo and pushed a lever to rewind the film.

"Hmm," Carlitos said while lowering the camera. "Shouldn't that scene be different?"

"How so?" Angelito looked at Olga, who was trying to make the child smile, while Manolo proudly stood next to his young wife.

"A bit upside down, no?"

"Maybe, maybe not. It depends on the lens from which you view it."

Carlitos smiled at Angelito. "I like your metaphor."

"Philosophy and photography, an inevitable couple."

"Are you going to the Grand Prix? Fangio will be driving." Carlitos asked.

"When is it?"

"This February. You should go and test your camera's ability to photograph fast-moving cars. It's why I'm holding on to my Leica."

"Excellent idea. *Oye*, do you mind taking several pictures of the family?"

"I'm happy to. It'll give me something to do."

"But you have to use mine."

"I'll use both. We'll see which one you like better."

Carlitos photographed the family gathering at different junctures of the night. Always trying to tie in the different elements of a good photo, despite the complaints of those being photographed. It wasn't long before he quietly considered the Japanese might have surpassed the Germans in this artistic field.

He and Olga were driving back to Tina's house when he saw her staring out the window wistfully. He knew she longed to be a mother and feared never getting pregnant. He reached over and held her hand to reassure her.

"I'm thinking of something new for this year," Carlitos said to her.

"*Sí?*" she replied and wiped a tear from beneath her eye.

"I want to run for Congress in June's election."

"*Ay*, Carlitos, that's wonderful!" she said with a big smile.

"Papá is organizing a new political party, *Partido del Pueblo Libre*, the Free People's Party. He thought it would be a good idea for me to join and run for Congress."

"It's happening!" Olga bounced in her seat. "I'm so excited. And of course, he wants you to run for congress. It's what you've been preparing for your whole life. My husband, the congressman. I love the sound of it, and I like the name of the party, *Pueblo Libre*. We need to free ourselves of Batista and all that is keeping us down."

"You know," Carlitos smiled. "He's been very supportive lately."

"Your father? Well, yes. He bought you this car."

"The car was for a practical reason. I can't help him with the campaign if I have to depend on the buses and risk being late, but it's more than the car. It's how he includes me. We strategize every day, and he listens to my ideas. In a few weeks we'll have the assembly of the party where he'll be nominated as the presidential candidate."

"Oh my God! Wait till Marisa hears about this!"

"Can you feel it, Olguita? These elections will be the start of a new life, a new Cuba."

"I wish you would have told me sooner. I would have announced it at the party."

"No. It's better like this. They'll know soon enough."

******

Nobody really knows how or when it happened, but at some point, it became obvious that Jenny, Manolo's pretty young wife, who grew up not too far from Olga and who, by all apparent markers, enjoyed a middle-class life, became a fanatic follower of Fidel Castro. She really was not part of the poor masses who cried oppression, nor was she raised by parents who were members of the Communist party. And yet, Manolo came to realize that the woman he married, and who was mother to three of his children, was a revolutionary.

He was sitting in his living room one Sunday morning, watching television, while Jenny breastfed their son, Sergio. Everything seemed quite normal for a growing family. The smell of coffee still lingered, and the joyful sounds of his two daughters playing in their room filled the house. Manolo stood and walked to the television set to raise the volume.

"Good morning," the handsome young man in front of the camera said. "I am Nicolás Bravo, and this is *Ante la Prensa*."

"Why do you want to see that show?" Jenny asked with a grimace on her face. "They're out of touch with the Cuban people."

"*El Viejo Márquez* is going to speak. I want to hear what he has to say, and there's always a great panel of journalists assembled on this show."

"With us today is Doctor Carlos Márquez-Sterling, founder and leader of the Free People's Party, soon to be nominated as the party's presidential candidate."

"I swear, Manolo, if I didn't know any better, I'd say you're in love with that man." Jenny said as she swiveled in her seat with the breast-feeding child. "Every time he speaks, you listen so attentively. Have you forgotten he was Tina's lawyer?"

"The man is my *consuegro*, in-law, and he is offering a solution to the mess we're in. I'd like to listen to him, if you don't mind."

"*El Partido del Pueblo Libre* has the attention of every citizen and journalist," the host spoke into the camera. "Could it be the answer to the political mess we find ourselves in? Please tell our viewers, Doctor, how is the Free People's Party any different from the *Ortodoxos*, the party you were a member of for so many years?"

The camera zoomed in on Carlos Senior, whose black hair was slicked back and he donned an elegant three-piece suit.

"He is handsome," Jenny said. "I have to give him that much."

"*Gracias* Nicolás," Carlos Senior began. "Unfortunately, the *Ortodoxos* have been infiltrated and sabotaged by Castro's 26th of July Movement and by those who want to abstain from the electoral process. The division in the party is too great. It's better to break off and begin something new. We, the Free People's Party, are committed to a free and fair presidential election. I am personally asking the United Nations to send a delegation to monitor the polling sites and I urge the Cuban people to cast their vote. Only through a large voter turnout can we free ourselves of the dictatorship in a peaceful and constitutional method."

"You see?" Manolo expressed. "He talks about peace and respecting the constitution."

"He's a bureaucrat. Of course, he's going to talk that way." Jenny pulled her child from the breast, wiped his mouth and began bouncing him on her shoulder.

"Yes, that is important," the program host continued. "Doctor, there is an anti-Batista group in Miami that calls itself *La Junta de Liberación*, the Liberation Council. They have endorsed Fidel Castro and the 26th of July Movement. What are your thoughts?"

"Miami?" Jenny gasped while feeding her son from the other breast. "Who cares what Miami thinks?"

"Once again, Nicolás, it's trading one tyranny for another." Carlos Senior replied. "The Cubans living in Miami are fools if they think Castro will restore the constitution and the democratic process. They sit in the comfort of air-conditioning and safety, while I'm here, actively working to save the future of this island and facing death threats from Castro's thugs."

"*Oye eso*, he's calling Fidel a thug. Did you hear that? The man is in the Sierra, putting his life on the line to fight Batista, and your in-law calls him a thug!"

Manolo didn't respond. His daughters ran into the living room, laughing loudly, forcing him to walk to the television set and raise the volume, once again, as the host asked Carlos Senior another question.

"We understand that Fidel Castro and Camilo Cienfuegos invited you to be part of the 26th of July Movement. They assert that if you join, they will make you the next president."

"That offer is not made in good faith. My road to the presidency is through the elections, not revolution."

"Good! We don't want you and we don't want your democratic process!" Jenny screamed at the television. "You fucking bureaucrat!"

"*Oye,*" Manolo complained with a surprised tone. "Relax. Why are you screaming and cursing? The girls are going to hear you."

Jenny, while adjusting the mouth of her infant son on her breast, rolled her eyes at him.

"The best thing Castro can do," Carlos Senior continued, "is to stop making death threats, stop intimidating citizens with his fear tactics, and allow for the elections to occur. And I assure you, the will of the people will make me the next president."

"Thank you, Doctor. It is always a pleasure to have you on our show. You are watching *Ante la Prensa,* and this is Nicolás Bravo for CMQ-TV."

"Are you really going to vote for that man?" Jenny challenged Manolo.

"Are you really *not* going to vote?"

"The elections are a joke. Fidel says they're not valid, regardless of who wins."

"The elections are the only way to move the country forward. Have you not been listening? It was explained just a minute ago."

"What about you? Are you not paying attention? The people don't want an election. They want Fidel," she said loudly while removing her son from her breast.

"What the hell is going on with you? Why do you want this revolution and Fidel? Do you want to go to the *Sierra Maestra* and be another mistress of his."

"I would," she screamed back while placing the crying child in the bassinet. "I would go to the Sierra and join the movement, but you got me pregnant, and now I have to take care of your three children."

Jenny grabbed her sandal and started smacking Manolo with it. He wrestled the sandal away, only to be smacked and punched by her hands.

She hit him in the head, which sparked his rage. With a blinding fury he jumped at her and stopped within an inch of landing a blow.

"Don't you ever hit my head again," he said with a raised fist. "Never, do you hear me? Never touch my head."

He was shaking with anger and feared losing control. He knew he had to get out of the house before he committed a regrettable, violent act. Jenny followed him down the stairs and, with tears in her eyes, screamed, "*¡Eres un maricón!* If you were a real man, you'd join the movement, you faggot!"

Across the street, people raised their heads to look as Jenny screamed insults at her departing husband.

Manolo, red faced from Jenny's punches, walked around the neighborhood, trying to cool down. He saw a group of men playing dominoes under a palm tree and decided to join them. Two steps later, Manolo was on the ground fighting off an attack of the neighbor's dog. By the time the domino players separated the dog from him, his pants were soaked in blood.

Manolín, who was working at *el taller*, learned about his father's injuries and promptly told his sister about it.

"Will you take me to my father's house?" Olga asked Carlitos in a whisper.

"Why are you whispering?" he asked in his usual loud voice.

"Shh! I don't want Mima to find out. You know how she gets. Anyway, can you take me? I won't be long."

"I don't have to go in, do I?" he almost whispered.

"No." She looked out the door to see if her mother had heard them. "Just drop me off, and pick me up later."

"So, what am I now, your chauffeur?"

"Oh please. C'mon. Don't get angry with me."

"Fine. It gives me a chance to visit the dog track."

Carlitos was a regular at the races. He had a betting system that, according to him, yielded a profit. Olga frowned upon his gambling but didn't object too vociferously, because when he did win, he shared generously. If Carlitos was a magnanimous winner, he was also a sore loser, angrily smacking his lips when the poor animals didn't perform as expected. It was with trepidation that Olga watched him drive away from Manolo's home.

"¿Sí?" Jenny stood at the threshold of her door with a blouse that was partially undone.

"I came to see Papá. How is he doing?"

"He's alright," she said as she stepped aside to let Olga in. The two women, less than a decade apart, stood at the bottom of the stairs inspecting each other.

"Were you breastfeeding?"

"No. The baby's asleep now. C'mon in."

At the top of the stairs, a small living room opened to the dining room and kitchen. Olga looked around and saw a book on the reading table.

"Wait here," Jenny said.

"Where are the girls?"

"With my mother. They kept climbing on the bed, and for Manolo's sake I sent them away for a few days."

Jenny stepped into the hallway and Olga quickly walked up to the table to read the cover of the book. The Communist Manifesto by Karl Marx and Friedrich Engels. She turned to see Jenny, smiling at her.

"Interested?" Jenny asked.

"No. Well, yes. I was curious."

"I can lend it to you."

"Thanks, but I would rather not."

"Okay, but if you ever want to know more about this, just ask."

Olga looked down, embarrassed.

"Your father is inside, waiting for you."

Olga hurriedly walked in without looking at her young stepmother. Manolo was sitting up in bed, freshly bathed, combed and splashed with a handful of cologne. His left arm and hand were bandaged.

"Olguita," he said with a meek smile.

She stood at the foot of the bed, unsure if she should approach him. He was pale, with sunken eyes. A bloodstained bandage over his lap showed beneath the thin sheet.

"Ay, Papá, what happened?" her voice revealed an urge to cry.

"One of those fluke occurrences in life. Come," he motioned to the chair. "Sit over here. Tell me about my in-laws and their political campaigns."

Olga began to cry as she sat next to him.

"*No llores mija.* I'm going to be alright. Really, I will."

"That dog could have killed you."

"I know. I know, but so could a dozen other things. These things happen. I just had bad luck on that day. That's all. I'll recover."

"I heard the dog bit you..." her head tilted toward his groin, "down there."

They both glanced down to acknowledge the bloodstained bandage.

"Yes, he did. I guess he heard mine is bigger."

Olga chuckled and wiped several tears from her face.

"Now talk to me about Carlitos and his run for Congress."

"There's going to be a convention where they'll announce the candidates and *el Viejo Márquez* for president. I thought that maybe I would have to buy a dress, but I still fit into my engagement dress."

"How nice! And Angelito told me he's going to the Grand Prix with Carlitos. They're taking photos. Will you be there too?"

"I think so. I didn't get to see it last year," she said. "Papá, can I get you anything? Are you in pain?"

"A little, especially when I move. But no, thanks. Jenny's taking good care of me. The doctor prescribed morphine, but I don't want to take any."

"Why not?"

"*Bueno*, I took one last night so I could sleep, but I rather deal with the pain."

She placed her hand on his good hand and squeezed. He squeezed back.

"You know, when I had the headaches, I suffered through pain much worse than this and I learned different ways to cope with it. You were young, but you might remember that I visited *un chino*, who did acupuncture."

"I'm not sure," she shook her head.

"Well, *el chino* taught me to meditate and contemplate."

"Is it like praying?"

"A little, but not really. It's breathing in rhythm and focusing on nothing."

"On nothing?"

"Sounds strange, right? What I want to say is that meditating puts me in a different state of mind. I don't know how to explain it, but I get a new way of seeing my life."

Olga sat quietly.

"The point is I've been using my time, here in bed, to meditate and contemplate. And I think I figured something out."

"Like what?"

"Well, just listen to me for a little bit. Try to picture what I'm telling you."

"Okay," she leaned forward and smiled.

"Our thoughts radiate outward, like sound. Think of a stone hitting water and the ripples it creates. Thoughts move like that. Can you picture what I'm telling you? We can't hear or read them, but dogs can. That's right, dogs can read our thoughts."

"How do you know that?"

"Think of *Blanquita y Negrita*. Don't they seem to know what we're thinking?"

"*Ay*, Papá, those two are so smart."

"They are. So, what I want to tell you is that right before the dog attacked me, I got into an argument. I was angry. No, I was furious, and as I approached the men playing dominoes my thoughts were violent. I think the dog sensed my energy vibrations and considered me a threat, which is why he attacked."

He examined Olga's expression to see if she was understanding his logic.

"Think about it," he said to her. "I've been to that house many times before. That dog knew me. There was no reason for him to attack, except that he picked up on the energy I was emitting. You don't think I'm crazy, do you?"

"No, Papá, of course, not. I'm listening. I just don't know what to think."

"Well, thoughts can influence. Think about the people who are peaceful and when you are with them, you also feel at peace. Why is laughter contagious, even when we don't understand the joke? Because an energy is radiating outward and it affects us."

"*Sí, sí.* I know what you mean. And you thought of this while lying here in bed?"

"Well, it's not my original idea. I heard it first from *el chino*, but now it makes sense. As I sit here, with nothing to do, trying to move my focus away from the pain, I've been contemplating the power of thought."

"*Coño*, Papá, you sound so smart and profound, like *el Viejo Márquez*. But just in case, don't throw away that morphine."

Olga and Manolo laughed and then Jenny stepped into the room. They turned and saw she had something to say.

"Your husband is here. He honked his horn."

Olga jumped out of her seat, alarmed.

"I have to go. Carlitos doesn't like to be kept waiting."

"Is that a new car he's in?" Jenny asked.

"Yeah, it's an MG. *El Viejo Márquez* got it for him so he could campaign properly."

"Hmm. Must be nice," Jenny said sarcastically and turned around.

Olga carefully leaned over to give her father a kiss on the cheek. He pulled her in.

"Remember, good thoughts," he said to her.

"Good thoughts," she repeated and then quickly left the room.

As she approached the car, she held her breath, afraid Carlitos' bets at the racetrack weren't fruitful, but then he smiled.

"You won?" she asked as he pulled away from the curb.

"Did I ever! I placed fifty pesos on Calamity, whose odds were twenty to one."

"And how much is that?"

"*Mil cocos*, a thousand coconuts!"

Olga bounced in her seat with joy.

"I couldn't believe my luck. Calamity looked like she was going to come in third, and then her sprint went into high gear. The speed of that dog!"

He leaned over and gave Olga a light kiss on the lips.

"We should celebrate," Carlitos suggested.

"*¡Ay, si!* Let's go see that movie, 'Gigi.' "

"Gigi? No, I don't think so. Well, maybe some other day. Tonight, we have to be at my father's house for dinner. We'll be reviewing the final details for the campaign."

"Oh. I'll tell Mima."

"Why do you have to tell her? She's not coming."

"No, but I'm sure she'd like to know. Who else is going to be there?"

"I'm not sure, but if I know my father there'll be other political couples."

That evening Olga and Carlitos dressed in semi-formal attire. The dinner gatherings with her father-in-law and his new wife, Uva, seemed too formal. His bid for the presidency elevated the bar of etiquette and decorum, forcing Olga to restrain her knowledge of funny limericks. The dinner was attended by several couples that Olga had never met, and who were only interested in discussing politics. To her right sat Sara Hernandez-Cata, Uva's sister and the only non-accompanied woman at the gathering. She was an artist whose interest in paintings of nude people made Olga blush.

"I swear," Sara said to Olga while the other guests spoke among themselves. "If I have to listen to one more comparison of Batista to Franco, I think I will scream."

"Why? Do you not think they're alike?" Olga asked.

Sara's eyes were set on a distant horizon, making her presence at the table seem as part of an unwanted compromise. Her hair was wildly loose, unlike the other women around the table, whose heads were perfectly coiffed. She wore a simple dress adorned by a colorful scarf, accentuating a natural beauty that must have provided a long line of suitors when she was younger. Olga sensed the most interesting woman in Havana was seated just inches away.

"Of course, they are. I just don't want to hear about it." Sara directed her eyes back at Olga and with a mentor-like tone continued to explain. "Only boring men with no imagination could think this to be an acceptable conversation starter. Unfortunately, I think we are surrounded by them." Sara then reached into her purse and took out a pack of Dunhill cigarettes and looked at Olga appreciatively. "How old are you?"

"Twenty-three and a half."

"And a half? You're not a child. You can stop saying 'and a half.' Only children speak like that. You're either twenty-three or twenty-four. Never half of one."

Olga nodded and looked down slightly embarrassed by her response.

"And you're also old enough to know that you should avoid men with no imagination. They end up being the same men who can't satisfy their wives in bed."

"*¡Sara, por favor!*" Uva interrupted her sister and frowned from across the table.

Sara rolled her eyes, took out a cigarette and smiled at Olga, who was holding back a giggle.

"It seems I'm being reprimanded for being too honest," she said. "Carlitos, can you light my cigarette?"

Carlitos, whose mood was heightened by the win at the racetrack, reached across his wife to provide a light without missing a syllable from the energetic conversation he was engaged in.

"The problem we're facing is of public opinion," Carlitos said to the guest across the table. "More and more people are losing trust in the democratic process. With every day that passes, Fidel and the revolution gain more sympathy, convincing the people he is the savior who will free us from a corrupt dictatorship. My father has a good plan and his campaign promises are refreshing, but we're fighting an uphill battle."

The guest sitting in front of Carlitos was an older, wiry man, Congressman León Ramírez, who listened patiently, waiting for an opportunity to speak.

"I traveled to the *Sierra* and visited Fidel in his camp," Ramírez said.

"Yes, I heard. Very brave of you. You were lucky to return without a scratch."

"You're right. Especially now that he's created a Revolutionary Tribunal. He's executing anyone who is dissenting, including his own soldiers."

"Because the only opinion that matters is his. He will rule by fear, or by mesmerizing his followers with fantastical dreams. I heard his speech on..."

"I heard it too," Ramírez interrupted loudly, "but this is not what I want to talk about."

"Oh, thank God!" Sara exclaimed while exhaling smoke. "Finally, somebody who does not want to talk about politics."

Ramírez glanced at Sara but did not waver from his posture. The separate conversations around the table ceased and everyone turned to look at Ramírez.

"Fidel is gaining ground," Ramírez said. He stood and looked directly at Carlos Senior. "He has troops moving to Las Villas with El Che Guevara, and he's launching a new radio station called *Radio Rebelde*. His message is one that makes sense. How can we have a fair election when Batista is the one coordinating it? Aren't we wasting our time?"

"I think I'm wasting my time," Sara said and placed her napkin on the table.

"This is no joking matter, madam," Ramírez said with a tone of offense.

"Who says I'm joking? I tire of all this political commentary. Carlos, please forgive me," she looked at Carlos Senior, "but this gathering lacks proportion. So, if you'll excuse me, I'm going to retire for the night."

Carlos Senior nodded and stood up. The men followed suit and stood as Sara departed. Olga looked at her with admiration, wondering how this woman developed such nerve.

"My question still stands," Ramírez said while the rest of the men returned to their seats.

"Are you being rhetorical, or can we offer an opinion?" Carlitos challenged Ramírez.

"Fidel has a valid point," Ramírez sat down. "And no, it's not rhetorical. Please say something that would satisfy my worried mind."

"Ramírez, that is why we're here," Carlos Senior replied from the other end of the table. "We need to speak louder and more often than Fidel. We need to convince the Cuban people that the solution to our crisis is through an election and not a violent revolution. Batista has sabotaged democracy, but it's no longer him that matters. It's the one who follows that should worry us."

Carlitos opened his mouth to speak, but his father raised an index finger and silenced him. Olga reached for her husband's hand to settle him.

"We are at an intersection riddled with crossfire," Carlos Senior continued, "From one direction, shots are fired by an incompetent, bumbling dictator. From the other, an ambitious tyranny that is terrorizing the populace. Our path is set before us. We must move forward, toward democracy. And like any war, the number of soldiers at the front lines matter. The more people who cross this intersection with us, the more likely we are to reach the other side. Ramírez, I need you to recruit soldiers, people who will speak for the election and increase voter turnout.

If the Cuban people vote in large numbers, neither Batista nor Fidel can do anything about it. We will win, I promise you."

At the end of the evening, after all the guests had left, Olga helped clear the table, while the maid washed dishes.

"Olguita, tell me, how is your family?" Uva asked while carrying several drinking glasses to the kitchen counter.

"*Bueno*, what can I say? My mother is good. She retired from teaching about two years ago, and she spends her time either in the garden and cooking amazing meals. Can't you tell by the way Carlitos has added a few pounds?"

Olga chuckled and Uva smiled.

"My father got attacked by a wild dog."

"No!" Uva responded with shock. "Is he alright?"

"*Bueno*, he's in bed, recovering. He got bit..." Olga motioned to her crotch.

"No! Poor man! Oh my god. I haven't heard of something like this in years."

"Neither have I," Sara said from the kitchen entrance. Olga turned with surprise and found her standing with a glass of scotch whiskey in her hand. "I wonder if that will affect his ability to..."

"Sara!" Uva protested. "You do not speculate such things."

"Why not? It's a natural question." Sara replied without hesitating. "If he had been bitten in the hand, I'd be wondering if he could use his fingers."

"Well," Olga offered. "I didn't ask him how bad it was."

The women were walking back to the dining table when Carlos Senior returned.

"*Y Carlitos*, where is he?" Uva said, meeting her husband at the table. He pulled out a chair and sat at the head of the table. Olga stood behind Uva, smiling, while Sara stayed a few paces behind.

"Outside, still trying to make his point and wearing down Ramírez."

Carlos Senior leaned forward and rested his head on both hands.

"You're tired, *mi vida*. Let me get you *un café*."

"No, no. It's too late for that. I just need to sit for a little while."

"Or maybe a glass of whiskey," Sara said with a smile.

Carlos Senior looked up and saw Olga, pleasantly smiling at him.

"*Ven*, Olguita. Sit here, next to me," he said, motioning her to the chair on his right and then looked at Sara. "Her smile is better than any glass of whiskey."

Olga's smile widened as she sat next to him. Uva followed and sat to his left.

"Well, I think I want a little bit of coffee, *un buchito*," Uva said with an uplifting tilt in her voice. "Olguita, do you want some too?"

"Sure. It sounds like a good idea."

"Well, if Piedad is going to make some, I'll have one too." Carlos Senior joined.

"Don't look at me," Sara said and raised her glass. "I can't imagine ruining my whiskey with the taste of coffee."

Uva looked at her with disapproval.

"Okay, okay. I'll retire once again before I say something that might rouse my sister."

"You're welcome to stay," Carlos Senior said to her.

"No, no. It's quite alright. I'm working on a painting and I should return to it before the paint dries."

"At this hour of the night?" Olga asked.

"Somebody here has to do something other than politics."

"Piedad," Uva called out.

"*Si, señora?*" The maid stepped into view.

"Prepare some espresso, three to be exact, if you please."

"Four," Carlos Senior corrected.

"No, I don't want one," Sara said.

"It's not for you," Carlos Senior said. "My son will eventually return."

"Oh, then I really should get back to my room," Sara replied while turning around. "I don't know if I could stand more political explanations."

A momentary pause lingered over them as Uva directed her attention to the maid, who was still waiting for an order.

"Four coffees, Piedad, if you don't mind," Uva said and the maid quickly retreated into the kitchen. Carlos Senior reached over to Olga's hand.

"Quickly, Olguita, is Carlitos doing better?"

"Yes, very much so. I think working as your campaign manager, and his own run for congress, has pulled him out of the depressed state he was in."

"*Bueno*, let's not talk about this," Uva said. "He's right outside. Did you know Olguita's father was attacked by a wild dog?"

"*¿Como?*"

Olga narrated an embellished story that had both in-laws at the edge of their seats.

"*Ay*, it broke my heart to see him in bed with bandages," she lamented. "He's very lucky that the dog didn't bite his face or do more damage."

The maid arrived with four cups of coffee, providing the pause for silence.

"I'd like your opinion on something my father said," Olga said to Carlos Senior, who consented to the question with a nod.

"My father has a spiritual side, one he developed when he used to suffer from headaches," she said. "He even meditates."

"Really?" Uva exclaimed with surprise.

Carlitos walked in and quietly joined the trio by sitting at the opposite end of the table.

"So, while lying in bed, recovering from his wounds, he's been meditating and he told me about a new insight."

"About what?" Carlos Senior moved his hand to speed her question along.

"Well, let me see if I can say it correctly. Thoughts are like waves, or energy, that move outward from our heads," Olga said, motioning with her hands and moving the air around her forehead. "Although we can't physically see these thought waves, they can influence."

"Yes, which is why sometimes people have the same thought at the same time," Carlos Senior said to her.

"Exactly!" Olga replied with enthusiasm. "The thing is that my father thinks the dog attacked him because the dog sensed his thoughts."

"What was he thinking?" Carlitos asked while reaching for the fourth cup of coffee.

"I don't know, but he said he was furious, and he thinks the dog perceived it and attacked him. I find the notion fascinating and I'm wondering what you think about it."

"About what in particular," Carlos Senior asked, "the dog or the energy of thoughts?"

"*No sé*. It's all so new to me. I don't know what to think."

"*Bueno*, Olguita, I was not there, and I haven't talked to your father, but we need to consider that maybe he was bit simply because it is the nature of dogs to bite. However, your father has touched upon a concept that has been discussed by mystics and philosophers for the last century."

Olga nodded and waited for her father-in-law to continue while Uva stood and went to the kitchen to supervise the maid.

"If you have one angry person in a room, a small room like this," Carlos Senior continued, "the anger of that single person can be disruptive, even if the person is well behaved. But if that person is in a large room, or an open space, like a ballpark, his anger is no longer disruptive. Why? Because it's a much larger space and the thoughts get diffused. The rules of proportion apply. If one hundred people are all angry and they're inside a theater, you better run. Put those hundred people in the ballpark, and they have to work in order to influence the others around them. They have to scream outrage, in hopes of creating a small mob. In every mob, there's always people who don't know why they're angry, but they enjoy the energy. Then there's those who realize it doesn't make sense and they step away. At some point, there's a critical moment where the mob might dissipate or unify. If the mob stays together, feeding this negative energy to each other, they become dangerous. Do you see where I'm heading?"

"Yes, but what does this have to do with my father's thought waves?"

"Because if you get enough people together, with the same thoughts, there is a magnifying effect, the small individual thought wave of one person can become a large community wave. Think of thousands of people, hundreds of thousands of people, all angry and living in close proximity to each other, and all suffering from discontent. Some of them know exactly why they're angry, but others don't. Some might be annoyed, others might be raging mad, but very few use the same language to describe the source of their discontent. They can't tell you why they feel the way they do, but they're part of a collective signal, a disturbance that is transmitted at a subconscious level. If this disturbance is amplified by radio messages, conversations with neighbors who complain incessantly, and their own life experience, then guess what Olguita?"

"What?"

"We have a problem, and that's actually what we're living through now. Batista has created a cauldron of anger that is boiling over. The mismanagement, violence and injustice have the people screaming and no one is listening. Which is why we need to keep spreading our message. We need to move the people toward hope and away from anger and fear."

"The mystical side of politics," Carlitos said to his wife with a tone of amusement. "All this from your father's dog bite."

"It's human nature," Carlos Senior corrected. "It's group dynamics and how mob mentality is formed. Many people, not all, are attracted to the energy, even when it's not in their best interest. When you scratch at the surface and ask why, they can't give a rational answer."

"Thank you," Carlitos said from across the table. "You just proved my point."

Olga and her father-in-law looked at him with surprised interest.

"You keep giving speeches about the constitution, and the people aren't listening. Why? Because people don't vote for a constitution. They vote for a person who is moving and inspires them. We need to appeal to the heart, and create energy. Group dynamics, like you said."

Carlos Senior leaned back in his chair and silently examined his son, who stood up to amplify his argument.

"The campaign has a catchy phrase, 'Not the past, nor the present, Márquez-Sterling for president.' But we need to make them afraid of Fidel's revolution. We need to create an energy against Fidel. That's how we'll win."

"Carlitos," Uva said, stepping into view. "It's getting late, and we're all tired. You'll have to continue strategizing tomorrow. Olguita, thank you for coming."

Olga stood and leaned over to give her father-in-law a kiss on the cheek. He lightly patted her on the shoulders and said, "*Bueno, bueno.*"

******

Fangio, an Argentine Formula One driver, was in Havana for the 2nd Annual Cuban Grand Prix. He was greeted at the airport by an American named Brown, who thanked him on behalf of the Grand Prix and President Batista.

"Shall we go on a tour of the city and review your schedule?" Brown asked while walking toward the car.

"Where are we going?" Fangio asked in a curious tone. "We're not going near the revolution, are we?"

"Revolution? Where did you hear that? There's no such thing."

"What about this man, Fidel Castro?"

"Well," Brown said. "There are some rebels, but they're not in the city. They're far away, in the mountains. Anyway, the army has them on the run. President Batista assures your safety. Did you not enjoy your visit last year, at our first Grand Prix?"

"Oh! That was a party!" Fangio said as he reached the car. "I enjoyed myself more than in any other Grand Prix. Which is why I'm here again, but I've heard about these revolutionaries and I just have to ask, is it safe?"

"Very safe," Brown reassured with a smile and opened the car door for him.

"Good. Then, let's go to a casino," he said as he plopped himself into the back seat of the limousine.

"Perfect," Brown said.

At the casino, Fangio played roulette, drank a multitude of Cuba Libres, gambled thousands of *pesos*, and posed for photographs with fans and casino workers. He returned to his hotel room accompanied by two young women, who were eager to make him feel welcomed. Later that evening, as he and the two women walked into the lobby of the hotel, a young man in a leather jacket, brandishing a pistol, confronted him.

"Fangio, you must come with me," the man said. "I am a member of the 26th of July Revolutionary Movement."

Brown, who was waiting for him at the bar, ran to the assailant and threw a marble paperweight toward the intruder, narrowly missing his head. The women screamed, and the rebel spun around to aim his gun at Brown.

"Stay still!" he screamed. "If you move, I shoot."

Brown raised his arms and watched as Fangio left with the young rebel to an awaiting car. News of the kidnapping spread quickly, and Batista deployed dozens of police units to search for the Argentine driver, who disappeared into the night without a trace.

The next morning, Carlitos read about the abduction of Fangio and eagerly went to look for his camera case.

"I didn't know the rebels were in Havana," Olga said to him. "Will it be safe at the racetrack? What if there's a bomb?"

"Olguita, *mi vida*, you don't want to miss this." He emptied his case and began to organize its contents. "What did I tell you last year when I came back from the race?"

"I don't know. What did you say?"

"That you should have been there."

"Oh. What are those?" she pointed at several small, plastic cases he lined up on the table.

"Film."

"How many pictures are you going to take?"

"As many as I can. But I have to save a roll for Fangio."

"Isn't he being held hostage?"

"Yes, but at some point, he'll be released," he said while tossing one case in the air. "That's what this one is for. So, are you going? *Vamos.* There's nothing like it."

"It seems dangerous with rebels kidnapping a driver, and all."

"That makes it ten times more exciting. It will be remembered as the race when Fangio was kidnapped. Even if you just sit in the stands, at a safe distance, it's electrifying." He put down the case and turned to her. "C'mon, you have to go," He begged and pulled her in close. "I won't enjoy it if you're not with me."

"You won't enjoy it?" Olga asked sarcastically.

"Well, not as much," he corrected and kissed her.

"Alright," she agreed in between kisses.

"Excellent!" he exclaimed and stepped back.

"So, what do I wear to a Grand Prix?"

Carlitos chuckled and walked away, knowing his wife would wear enough clothes to reveal her youthful beauty, while still protecting herself from the cool February winds that were certain to blow through the *Malecón.* They drove to Angelito's house in Carlitos' new MG. She relinquished her seat and moved to the back, where she barely fit, allowing the two men to compare cameras and shutter speeds.

The morning sun shone on the two-hundred-year-old buildings of central Havana, remnants of an era when Spain invested heavily in its prized colony. Two centuries later, frazzled electrical wires curled out of their corners, like unshaven armpits. Chipped paint, bleached and streaked with the morbidity of a lopsided economy, speckled the decomposing buildings. Clothing lines with thin shirts and stained undergarments hung between the windows and balconies. The residents, although innately beautiful, looked from their graying balconies at a display of wealth that made them feel ugly. One by one, the extravagant Formula One race cars and wealthy drivers wearing shiny outfits, slowly drove to the starting gate, just one block from their impoverished homes. The residents looked in awe at a sport and a life so far removed from reality that it bordered on being offensive, as if saying, "Take a look at what you will never be."

It was there, in the contrasts of her privileged life against hopeless expressions, where Olga heard the whispers of the revolution. In every sigh and exhale, "Fidel." In every mother, nurturing a barefoot child, "Fidel." In the creaks of splintered doors hanging on rusted nails, and in the dreams of men who longed for change, "Fidel."

Carlitos parked within walking distance of the race while Fangio was being taken to a new safehouse. The racecar driver did not have any training in hostage negotiations, but he instinctively knew to make friends with his captors. They joked, told stories and drank rum together. A young rebel, motivated by the desire to impress the hostage, fetched his mother for the sole purpose of getting her to cook a homemade dish of *carne con papas*. Fangio joked that these revolutionaries will kidnap anyone, including their own mother. It was a joke that spread through the rebels, and weeks later Castro, himself, repeated it in a motivational speech.

The rebels behaved more like hosts than aggressors, stealing a television set so their new Argentinian friend could watch the race and explain the dangers involved in the sport. Ironically, within minutes of his lesson, a race car skidded into the crowd, killing thirty spectators and seriously injuring the driver. The tragedy brought the race to a quick conclusion and the rebels gladly returned their hostage to his hotel, giving him hugs before parting ways. In an interview to dozens of reporters Fangio spoke well of the rebels and their cause, going on to endorse the revolution by saying, "I hope they're successful in ousting Batista." His support was heard in Washington DC, and a new sympathetic light was cast on Fidel Castro.

Days later, Carlitos was in Tina's living room, trying to determine which photos best captured the feel of the race. Similar to car parts strewn over a garage floor, Carlitos had photos scattered over the furniture.

"All these photos, and not one of Olguita," Tina complained.

He was on the floor, leaning against the sofa, comparing photos of Fangio at the interview.

"Look, in this one, he's saying how the rebels cooked for him. You can almost see how he was still savoring the meal."

"Don't you have a campaign to run?" she asked with a sneer. "Shouldn't you be doing something other than taking pictures of little cars?"

Carlitos stood to face his adversary. He knew she was not going to listen to his explanation of the historical relevance captured in those photos. He knew his mother-in-law only cared for the restoration of her living room to its previous condition. So, he smacked his lips and began gathering the photos.

"I've taken plenty of pictures of your daughter, for your information," he said while placing the photos in a folder. "Don't worry, I won't mess up your living room anymore. Besides, we need to leave soon."

"Are we leaving?" Olga asked from the hallway. "Do I need to get ready?"

"*A donde van*, where are you going?" Tina asked.

Carlitos looked at Tina and walked away without answering.

"*Artística Gallega*," Olga offered as she stepped aside to make room for her husband.

"Fancy place," Tina nodded. "Are you going to the casino?"

"No, Mima. It's the assembly of the political party. *El Viejo Márquez* is accepting the nomination as presidential candidate."

"Is that today?"

"Later, around six o'clock."

"What are you wearing?" Tina asked while Carlitos crossed the hall.

"The black dress. It's a formal event, you know. Carlitos even has a new suit for the occasion. His name is listed as one of the congressmen."

"Very exciting. I wish I could be there," Tina said with a sarcastic tone, feigning injury for not being invited.

"But you can't," Carlitos retorted loudly from the bathroom.

Artística Gallega was in the center of the city, not far from the capitol building. It housed a restaurant that served Spanish food, a ballroom, a casino, an outdoor garden with several fountains, and most importantly, a convention hall. It was the perfect venue for the inaugural assembly of the Free People's Party. By forming the political party, Carlos Senior managed to attract a lot of big-name politicians, who wanted to disassociate themselves from Batista and the rampant corruption. When Olga and Carlitos arrived, the convention hall was buzzing with the overlapping conversations of hundreds of people all dressed in their finest.

"*¡Ay, Dios mío!* Look at all the people here!" Olga said as she held on to Carlitos.

"I didn't think they would all come. This is really something."

A young woman, wearing a tight and slightly revealing outfit, walked toward them with a tray of drinks. Older men ogled her as she walked past them, but she kept her poise and smile. Carlitos waved her away before she got too close.

"Why?" Olga protested. "I'm in the mood for a little drink."

"Don't ever accept a drink from a wandering tray. Always go to the bar and watch them make it for you. Besides, tonight we should stay away from mixed drinks."

"You make it sound dangerous."

"There's too many people here, and not everyone may be a friend. A mixed drink is the easiest sabotage."

"*Gordo*," a familiar voice called from behind.

Carlitos turned around to see Cristóbal and Oscar Jorge, smiling handsomely.

"Don't you look lovely tonight," Oscar Jorge said as he kissed Olga on the cheek.

"*Gracias*, and you both look very handsome," she replied and leaned forward to receive a kiss from Cristóbal. "Where's Marisa? Don't tell me you left her at home."

"Life with toddlers is not easy," Cristóbal answered, "but don't worry. My mother is watching the babies. Marisa is in the back, by the bar, with Matty and Gloria."

"You see all these people?" Olga commented while looking around.

"Well what do you expect," Oscar Jorge replied. "Free food and drinks, and a chance to play some roulette? I'm surprised half of Havana isn't here."

"Whose paying for all this?" Cristóbal asked.

"We're sending the bill to your newspaper." Carlitos chuckled.

"Yeah, right!" Cristóbal smiled. "*El País* is doing well, but not for all this."

"Sugar money," Oscar Jorge said. "You see, over there is Julio Lobo."

"Who's that?" Olga asked.

"Who's that?" Cristóbal repeated, shocked at the question and then began to laugh. "Only the richest man in Cuba, owner of at least a third of the sugar industry."

"He's been a client of Papá for many years," Carlitos offered.

"Where is your father?" Oscar Jorge asked.

"Closer to the front of the room," Carlitos tried to see over the people, "probably shaking hands with all the donors. Is that Manuel, my brother, up there?"

"Of course," Oscar Jorge responded. "He and Gloria arrived early."

Olga focused on a group of men near the stage. A tall man, American looking, was among them.

"And who's that over there, he looks familiar." Olga asked Oscar Jorge.

"Who are you talking about?"

"*El Americano* up there, near the sugar man."

Oscar Jorge laughed. "Julio Lobo," he corrected her.

"Yes, near him. You see him. He's taller than most men and his hair is light."

"Yes, I see him. I'm not sure."

"Who are you looking at?" Carlitos asked.

"That *Americano* over there," Olga pointed. "He looks familiar to me."

Carlitos immediately knew who Olga was referring to. It was Brown. He looked down, shook his head and smacked his lips.

"Where do I know him from?"

"From the casino. He's the man who got us free drinks."

A group of men walked through the crowd. One of them had a lit cigarette hanging from his lip and accidentally stepped on Olga, who immediately complained.

"Watch where you're walking," Carlitos reprimanded the man. "And extinguish that cigarette before you burn somebody."

The man shrugged his shoulders and continued to make his way through the crowd.

"It's too crowded," Olga complained. "Maybe we can go outside and see the garden."

Carlitos leaned forward, indicating he didn't hear what she said. Olga repeated her suggestion a bit louder only to be met by three shaking heads.

"This is where it's all happening," he replied. "Besides, pretty soon they'll call me up to the stage with the other candidates. Do you want to join Marisa and the other women?"

"C'mon, I'll take you to her," Cristóbal offered.

Olga looked at Carlitos, who nodded at her and then turned to talk to Oscar Jorge, who playfully winked at her before giving Carlos his attention. She laughed, not having been winked at before.

"What?" Cristóbal asked with a smile.

"Oscar Jorge, he's such a flirt."

"He's a charmer. Look, there's Marisa. You see her?"

Marisa was standing with Gloria and two other women, all of them laughing, each holding a glass of white wine. They greeted Olga warmly as Cristóbal quickly returned to join the men. Olga felt an immediate relief from the noise and congestion.

"Have we separated ourselves from the action?" Olga asked Marisa.

"Maybe it's our natural aversion to cigarette smoke."

"And dirty old men," Olga pointed out two balding men who were staring at the rear end of the woman carrying a drink tray.

"Gloria was just telling me about her wedding," Marisa said. "It must have been lovely!"

Olga smiled at her sister-in-law. "Manuel is a lucky man."

"Thank you," Gloria blushed.

"Where did you honeymoon?"

"Miami Beach. We stayed at the Fountainbleu, on the beach."

"*Damas y caballeros*, your attention please," the Master of Ceremonies spoke into a microphone. "Ladies and Gentlemen, let's begin with the business of the evening, so we can continue with the celebration afterward. There will be plenty of music to follow, but please settle down so we can begin."

Olga had a good view from where she stood. Her father-in-law was on the stage with the other candidates. Manuel was sitting off to the side.

"Where's Carlitos?" Marisa asked.

"Probably still on the floor," Olga answered, "debating political theory with some poor fellow who doesn't know he's outmatched."

"I've seen him get like that." Marisa smiled. "When that happens to me, I have the perfect exit." She changed her expression to a deep concern. "I just say: 'I think I hear the baby crying. Excuse me.'" She turned and pretended to leave.

"Brilliant!" Olga laughed. "One more reason to have children."

"Oh, they're good for most excuses. 'Sorry, I can't. The baby has a slight fever.' Nobody can get offended, and if they do, well then that's the sort of person you don't want as a friend."

Olga laughed as the woman with the tight outfit and a tray of drinks approached them.

"Excuse me," Olga called her.

"*Si*, rum and soda or white wine?"

"Not sure, but tell me, woman to woman, is there anything wrong with these drinks?"

The server was defending the quality of the drinks when a chant arose at the front of the room, "Death to the elections!" Thirty or more men loudly repeated the chant as another group of men rushed the stage from behind. A brawl ensued on the floor as the disrupters attacked the audience. Olga, Marisa and the women near them moved further back in search of safety.

"Death to Batista! Death to Márquez-Sterling!" The men yelled as they rushed toward Carlos Senior with knives in their hands. Having been warned of the strong possibility of troublemakers in the audience, the presidential candidate arrived at the convention with a .45 caliber gun tucked in the back of his pants. There was a scuffle on the stage as Osvaldo, his bodyguard, used a chair defensively, giving Carlos Senior the opportunity to fire a warning shot at the ceiling. The deafening sound of the solitary gunshot surprised everyone, and soon after the security guard and police officers apprehended the assailants. Luckily, no other shots were fired, and few people were injured. Olga, Marisa and Gloria, still hiding in the back of the room, were stunned and horrified. Carlitos and Manuel hurriedly returned to them.

"Are you okay?" Carlitos asked Olga. His tie had been pulled apart.

Manuel, who wasn't wearing his glasses, tried to reassure his bride.

"*Y tu, mi amor*, are you hurt?"

"Not at all. What about you? What happened to your glasses?"

"They fell during the scuffle." Manuel touched the bridge of his nose.

"Where's Tobi," Marisa asked Carlos. "Do you know if he's alright?"

"I saw him. He's talking to a reporter from his newspaper. He's fine."

"We should get out of here," Olga nervously suggested as dozens of people were making their way to the exit.

"Not yet," Carlitos said. "We have to make sure Papá is alright." He turned to his brother. "We should go up there. Come with me."

Not wanting to push against the crowd, Carlitos and Manuel walked the perimeter of the room, alongside the wall, to reach the front. Olga, Gloria and Marisa followed him.

"People," the Master of Ceremonies called into the microphone. "People, please calm down. Your attention, please. The police have the rioters in custody. All is under control. We must continue with the business of the party, the business of democracy. We must continue, or else Fidel and his thugs will have won."

The crowd became almost immovable as the spectators turned their attention to the stage. Olga and her companions watched from the far wall as Carlos Senior stood next to the Master of Ceremonies. He seemed taller than ever, unshaken and resolute. She felt a surge of pride and began to shed tears. Marisa looked at her, knowingly, and also began to cry.

"People of Cuba," the Master of Ceremonies said into the microphone. "It is time to speak with one voice against the forces that are tearing our island apart. We will not be silenced by thugs who want to hijack the country."

The room grew silent as everyone fixed their attention on him. The Master of Ceremonies looked at his audience and with a loud voice, wanting to be heard near and far, lifted his arms and proclaimed: "We the Free People's Party embrace democracy and the next president of our republic, the man who gave us our constitution and who will save us from tyranny, Dr. Carlos Márquez-Sterling."

The crowd cheered and applauded as Carlos Senior stepped forward. Olga, Gloria and Marisa, clapped enthusiastically, with tears running down their cheeks.

"Thank you. Thank you," Carlos Senior said as the people quieted down. He examined the crowd, their hopeful faces amid the traces of a violent disturbance, and caught sight of his two sons, making their way to him. His face became stern. With the rhythm and cadence of a prophetic preacher, he spoke into the microphone.

"There are many who don't understand why we are here, but we do. There are many who don't think we should continue forward, but we will. There are many who are disheartened and have given up, but we haven't. There are those who resort to violence and fear tactics, hoping we will turn and run, but we will stand our ground. We stand together for a new Cuba, and I accept this responsibility you are entrusting to me, to lead this island we love to a future that is within our grasp, a future where freedom, peace and prosperity reign."

The crowd applauded, but the presidential candidate kept a stern demeanor as he faced his audience. He turned and saw his sons reach the stage, looking at him with pride in their eyes.

"The future of Cuba is in our hands," he said, extending his hand to Carlitos and Manuel and then toward the audience. "The importance of what we are doing has become evident tonight, in this very room. You have witnessed it. By storming this assembly, by invading our democratic process, Fidel has revealed what he fears most, Democracy, which is why we need to implore our neighbors, friends and co-workers to vote. It is the only way forward. Should we falter, should we surrender to evil and the corruption that has afflicted this island for too long, then Cuba will cease to be free. It will be the death of democracy in Cuba if Fidel Castro takes over. We will not waver. We will not be deterred until the election is won."

Carlitos and Manuel stepped onto the stage as the people cheered effusively. They turned toward each other, and in a rare display of emotion, hugged. Olga, Gloria and Marisa held hands and cried with joy as competing chants and acclamations echoed in the room. The run for the presidency had begun and with it the hope for a new era.

Later that evening, when Carlos Senior was in the comfort of his home and Uva was helping him undress, they saw how close the assailants had been to killing him. The back of his suit jacket, shirt and undershirt had been sliced by a knife and a small red scratch ran down the length of his back.

CHAPTER 14

Olga

January 8, 2021
St. Petersburg
It was after ten o'clock at night, late enough for my mother to have been asleep for a couple of hours, when a distant complaint competed for our attention. Maria and I were watching a commentator analysis of the U.S. Capitol being stormed by radical Trump supporters. It had been an emotionally disturbing week as our outrage grew with new video footage.

"*¡Ay, ay, ay!*" I could hear the muffled voice.

Maria muted the television and we focused our attention, unsure of what we heard.

"*¡Ay!* Get them off! *¡Ay!*"

I leapt from my seat and ran to my mother's room.

"*¡Ay, ay, ay!* Get them off me! Get them off me!" My mother screamed from her bed as she frantically slapped an invisible enemy from her skin.

I pulled her bedcover to examine the situation.

"I'm here. Everything is okay. I'm here," I tried to reassure but she continued to kick and squirm inside the bedsheet.

"*Quítalos,*" she cried out repeatedly. "Get them off me!"

Maria began swiping at her legs, brushing off a non-present threat. I joined in the effort and soon my mother ceased to struggle as her cries for help became a sob of grief.

"There," Maria said. "They're all gone. All gone now."

"Mama, you're okay," I reassured her. "You're safe in bed."

With tears still puddling under her eyes, my mother looked around and saw me for the first time. She then turned and saw Maria, who smiled at her.

"It was a bad dream," Maria softly said. "You were dreaming, but it's okay now."

Several minutes later, while seated at the edge of her bed and sipping chamomile tea, my mother was breathing easier.

"Mama, what happened? What did you dream?" I asked from the chair next to her.

"It was the cockroaches!" she said. "They were all over me, crawling up my legs."

I nodded and she sighed, handing the teacup to me.

"It felt so real."

"Well, you know it was just a dream, a nightmare, right?"

"The worst kind to have. I need to lay down," she said as her body surrendered.

"That's a good idea," I replied and turned on the night light.

"No, no, no. Turn that off. It bothers me."

I stood by the doorway looking at her fall asleep as Maria approached.

"That's it," I whispered. "No more evening news for her."

"We'll watch comedies instead."

"Anything as long as it keeps her mind away from Trump and the insurrection. Even if I have to watch an entire season of 'Two and a Half Men.' "

Five o'clock became the boundary. No more talk of politics after that hour.

CHAPTER 15

El Che Guevara

1959
Havana, Cuba

The evening crickets had gone quiet and a half moon glowed over Havana. Outside, *Negrita y Blanquita* sat at attention, incessantly scanning the night for signs of feline prey. Olga was sleeping in the guest room when the phone rang. The ringing sounded distant at first, only to become louder as her consciousness floated to reality. She sat upright, alarmed, and ran to the phone sitting on a small table next to the hallway. Tina was opening her door when Olga lifted the receiver.

"*¿Alo?*"

"Olguita?"

"*¿Sí?*"

"It's me, Oscar Jorge."

Olga stepped into the kitchen to look at the clock hanging on the wall. It read 2:45 a.m. She returned to the living room, adjusting the cord as she walked.

"What's the matter?"

"I need to speak with *el Gordo*."

"Who is it?" Tina whispered while pulling a robe around her shoulders and standing next to Olga.

Olga shook her head.

"He's asleep."

"Can you wake him?"

"He's sick with mononucleosis. He's in bad shape, with a high fever. What's going on?"

"Who is it?" Tina asked again, this time a bit louder.

"It's Oscar Jorge," Olga said to her with annoyance. She placed the receiver on her shoulder to shield it from her voice. "I'll tell you later. Let him speak." She returned her attention to the caller. "Sorry, Oscar Jorge. You woke up the house, and my mother wants to know what's happening."

"Batista has fled the island. He got on a plane with Orlando Piedra at midnight."

"What? He left? I don't understand, and the colonel left with him?"

"Many of the generals are also leaving, like rats."

"But, but...."

"The police are removing their uniforms and abandoning the patrol cars."

"What does this mean?"

"It means there's no one in charge. The city is defenseless, and the rebels will be here in the morning."

Tina pulled at Olga's sleeve.

"Batista has fled the island," she said to her mother and then turned her attention to him. "What about *el Viejo Márquez?*"

"He must know, I'm sure."

"What do we do?"

"I'm not sure, but just in case, don't leave the house. Will you tell Carlitos?"

"I'll tell him in the morning. *Ay,* Oscar Jorge, please be careful."

"I will. Go back to sleep. We'll talk again tomorrow."

Olga placed the phone down and looked at Tina.

"What's happening?"

"El Che Guevara is marching into the city and will be here in the morning."

"*¡Ay, Dios mío!*"

The two women looked at each other, unsure of what the future held. Olga opened the bedroom door to wake Carlitos but chose to silently stand over him and place her hand on his forehead.

"Does he still have a fever?" Tina whispered.

"He feels warm, but not like before."

"Put a cold compress on his head."

"I have one," she replied while placing a damp towelette on his head.

"Get some sleep," Tina said from the doorway.

"I can't sleep now. I think I'll just sit here for a bit. You go. I'll see you in the morning."

Tina closed the door and returned to a dreamless sleep. The sound of crowing roosters woke her. The morning light was peeking in through the window. She momentarily forgot the news of the fleeing dictator and the threatening army, allowing one last anxiety-free moment to exist in her mind. She percolated coffee and sat to drink a small cup. Olga stepped out of the room, holding a thermometer in silence before Tina jumped in her seat.

"Oh my God, I just remembered. Batista left the island. El Che Guevara is on the move."

"Yes, we got the call last night."

"I woke up with no recollection of the call, until I saw you. What are we going to do?"

"Nothing," she looked at the thermometer.

"We should get the newspaper. Put on the radio. See what they're saying."

Olga didn't move and Tina noticed she was exhausted.

"You didn't sleep well?"

"I did, until the phone rang. I've been awake since then."

"How is Carlitos?"

"His fever is out of control," Olga said.

"How bad is it?"

"Forty," she examined the Celsius markings on the thermometer.

Olga stepped back into the room and stood at the foot of the bed. Tina joined her, with the cup of coffee still in her hand.

"Let me look at that." Tina put her cup down, reached for the thermometer and walked to the window to examine it in the light.

"It's almost forty-one," she said with narrowing eyes. "Maybe we should call the doctor."

"I don't know. He was here just two days ago. Will he say anything different?"

"Don't call him," Carlitos said in a weakened voice. "It's New Year's."

"*Pero*, your fever is out of control."

"I know. It's what happens," Carlitos said while turning in the bed. "He told us it would be like this. I just have to ride it out. Let the man enjoy the New Year."

Olga turned to look at Tina.

"You haven't told him," she said to her daughter.

Carlitos tilted his head toward Tina. Olga shook her head.

"Tell me what?"

"Oscar Jorge called last night and said Batista got on an airplane at midnight. He's fled the island. The military and the police are running too."

Carlitos sat up and looked at Olga.

"He also said El Che Guevara and his troops would be here by morning."

"*Ahora sí que le entro mierda al piano*," Carlitos said softly while sinking back into bed and pulling the sheets over his shoulder.

"You don't seem too concerned," Tina said.

"I'm too sick to care. Besides, I suspected this would happen. Cristóbal warned me."

"Cristóbal?" Olga said, surprised. "What did he know?"

"His family owns a newspaper," Carlitos replied with annoyance. "They're in the business of knowing things." He turned to look at Olga, who was dumbfounded. "On December 30th Batista's wife and children all left for Spain. It's obvious he'd leave shortly after."

"So, what do we do?" Tina asked.

"Nothing," Carlitos said. "Without an army to fight, there's nothing anyone can do."

"What about the doctor?" Olga asked.

"You want to risk his life?" Carlitos replied with a stronger tone of annoyance. He turned and pressed his head against the pillow. "It's best if we all stay indoors."

Tina stepped away as Olga looked out the window. The roosters were still crowing, and her two dogs were walking back to the house, presumably from a hunt.

"And bring me another aspirin," Carlitos ordered as he closed his eyes.

******

C'mon, drive faster!" Jenny snapped at Manolo. "They'll be here soon."

"Woman, I'm going as fast as I can. Do you want us to end up in an accident?"

He looked through the rearview mirror of his cream-colored convertible to check on his daughters, still seated in the back seat. The top was down, and the girls had their hands raised, trying to catch the wind. Jenny sat in the front passenger seat with their toddler son on her lap, as they sped to the eastern edge of Havana. Soon the scenery changed from residential to rural. Tall grass and sugarcane lined the road on either side. Small wooden homes and broken-down shacks speckled the vast expanse of undeveloped land. A slow-moving coal truck blocked the street and forced them to slow down.

"Oh my God! Can't you go around the truck?"

"I will. Relax! I need to check for oncoming traffic."

"You're such an old man!"

Manolo slowly went around the truck and began looking around as if lost.

"What's the matter?" Jenny asked.

"I don't think we should go much further. They're bound to pass through here."

Jenny stood while holding the top of the windshield and searched the horizon.

"Look, I think that might be them," she pointed at a caravan of trucks and people coming over a distant hill.

Manolo pulled the car over to the side and stood to look.

"Mama, what's happening?" Lily, her oldest daughter asked.

"El Che is passing through with his army. Today is an important day," she said enthusiastically.

"Because it's New Year's Day?"

"No, because today is the day that Fidel is liberating us from the evil Batista."

Manolo parked the car at a safe distance from the road, while still giving his wife a full view of the approaching parade. A young man, riding a mule, approached them.

"*Señora*, excuse me," the young man called Jenny from his mule. "Who are those people coming from the other side of the hill?"

"That's El Che Guevara and the 26th of July Movement," Jenny replied. "Have you not been listening to the radio?"

"We don't have a radio. Is Fidel there?"

"No, not yet. I think he's making his way and he'll be here later this week. Bring your family. You don't want to miss this."

"Oh my! I'm going to tell my wife and kids. Thank you!" The young man said with a smile and dug his heels into the mule to announce the arrival of the liberating army. It wasn't long before the side of the road was lined with nearby residents who wanted to catch a glimpse of El Che Guevara and his troops.

Like people at a drive-in movie, Manolo and his family sat on top of the back seat to watch the passing army. His wife was bouncing with excitement, waving at the rebels, as a growing fear took hold of him. Men wearing olive green uniforms, scraggly beards, and a scowl on their face, passed by on foot and trucks. Many had rosary beads hanging around their neck. All had long guns and a fierce look on their faces.

"*¡Viva Fidel!*" Jenny screamed loudly at the passing troops as she waved to them. A pair of rebel soldiers saw her and waved back.

"Here, hold the baby," she stood and passed her son to Manolo.

"*Compañera*," the first rebel said, waving back.

Jenny tilted her head and swept her hair back, while smiling at the men.

"*¡Oye, guapa!*" the second rebel called out.

Manolo stood and pulled Jenny down.

"What are you doing?" he protested.

"I'm welcoming the troops. What's wrong with you?"

"What's wrong with me? What's wrong with you? Those men are dangerous."

The rebels looked at Jenny arguing with Manolo and laughed among themselves as they continued their march with the rest of the troops. Jenny turned from Manolo and screamed once again, "*¡Viva Fidel!*"

The procession of rebel soldiers moved aside for the caravan of Jeep trucks. Jenny looked on with interest, trying to decipher which one of the passengers was el Che Guevara. Eventually, the children complained of hunger, forcing Jenny to put aside her adulation and to seek a nearby open-air café.

"I don't like the look of things," Manolo said while handing his daughter a *frita* for her to eat. "These men are itching for a fight."

"They're rebels," Jenny said. "Of course, they look like that." Her mouth was full, and Manolo saw chunks of meat swimming over her tongue. "Did you think they were going to be refined and well mannered?" She continued to eat, making smacking noises as she chewed.

"I think it's going to be dangerous," he said as he broke a small piece of his *frita* for his son. He watched the toddler try to chew the ground beef. "The whole situation is out of control," he continued, "I'm afraid there's going to be a lot of innocent people caught up in this mess. Don't you think?"

"This is a revolution, Manolo," she said after swallowing. A drop of grease stained the side of her mouth. "We're all going to have to make sacrifices, and those Batista supporters, they better run."

"It's not just the *Batistianos,*" he said calmly, trying to not incite a passionate response from her. "We'll all be in danger. *El Viejo Márquez* said it."

"There you go again quoting that bureaucrat. Let me tell you, I plan on joining the movement as soon as I can, and I think you better too."

Manolo remained silent as he methodically broke another piece of sandwich for his son.

******

He was told to sit, but Carlos Senior preferred to stand. He was in one of the interrogating rooms of the eighteenth-century Spanish fort, *La Cabaña*. The thick walls, meant to withstand canon blasts, were rustic and damp. A solitary window supplied the room with morning light, wisps of sea breeze and the sound of breaking waves. A single light bulb, hanging from an electrical wire, partially illuminated the hallway that echoed with the sounds of jailed men who had given their support to Batista, an act considered to be against the revolution and punishable by death.

Carlos Senior observed young men, trying to grow beards on adolescent cheeks, wearing uniforms that were too large, holding rifles they didn't command, and upholding philosophies they couldn't articulate, walking excitedly as if it were the first day of class. Across from him was a handsome, long-haired and bearded Argentinian doctor turned rebel, *el Che* Guevara. He wore the revolutionary colors - olive green, a rosary around his neck, a blood stain on his shoe and a smirk on his face.

"C'mon Doctor, have a seat," *el Che* said while pulling a chair out. "You're the one person I've been wanting to meet. Everyone else..." he paused and looked behind him with a bored expression. "...we'll just throw in jail."

El Che scratched his beard before sitting down unceremoniously. He motioned at Carlos Senior to accept his offer for dialogue. The disturbing sounds of a commotion echoed through the fort as desperate men struggled against their jailers.

"Why am I here? I wasn't part of the Batista regime," Carlos Senior said while sitting down and looking directly at the man who would decide his fate.

"Don't worry, Doctor. We know you are not the enemy. If you are guilty of anything, it's of a political mistake, and those are paid in the political arena."

"You still haven't told me why I'm here."

"I guess I want to see why we shouldn't kill you."

"What's stopping you?"

"I don't know that anything is stopping us. Have you not noticed? We're running the whole island. Nothing is stopping us. I choose to keep you alive..." he paused again looking at something behind his prisoner and then refocusing his attention. "...for now."

"It's the people, isn't it? They wouldn't approve."

An eerie silence interrupted the echoing sounds of tumult.

"Approve? Do you still fill your head with silly dreams of democracy? Do you? It's not the people. It's Fidel. He thinks you might be of service. We know you're popular and should you die, there will be some mourning. You're right, to some degree, but eventually the triumph of the revolution will move every grieving heart."

In the hallway behind *el Che*, two rebel soldiers dragged an unconscious man with a bloody face to a nearby cell. Carlos Senior leaned forward to turn the tables on him.

"What are you going to do when Fidel's envy is directed at you? I was his professor and I know the psychosis that festers in his head."

"Yes, we were all laughing at that: the professor who offers his student the opportunity to participate in a corrupt democracy. You really don't know your student. Do you really think Fidel was going to place his name on a ballot? Do you really think he would enter a debate stage and stand on a little podium to answer questions posed by Nicolas Bravo? Ha!" *El Che* laughed and ran his fingers through his beard. "I will tell you this much, had Batista not fiddled with the election and allowed you to win, our revolution would have had a considerable challenge to overcome, but make no mistake our revolution was destined to win."

Carlos Senior shifted his weight in his seat, revealing a discomfort.

"You are aware the election results were manipulated, right?" *El Che* asked. "We found the paper trail. *El Coronel* Orlando Piedra and the other generals were behind it. Ha! Fine system you had, putting the thieves in charge."

Carlos Senior looked away and dug his fingernails into the palm of his hand. *El Che* leaned back in his seat, enjoying the discomfort he was inflicting, when interrupting sounds of another scuffle ensued in an adjoining room.

"What is going on?" *El Che* yelled out.

The scuffle of men wrestling for control became louder. *El Che* stood with a gun in his hand and crossed the hall to see what the commotion was about.

"Hold him down," his commanding voice echoed through the halls of the fort.

"Hold him, I said!"

The sound of a solitary gun being fired echoed throughout the fort. It was followed by the soft thud of a body hitting the floor. El Che returned with a smile and a smoking gun.

"His face," *el Che* chuckled. "Funny, the look on men's faces when they realize they're about to die. Anyway, where were we?"

Carlos Senior kept silent as his captor looked at him, the smoking gun still in his hand.

"You know, I heard some of your speeches on the radio and I watched several of the interviews you gave. You offered a hopeful vision, but you left out a lot of details. So, now that we're here, together, I want to ask you a few questions. I hope you don't mind."

Carlos Senior sat still, his demeanor expressionless.

"Doctor, how would you have negotiated the casinos run by the American mafia? Would you have allowed them to continue their control of an industry that pushes young women to prostitute themselves for the entertainment of race car drivers and Americans from New York? Huh? These Americans, who rape the economy and your women, come here to play at the expense of the people's dignity. They think they own the island. Own *you*." *El Che* pointed at Carlos Senior with his gun. "Would you have continued to give them free reign over the economy?"

Carlos Senior remained silent while *el Che* used the gun as an extension of his hand, waving it around to emphasize his point.

"What about the brutes who dare call themselves police, servants of the people? Would you have faced a law enforcement system that sells drugs while wearing a badge? How would you have removed their immunity and held them accountable? Would you have continued to meet with murderers, like Orlando Piedra, who kill and torture in the name of law and order? What about the corruption inside your Congress, politicians who sell their vote to the highest bidder? Would you have continued to bribe them into good behavior? All that money, flowing through the system and into men's pockets, would you have taken some for yourself? Maybe you already have."

Carlos Senior looked at the gun being pointed at him.

"You see Doctor, there's too much money and everyone wants their percentage. It's how the system works, right? So, who's in charge, the elected official or the money that got him elected? There's so much money flowing through this island that even the Americans want to be in the game. Yeah, you left those details out of your speeches. Very convenient."

El Che stood and began walking around the room, waving his gun the way a professor waves a pointing stick.

"For instance, how do you stop the sugar industry from redirecting the island's wealth to bank accounts in Florida and Barcelona? Did you accept money from the sugar industry for your campaign? Isn't Julio Lobo your client? Hmm. It's an interesting dilemma. How would you have done any of that? I don't think you could have. You wouldn't have been able to. It's too much. You had your chance to nip it in the bud twenty years ago, when you were debating the island's constitution, but you didn't. Now, it's too big of a problem for you or for any other president. Only a revolution can do it. The American experiment of democracy has failed. It failed Cuba and it failed you."

El Che paused his monologue to re-holster his gun. He spun the chair around to sit with his chest against the backrest and his legs spread apart.

"Do you know why the Americans fear *comunismo*?" *El Che* continued. "Allow me to explain. Communism is the cure against the evils perpetuated by a capitalistic system that promotes slavery over freedom, profit over people, stock market over the common good, corporate wealth over moral virtue. Communism faces the hypocrisy of an American constitution that claims 'we the people' while denying Blacks the means to live with dignity. Communism exposes the modern-day slavery of industry workers, and the fat politicians getting rich from it all. Doctor, the cure has arrived," *El Che* opened his arms wide and smiled, "*comunismo*."

Carlos Senior smiled for the first time since meeting his jailer. The smile revealed amusement at the idea that he would be lectured by a thug. *El Che* saw his smile and raised an eyebrow.

"What you are describing are not the sins of a democratic system, but rather the failings of men in power," Carlos Senior replied. "Those shortcomings in governance occur in every nation and in every system that does not place controls over men in power. Power needs to be regulated and directed, or else it will only serve itself. The court system is to democracy what pruning shears are to a gardner. Power, like weeds, will grow out of control, until it is held accountable by an independent corp of prosecutors and judges. Where men fail, the constitution succeeds. That is how I would address all those problems you listed. Not through violence, firing squads and fear, but through the proven instruments of the democratic institutions."

"*Ay*, Doctor, I never took you for a fool," *el Che* said, a broad smile breaking over this face, "but you are beginning to sound like one. Regulations, really? Court system?"

"Let me ask you a question, do you know why *comunistas* fear democracy?"

Carlos Senior didn't wait for *el Che* to respond.

"Allow *me* to explain. Democracy is the hand that peels away at the lies. Democracy exposes the truth about communism, a system that is inherently oppressive. The first lie to be peeled is the lie to the people. Communism tells them they will all be equal, but it does so by reducing them to the lowest common denominator. Instead of elevating men and women to their highest potential, communism removes their path for personal growth. Next, it lies to the child-carrying mother, assuring her the State will raise her children, but instead it turns infants into hollow beings, devoid of dreams and creativity. It lies to every father, telling them they need to work for the State, when in reality they are working for fat men who sit in the politburo. It lies to the world, claiming high educational rates, while the children grow up to be inept dependents of the State. It lies to the mirror, claiming political virtue is driving the cause, when in reality it's all about the greed for power, property and wealth it didn't earn. And the biggest lie of all is at the core of this infested system. Communism claims to be the cure to the world's ailments, the grand liberator, while keeping people subjugated, robbing them of their God-given right to determine their own future."

Carlos Senior leaned back in his chair. "Fidel fears democracy because he fears losing to a better man, a better idea, a better way forward. He's not a communist. He's just another power-hungry man. I dare you to disagree with him and have a different idea. Go ahead. You'll see he can't handle it, and soon you'll find yourself dead with your face in the mud."

El Che kicked his legs in the air and laughed.

"You seem to forget who is holding the gun, Doctor," he patted his holstered gun. "I'm not going to end up in the mud. That fate will most likely be yours, but as I said before, not today. No, today you get to go home. That is where you will remain, confined to the four walls of your house, which I have seen, and I think will soon make a fine house for one of our leaders. Take care of it, because as of today it no longer belongs to you. It belongs to the revolution. *Viva la revolución.*"

A disturbing, clanging sound echoed through the fort. *El Che* stood, looked at his prisoner and smiled.

"I knew I would enjoy talking with you." He looked in the direction of the clanging sound. "Let's see where we go from here. Somebody will take you back and from now on two men will be assigned to watch over you. Welcome to the new Cuba."

******

It was one of those strange pulls of the subconscious mind, compelling Manuel to look behind him when there was no reason to stop facing forward. He and Gloria were visiting Carlos Senior, eager to present their newborn child when, for some reason, he turned around to look at the apartment building that stood behind Uva's home. There, on a top floor balcony, looking down at him, was his cousin, *el Canalla*.

"*¡Ay Dios mío!* Let me see this precious child," Piedad, the maid, said and welcomed them inside.

"Come in quickly," Uva ordered. "Don't linger in the doorway. Come in!"

Manuel and Gloria pushed the stroller over the threshold, slightly startled by Uva's tense command and the darkness of shuttered windows. As they entered, they found a house full of guests, energetically talking among themselves.

"What is going on?" Gloria asked Piedad. "Why are there so many people here, and why are the windows shuttered?"

"I don't want anyone looking in," Uva stood with her arms crossed and then turned her attention to Manuel. "Your father has been arrested. He's been in *la Cabaña* since last night."

"*¿Como?* Why didn't you call me?"

"Because the phone lines are compromised. They came yesterday to arrest him, and they knew he was here. Somebody is listening to our calls."

"It's not the phones," Manuel said.

Uva waited for his explanation.

"It's Bernardo. I just saw him. He's in the apartment building over there. The Scoundrel must have tipped them off."

"No!" Gloria responded in shock.

Uva glanced at the baby and half smiled.

"She chose one hell of a time to be born," Uva commented while standing over the child and appreciating her newborn beauty.

"Do you want to hold her?"

"No, I'm too nervous. I can't stop thinking about Carlos," she said and began to cry. "We need to go to *la Cabaña*," Manuel replied.

"That is why our friends are here," Uva stated. "We're trying to decide the best way to approach the situation without getting thrown in jail ourselves."

"We should call Carlitos," Manuel offered. "He knows how to raise hell."

"But is that what we want at this moment, a hell raiser?"

Manuel paused to wipe his face, which had started to emit beads of sweat.

"Well, someone has to find out what's happening," Manuel said. "We won't get an answer by staying here."

"I agree," a tall woman commented. She came from behind, smoking a long-tipped cigarette. Manuel recognized her as Uva's sister, Sara. "Let's call Carlitos and if he agrees I'll go with him to *La Cabaña*," she said while slowly approaching the group. Manuel could not keep his eyes off the woman, now in her fifties, but retaining a sensual beauty that was timeless.

"You?" Gloria asked, almost laughing.

"Yes, me. I'm not afraid. I was in Barcelona during Spain's civil war. I've seen men at their worst and these teenage boys trying to grow a beard, pretending to be soldiers, are absolutely laughable. They don't scare me."

"*Dale*, Manuel. Call Carlitos." Uva ordered.

At Tina's house, Carlitos was seated in front of the television set with a blanket around his shoulders, and a thermometer in his mouth. His eyes were glazed by a fever, his body ached, and the need for sleep was taking over. Olga was reading the thermometer when the phone rang.

"*Alo*," she said into the receiver.

"Olguita, it's Manuel. Did you hear the news that Papá was taken to *La Cabaña?*"

"No, I didn't know. That's terrible! What's going to happen?"

"Well we have to get him out. Can I talk with *el Gordo?*"

Olga turned to see her husband asleep on the sofa, his head tilted back and his mouth wide open, ready to emit a snore.

"He's in the bathroom, tell me and I'll relay the message."

"Okay, good. Tell him that Papá is in *La Cabaña* and that we need his help to get him out. Maybe he can go there and find out what's happening. Who knows, I'm thinking *el Gordo* might even have a connection from his many adventures and involvements."

Olga bit her lip and looked at her sleeping husband.

"*¿Alo?* Olguita? Did you hear what I said?"

"Yes, one second. I'll be right back."

She placed the phone down on the table and walked over to Carlitos. With a caress on his arm he stirred and looked at her.

"*Gordo*, do you want to go to the bedroom and sleep?"

"No, leave me here. I'm tired of the bed."

"Can I get you anything? Can I turn off the TV?"

"No, no, no. Leave it on. I like the sound of it and just let me rest. I'll be alright."

She stepped back and witnessed his immediate immersion into a deep sleep. Within seconds he was snoring again.

"Manuel?" Olga spoke into the phone.

"*¿Sí?*"

"Bring a car to the house. He'll be ready."

Manuel hung up the phone, turned to Uva and announced his brother was going to face the rebels to demand the release of his father.

"I'm going too," Sara said while exhaling cigarette smoke.

"Fine," Uva said and with the force of a drill sergeant she called out for the butler and lifelong servant.

"Agustín!"

The servant stood at attention, like a soldier being commanded to war. Several minutes later, their onyx black, 1957 Chevy Bel Air was at the front of the house, and Agustín was holding the passenger door open for Sara. They arrived at Tina's home in *Víbora Park*, only to find Olga standing on the front porch with her purse in hand.

"Let's go," Olga said to the butler and the artistic, non-conformist socialite.

They looked at her with open mouths, unsure of what was transpiring.

Olga sat in the car, placed her purse on her lap and looked at the home's front door, afraid that her mother might come out and order her back inside.

"Vamos!" She said with urgency. "Let's get *el Viejo Marquez* out of jail."

Sara smiled and then chuckled. Agustín looked at her, awaiting instructions, but the artist woman only continued to laugh.

Olga looked at the front door of her home, and with increased urgency said, "*Vamos, vamos.* We shouldn't be wasting time."

"*Señora?*" Agustín asked Sara.

"Drive on, Agustín. Take us to *la Cabaña*."

Olga sighed, while Agustín faced forward to drive the two women to the old Spanish fort. The streets of Old Havana were empty. On most corners stood a rebel soldier with a long gun. Many of them were young, desperately wanting to grow out their beards.

"So, what did you do with your husband?" Sara asked while assessing the young woman next to her.

"He's asleep, fighting a fever from mononucleosis."

"Well, I must say, you certainly have surprised me."

"Would you have preferred my husband to be the one seated next to you?"

"I'm not sure. This might be a better arrangement. I won't have to contend with a man who thinks he needs to be in charge."

Olga and Sara looked out their windows at the young men recruited by the revolution. An older and more seasoned soldier, with a full beard, was handing out rosaries for them to wear over the olive green uniform.

"Where did they get the uniforms?" Sara asked as she looked out the window.

"Pardon me, ma'am?" Agustín replied.

"The uniforms, where did they come from? An entire army is being supplied with uniforms and rifles. Who's paying for it? It seems to me this revolution has a patron."

Agustín remained silent, gripping the steering wheel tightly as he maneuvered the large car through narrow cobblestone streets that occasionally were cluttered by abandoned police cars. *La Fortaleza de San Carlos de la Cabaña* was near the center of the city, next to the bay, on a hilltop, where it stood vigilant over the waters that led to Havana. Agustín parked at a short distance from *la Cabaña,* where he could keep an eye on the vehicle while accompanying the women up the hill to the guarded entrance. A dozen rebels stepped forward, almost in unison, marching toward an empty field where they could practice their marching. Olga flinched, almost jumped, at the sight of them, but Sara grabbed her hand, and steadied her nerves.

"Stay close to me," Sara said to Olga while keeping her eye on the entrance above. "Most of these soldiers are still boys, and they will respect the voice of a strong woman."

Olga closely observed Sara, who walked as if she owned the ground beneath her feet.

"Excuse me," Sara asked an indifferent bearded rebel. "I'm here to pick up Dr. Carlos Márquez-Sterling."

"Who?"

"Dr. Carlos Mar...."

"I don't know who that is," the rebel guard interrupted.

Sara looked around at the other rebels. Many had fully grown beards. A car drove up to the gate. The driver, wearing an olive green uniform, was starting to grow his beard. In the back seat were two civilian men, partially unconscious and with bloody faces. He exchanged a few words with the guard, who opened the gate to let him pass.

Sara and Olga approached the guard for a second time, whose annoyance seemed to grow at their presence.

"Excuse me. We're here to get Dr. Carlos Márquez-Sterling," Olga said loudly in her best authoritative tone. "We know he's inside. Can you speak with someone who will..."

"Is he part of the movement?"

"Not your movement," Sara took out a cigarette. "Do you have a light?"

"If he's inside and he's not a *compañero* then he's not coming out. You understand what I mean? Now move along."

"How about a light? Can I have one?" Sara asked with indifference.

The guard looked around and flicked his lighter under her cigarette.

"Were you in the *Sierra* with *el Che*?" Sara asked and inhaled.

"Yes, and with Raul too."

"So, then, you're a man who understands," she said while exhaling.

She stepped back and looked at the guard appreciatively.

"A man with your experience has the authority to send a messenger, possibly one of these skinny teenagers, to find out about my friend, Dr. Carlos Márquez-Sterling."

"We really can't go back without him," Olga added and then looked at Sara, who half smiled and gave her a knowing wink.

The guard assessed the two women before him, looked behind him once more and then leaned forward to whisper, "Let me see what I can do."

He called a young recruit and spoke to him inaudibly. The young recruit looked at Sara menacingly while listening to the instructions of the guard.

Agustín stepped forward and whispered into Sara's ear, "Maybe we should try something else. I don't think this will turn out well."

"We're not going anywhere," she replied.

The young recruit turned and marched toward the two-hundred year old edifice behind him. Olga stepped forward with the intention of thanking the guard, but Sara pulled her back.

"Just stay here with me. We'll know more soon enough."

Time passed very slowly for Olga. The minutes were oppressed by the growing humidity, and the midday sun punished those who dared to linger under it. Had it not been for the sea breeze, which blew with constant force, she probably would have fainted from the heat and stress. Her companion, however, seemed unmoved and unpreoccupied. Sara entertained herself by speaking with several soldiers, learning their names and city of origin. It was one young soldier, named Mateo, the youngest son from a family Sara was familiar with, who took the liberty to warn them of the dangers that lay beyond the entrance gate.

"*Señora*, you should leave these premises," the young recruit whispered. "It's not safe."

"*¿Como?*" Sara replied in a loud voice.

"There are men here, not too far away, who would arrest you and use the prison as their excuse to do...."

"To do what?" Olga asked with an air of defiance that did not hide the fear in her eyes.

"You know.... Things. I've seen it. Believe me, you should leave."

"*¡Ay, mijo!* These men don't scare me," Sara said and pointed at the entrance guards. "Shame is what they'll feel if any of them places a finger on me."

The entrance guard saw Sara's aggressive posture and somehow did not think she was allowed to have such a stance. With furrowed eyebrows he approached Mateo and pulled him aside. "Recruit, what's going on here? What are you talking about with these women?"

Mateo snapped into attention and replied loudly, "Sir, I am telling this woman here she should go home. This is no place for civilian women."

"I'm not going anywhere until my friend, Carlos Márquez-Sterling comes out."

The entrance guard looked at Sara and Olga, and with an air of annoyance told Mateo to get them out. Mateo raised his rifle with both hands and stepped forward.

"Can't you understand that you have to leave," he said to the women.

"And don't you understand that we can't," Sara stood her ground.

"Look, there he comes," Olga pointed at her father-in-law, who was descending the hill and approaching the gate.

Mateo looked back, but only saw the disapproving look of the entrance guard, who insisted his order be carried out. The young recruit stepped forward once again, this time pushing the mature woman standing in front of him.

"No. No. No," Olga yelled, stepping in between them. "You don't have to do this."

Mateo, now annoyed, pushed Olga who in turn displaced Sara, and it seemed they were both about to fall when a commanding voice from several yards shouted, "Stop!"

The young recruit and the entrance guard turned to see Carlos Senior walking toward them. Behind him were two young rebels with unshaven faces.

"Stop. She's here for me," Carlos Senior handed the guard a yellow slip of paper.

The recruit lowered his rifle, waiting for the guard to direct him. The guard looked at the two rebels behind Carlos Senior, and read the note. With reluctance, the guard told the recruit to step aside.

"Are you okay?" Carlos Senior asked Sara.

"I am. And you?"

Carlos nodded and looked at his daughter-in-law. "What are you doing here?"

"We came to get you," Olga replied.

"Agustín," Carlos Senior acknowledged. "Let's go home."

Agustín looked at the two rebels standing behind Carlos Senior.

"They're coming with us," Carlos Senior said. "I'll explain later."

"Why?" Sara said while tossing her cigarette on the floor.

"I'm under house arrest."

Inside the car, the escorting rebels sat in the back seat with Carlos. They emitted a stench that forced Sara to lower the window. She turned to look at them with disgust.

"Does anyone in this July 26 movement ever bathe?"

"Sara, please," Olga whispered to her.

Sara let out a solitary hackle, lowered the window further and leaned her head out.

"Agustín, drop me off at the corner," Olga said. "I'll take a bus home."

When the car stopped, Carlos Senior got out to give Olga a hug. He held her close, while she awkwardly hugged him back, unaccustomed to his physical proximity.

"Thank you for coming to get me," he whispered in her ear, "but from this moment forward please keep your distance. I don't know how this will end and I couldn't forgive myself if anything were to happen to you."

Olga did not reply, but her eyes eloquently expressed what words could not. He wiped her tears and got back into the car.

"Agustín, to the house," he commanded and faced forward with the intention of not having to see Olguita on the street corner.

When they arrived, Uva and her three daughters greeted them at the door. Uva looked at the two rebels standing behind her husband and very quickly welcomed them with a smile.

"*Hola*, come in. Can we get you some coffee? Piedad, please make more coffee."

The rebels walked in, staring open mouthed at the luxurious home.

Gloria, Manuel and several other friends approached Carlos Senior.

"Why are these men here?" Manuel asked.

"They needed a bit of culture," Sara answered sarcastically while going up the spiral staircase. "But please get them some cologne before we all asphyxiate."

Carlos Senior looked at Manuel and motioned him to approach while the rebels gazed at the art hanging on the walls.

"This situation can escalate very quickly," he whispered. "It's not safe. Don't come back and by all means use your common sense."

"*Pero*, Papá..."

"No buts. Do as I ask and don't worry about me. I'll find a way out."

"Here we are," Uva said with a smile while bringing two cups of espresso coffee.

"Thank you," a rebel said and accepted the cup.

"You're most welcome," she replied. "And what is your name?"

"Antonio."

"And you are?" she asked while handing a cup to the other.

"Juan."

"Well, Juan and Antonio, please have a seat. I'll be back soon."

"Agustín," Carlos Senior said. "Open the windows. Let some light and air in."

"By all means," Sara said loudly from the top of the stairs. "Let some air in."

Uva looked at her sister with annoyance but did not say a word. She walked with Manuel and Gloria to the front door, while the two rebel soldiers carefully sat on the living room sofa, sipping their coffee.

"Uva, what are you going to do?" Gloria asked.

"Whatever it takes." Uva's eyes filled up with tears. "Now go."

As Uva closed the door, Manuel could see his father staring at the unwanted guests.

******

Olga and Tina did not venture out of the house for eight days. Not only were they terrified of the patrolling rebels, but Carlitos was not recovering from the virus. His fever spiked every evening, his head ached most of the day, and to make matters worse, he broke out into a rash. It wasn't long before they ran out of aspirin, rubbing alcohol and most ingredients needed for homemade remedies. Eager to do something, she called Oscar Jorge.

"The doctor says there is a new medicine called Panadol," Olga said into the phone. "It's for children, but it may help with the fever."

"Yes, I've heard of it," Oscar Jorge replied. His deep voice was reassuring. "I didn't know *el Gordo* was in such bad shape. I'll be right over."

"Thank you."

Olga stepped into the living room, where Carlitos sat with a blanket wrapped around him. His eyes were swollen, a rash covered his neck and his body shivered.

"Oscar Jorge is coming to take me to the pharmacy."

Carlitos nodded and tried to smile but the shivering prohibited it.

Thirty minutes later Olga was still waiting for Oscar Jorge.

"*¿Alo?* Matty?" Olga called his home. She paced in the kitchen while fiddling with the long cord. "Is Oscar Jorge still there?"

"No," Matty replied over the loud cry of an infant child. "He left some time ago."

"Why is Oscarito crying?"

"*Ay, mija*, he's teething and he's miserable. I asked Oscar Jorge to get some ginger root. I rub it on the baby's gums and let him chew on it. Can you believe it makes him better?"

"Oh, I didn't know that was good for babies. Well, maybe he stopped at the *bodega* first. He's probably on his way. Thank you, Matty."

Olga opened the front door and stood on the front porch. She scanned the street and saw Oscar Jorge, at the corner, standing by his car while a rebel soldier inspected his identification. The young soldier was frail in contrast to the young lawyer's athletic build.

"Oscar Jorge," she called out and began to walk toward him.

He was smiling affably at the rebel soldier, as if trying to make one more friend, knowing charm was always his best strategy. The irascible soldier had softened and was no longer suspicious. The distant sound of Olga's call got their attention. Oscar Jorge turned around to see her walking towards him while the soldier rested the rifle against the car.

She was waving her hand when the shot rang out and her heart jumped at the sound. Oscar Jorge placed his hand over his neck and fell to the ground. The young soldier was looking at his weapon, unsure how it had misfired.

"No!" Olga screamed and ran towards him. "No, no, no!"

He was gurgling with blood spurting from his wound. The soldier kneeled to help, but didn't know what to do. Olga reached her fallen friend and held him as his blood spilled onto the street.

"I don't know what happened," the young soldier said. "I was leaning the rifle against the car, and it fired."

Olga looked at him with terrified, wide eyes, and saw he was a teenager.

"I swear I didn't mean to do it."

"Get some help. Get help!" she commanded.

The young rebel ran towards the next intersection, where other soldiers stood next to a parked truck, while Oscar Jorge struggled to keep his hand on his neck. Olga tore her dress and used it as a bandage over his wound. Bright red blood pooled on her hand and lap.

"*No te mueras*. We're getting help. You can't die," she said and held him tenderly as he struggled to breathe.

The young soldier returned with two other soldiers and the truck. Olga stepped aside as they lifted him and placed him on the truck.

"Do you have his identification?" she asked the young soldier.

"Yes, right here," his adolescent voice cracked.

Olga stood on the street watching the truck drive away. She abruptly bent over, as if punched in the midsection, unable to breathe. Neighbors rushed forward, took her home and placed her in Tina's care. Later that day, Cristóbal came to visit. Olga was coming out of the bathroom, her hair wet from the shower. She stood silent as Cristóbal told the story of Oscar Jorge dying while soldiers drove around in circles looking for a hospital they never found. Olga's vision darkened. A heaviness pressed against her chest and she collapsed.

The weeks that followed were swallowed by a pit of despair. Carlitos recovered from his illness, while Olga fell into one. She stopped eating and confined herself to bed. There was no remedy for the ailment that afflicted her heart. Carlitos tried to be supportive, but any word of comfort only made her cry more. He went to visit his father but was told to stay away for his own well-being. He visited his brother, but the loud cries of his newborn niece ended his visit prematurely. He did learn one infuriating fact: his cousin was the informant that led to their father's arrest. Anger, a familiar fuel, drove Carlitos to find his cousin, *el Canalla*.

Bernardo was sitting in front of his living room window when he saw Carlitos walking toward the apartment building. He knew he had to run, but he made the mistake of packing a few things, giving Carlitos the time to reach him. With the nimbleness of a slippery snake, Bernardo managed to elude the grip of his cousin, who was determined to throw him off the side of the building. He jumped over furniture and ran from his overweight aggressor, knowing his frail body would be no match against the fury that chased him. Like a mad bull, Carlitos battered the furniture in the apartment and eventually landed one blow on Bernardo's jaw, snapping it in two. Running for his life, the scoundrel reached his aunt Silvia and begged for sanctuary.

"Bernardo, *canalla*, come out!" Carlitos shouted outside his mother's door.

"Leave us alone," Silvia screamed from inside the locked door. "I'm calling the police."

"The police have fled," Carlitos reminded her. "There's no one to help."

Silvia feared her son's rage and secured every window and door against his possible intrusion, while Bernardo cowered in the living room, nursing his jaw with ice. Eventually, the menacing threats faded and the pounding on the door ceased, but Bernardo did not leave his sanctuary. His cousin was patiently waiting outside.

Olga received the phone call that alerted her to what was happening.

"It's for you," Tina said as Olga slept in bed.

"I don't want to talk to anyone."

"I think you better take this call."

"Who is it?"

"Just take it." Tina extended the phone, but the cord wasn't long enough.

Olga stood and walked over to her mother, who handed over the receiver.

"*¿Alo?*"

"Olguita?"

"*Sí.*"

"It's Silvia. Carlitos is here, outside my door, trying to break in."

"Why?"

"Well, it's his cousin, Bernardito."

"I heard what he did."

"I need you to get Carlitos to stop. He's going to be arrested by the *milicianos*, and these people will shoot him, especially when they learn he was elected to congress."

"So, what am I supposed to do?"

"Bernardito needs medical attention. I have to take him to the hospital. Come get your husband."

"I see."

"Do you hear me? He'll be labeled counter-revolutionary and sent to the firing squad."

"What about you? What will you be labeled, Mother-of-the-Year?"

Silvia remained silent while Olga waited for a response. The standoff between the two women lasted an eternal minute.

"What do you want me to say?" Silvia surrendered.

"I'll be there," Olga replied and hung up the phone.

"Get me Manolín," Olga said to Tina. "I need his help."

Manolín drove Olga to Silvia's home. Carlitos sat across the street, keeping watch over the front door. Manolín got out of the car and approached his brother-in-law.

"I'm here to take you home."

Carlitos didn't acknowledge him.

"Do you remember when you found me at the whore house and took me home? I never really thanked you."

"Is that why you're here, to thank me?"

"You never told Mamá. I was certain you were going to, but you never did. So, it's my turn to return the favor. C'mon. Let's go home."

"There's only one entrance and one exit from that house," Carlitos said while intently looking at the front door. "I'm going to sit here and wait this one out."

"If you stay here much longer, you'll end up in prison." Manolín placed his hand on Carlitos' shoulder. "*Vamos*. Mamá is preparing your favorite, beef stew."

"Get your hand off me," Carlitos whispered with clenched teeth.

Manolín backed away and returned to the car.

"He's not coming with me," he said while sitting behind the steering wheel.

Olga sighed. She had bags under her eyes and disheveled hair. She got out of the car and walked toward her husband with pronounced exhaustion.

"I can't do this," she stood next to him.

Carlitos was confused by her statement.

"I can't do this," she motioned to Silvia's door. "I don't have the strength. I'm hanging on by a string. So, I need you to walk away and come with me. I know how much you hate that man but please do this for me. If you don't, rebel soldiers are going to arrest you. God knows what they'll do, and I don't have the strength to deal with it. I just don't. So, please get in the car and come home."

Carlitos straightened his posture and looked at Olga straight in the eyes. A moment of silence stood between them, and then he lowered his gaze.

"Give me a minute," he calmly said, "I'll be right there."

Carlitos walked over to his mother's door, stood beside it and placed his hand on the wood, knowing his cousin was on the other side.

"Bernardo, *canalla*," he said in a measured tone. "You've been saved by God's mercy, but if I ever see you again, you better run, because I will strangle you."

******

In the weeks to follow, CMQ TV gave live broadcasts from *la Cabaña*, where men were sent to face the firing squad. Some held government positions, others were part of Batista's police force, and all were executed before a live television audience. Manolo and Jenny were walking to the recruiting office outside *La Cabaña* as the television crew was leaving.

"*¡Que barbaridad!* How savage!" One of the newscasters muttered as he walked past Manolo and Jenny, carrying a camera and tripod on his shoulders.

Jenny shot him an unfriendly look, but the man did not notice.

"This is what we do now," the other crew member said. "Film the killing of innocent people and call it revolutionary justice."

"Excuse me," Jenny walked up to the newscasters. Manolo followed.

"Yes?" They were putting the equipment down.

She paused and looked at them.

"How can we help you?" They looked at her and Manolo.

"No. I just want to get a good look at you," she said, "and I want you to remember my face. In this revolution no one is innocent, especially CMQ Radiocentro."

Shocked at her threat, the men shot a look at Manolo, but he lowered his head and looked down.

"*Vamos,*" she stepped toward the building. "The revolution needs us."

Manolo remained outside while Jenny applied for a new profession in the revolutionary army of the July 26th Movement. She traded her dresses for an olive-green uniform. Days later CMQ TV and Radiocentro were taken over by rebel soldiers and claimed as a necessary extension of the revolution. Jenny was with them. Dozens of employees were deemed guilty of conspiring against the revolution and sent to *la Cabaña* to face a firing squad.

In the weeks that followed, Jenny quickly rose in the ranks of the movement. Manolo quietly watched as she attended community meetings, where she proudly extolled the virtues of the revolution. He stood by as she instructed people how to root out the capitalistic evils that would undo the revolution.

"Keep a watchful eye," she taught. "The worms from a rotted and corrupt system are still with us. It is your job to find and expose them before they infest the revolution."

Manolo kept silent as Jenny turned neighbor against neighbor, and the prison cells of the *la Cabaña* overflowed with people accused of committing crimes against the revolution. He followed her to neighborhood meetings held in empty lots and school cafeterias, and listened to her motivate housewives so they might become the eyes and ears of the revolution.

"If you see suspicious behavior, let us know. It is up to you to uncover the counter-revolutionaries hiding among us. We must root out those who work against the good of the revolution. They will talk about violations against their individual liberties and rights. They will try to turn you against the vision of *el Comandante*, but you must remember they are *gusanos*, worms who do not deserve to live among us."

It was in one of those gatherings that a bearded revolutionary soldier stared at Manolo menacingly. The anger in the soldier's eyes caught Manolo off guard, but he chose to stand his ground and look back.

"You don't remember me, do you?" the soldier approached.

Manolo studied him momentarily and then opened his eyes wide in recognition of who stood before him.

"Yeah," the soldier smiled. "It's been a long time."

"Rubio," Manolo whispered, "the pervert."

"No, no, no. How about a little more respect? I fought with Raul Castro in the *Sierra Maestra*. I'm a hero of the revolution. Can you see the scar on my face?"

Manolo looked at the scarred cheek and recalled how he pummeled the man while his brother-in-law wielded a knife.

"I have to thank you for it," Rubio declared. "It's a reminder of how the bourgeois compensated me for slave labor."

Manolo did not reply.

"I'm actually surprised to see you here," Rubio said. "I wouldn't have thought you'd be a supporter of the revolution."

"Rubio," Jenny approached with a smile. "I see you've met my husband."

Rubio smiled and nodded. "Yes, yes. I was just asking him if he knew about the little neighborhood in Boca Ciega, the playground for *Batistianos* and bourgeois worms."

"You are so right!" Jenny exclaimed. "I've been to that beach," she said as she turned to speak with a community member.

"I want you to know," Rubio stepped forward and got within an inch of Manolo. "Boca Ciega is my birthplace. I'm the native, the one who belongs there. Yet, you and your kind managed to cast me out." Rubio stepped back and smiled. "But it's okay. I'm going back to reclaim it for the revolution."

Rubio glanced over at Jenny.

"I see you married well after Tina kicked you out," he said. "You and your type always seem to get better than you deserve, but don't think your marital status will protect you for too long. One day I'll expose you for the worm that you are."

Manolo didn't know how to respond to the threat and was saved from saying something regretful when his toddler son came running, interrupting the conversation by pulling on Manolo's thumb. He knelt to pick up his child, and turned to face Rubio, but the man had stepped away. He was standing next to Jenny, who was still running the meeting.

Later that week, Manolo called Tina at her house in *Víbora Park*.

"I'm calling to see how you are doing," Manolo said.

"How do you think we're doing? We're terrified of what's happening. I hear that teenage boys are being forced to join the revolution. Every time Manolín leaves the house, I don't rest until he returns. "

"I have some bad news."

"Oh no, what's happened now?"

"Don't go to Boca Ciega. It won't be safe for you."

"Why?"

"Rubio is there, and he's a *miliciano*. I suppose he's taking over."

"I have a deed for that house. We bought the parcel of land and built the house. It's mine. And now you're telling me I can't go to my own house!"

"Tina, it's crazy. All it takes is for one of them to be suspicious, and you can be accused of counter-revolutionary sympathies. They'll call you a worm and that will be the end."

"The end of what?"

"I don't know, but that beach house is not worth you going to prison."

Tina was silent.

"I don't have much time. Jenny will be back soon. Do you understand what I'm telling you? Don't go to Boca Ciega."

"I heard Jenny is in deep with the revolution. Are you going to be a *miliciano* too?"

"Don't be ridiculous."

"I'm serious. Do I have to worry?"

"I have to go."

Manolo placed the receiver down before Jenny walked in through the door. She was carrying a large box full of children's shoes and clothing.

"Look what I got," she said with a smile.

"Where did that come from?"

"We closed down Ultra. The owners and the managers are all worms. I heard *el compañero* Suarez was putting together a troop to close it down, and I asked to be included. So, I went. It was amazing! You should have seen the employees trying to run away."

"And they let you take these?" Manolo lifted a girl's linen blouse.

"I got these shoes for *el niño*. See if they'll fit him."

Manolo looked on as his soldier wife examined the spoils from the raid on one of the best stores in Havana. Apparently, looting in the name of the revolution was state sanctioned.

*****

Uva watched with horror as two long-bearded, scowling *milicianos* tried on shoes in her husband's closet.

"Who shines these shoes?" The *miliciano* asked her.

"My husband shines his own shoes."

"He should put a shine on my boots," said the other and then let out a hackle.

The first *miliciano* donned a pair of shiny black shoes and walked around the room. "What do you think? Classy, no?"

"You still look like a *güajiro*," his partner replied with a laugh. "Country boy."

"I don't know. I'm feeling rather grand in these."

The other *miliciano* stood and walked around in shiny brown shoes.

"I think these are big on me. Your husband has long feet," he said to Uva.

"We can get you some paper to stuff the ends," Uva suggested.

Carlos Senior walked in and looked at the men in his room.

"Look, there he is!"exclaimed the *miliciano* wearing his brown shoes. "*El Señor patas largas*. I guess you need big feet to stand on your big words."

The men laughed at the joke as Carlos Senior looked on in silence.

"I heard you're good at giving a polish," the *miliciano* wearing his black shoes said as he stepped into the hallway and gave Carlos Senior a pair of muddy boots. "If you do a good job, you just might prove your worth to the revolution."

Piedad and Agustín walked in and gave Uva and Carlos Senior a wide-eyed look. Uva nodded at Piedad who then returned the gesture.

"Do you gentlemen want some coffee?" Uva offered nervously.

"Oh, I think you can offer more than coffee," the *miliciano* with black shoes suggested. "What else do you have?" he looked hungrily at Piedad.

"Piedad, serve these gentlemen a plate of beef stew. Agustín, take them down to the cellar so they can choose a bottle of red wine."

"*¡Ahora sí!* Now you're talking!" The long-bearded men followed Agustín to the cellar while Carlos Senior stood with two pairs of muddy boots in his arms.

"The car is out back," Piedad whispered.

Uva's eyes watered as her husband stood still, waiting for the men to descend the stairs. When their voices faded, Carlos Senior dropped the boots and briskly walked to his study where a briefcase and a loaded gun were waiting for him. Uva quietly followed him down the rear set of stairs and out into the courtyard. The sound of an idling engine signaled his escape route. Carlos Senior stopped, turned to see his wife holding back the tears, and exchanged three seconds of silence with her. The distant sound of men trying to open a bottle of wine cut through the courtyard, making him jump. He leaned forward and kissed her.

"Tell the girls I love them."

He jumped into the back seat of the awaiting car, lying face down and covered by a blanket, unsure if he would safely arrive at the Venezuelan Consulate. There he hid until it was deemed safe for him to leave the island. Ten days later he boarded a cargo plane to Caracas, where an embassy official provided a couch for him to spend the night. Knowing El Che Guevara had contacts in Venezuela, Carlos Senior didn't sleep that night and kept his gun close at hand. It wasn't until the following day, when he arrived in Washington D.C., that he was able to speak freely. He warned government officials of what was happening on the island. He begged for an intervention to restore democracy, but his words fell on deaf ears. It didn't take long for him to realize his thick Cuban accent was the obstacle to his credibility.

******

Tina was in the kitchen, washing dishes, as Olga and Carlitos quietly packed their bags. The voice of a journalist, narrating the trial of seventy-two police officers and soldiers from the Batista regime filled the house. Manolín sat in front of the television with his girlfriend, Teresita, watching the black and white images of bearded *milicianos* lining up the accused. Carlitos paced between the bedroom and living room, unable to watch the flagrant disregard to legal process, but too invested to not follow.

"What will they allow us to take?" Olga asked.

"One suitcase, five hundred dollars each," Carlitos answered as he walked back to the living room, "and nothing the revolution would consider valuable to the state."

Tina stepped into the room to survey their packing process. On the bed there were folded clothing, undergarments, short towels and bathing suits.

"Why the bathing suits?" Tina asked.

"I'm hoping we'll get to stay at the beach for a night or two," Olga replied. She turned to Carlitos, who was returning from the living room. "How long do you think we'll be there?"

He looked at her and then at Tina. He smacked his lips and then stepped out to look at the television set again.

"Look, Raul Castro is approaching the microphone," Manolín called out.

Tina and Olga quickly returned their attention to the television set and stood next to Carlitos nervously.

"Tina, *siéntese*, please sit," Teresita offered her seat on the sofa.

Tina shook her head and remained still, watching the image of seventy-two beaten and despondent men, many of them not much older than her son.

"If one is guilty," Raul Castro screamed into the microphone. "All are guilty. I condemn them all to be *fusilados*, death by firing squad."

"*¡Ay, Virgen Santa!*" Tina exclaimed.

"They can't just kill them like that!" Olga protested. "Can they?"

"Manolín, turn that off," Carlitos softly asked. He then looked at Olga and pointed at the television set. "They can do whatever they want, and nobody is going to stop them." His voice raised a little louder and his eyes wider. "You want to know how long we'll be gone? I don't have a fucking clue." He threw his arms up in the air and stormed into the dining room. "So, pack your dresses and bathing suit, because if we stay here, I'll be part of the next group of men on that screen."

"Carlitos, please," Olga's voice broke. "They'll hear you outside."

"*¡Al carajo!* To hell with it all," he screamed at the immobile family who stood petrified in the living room. "You don't get it, do you?" He looked at them, wide eyed. "Don't you see? It's the end." His voice cracked and tears flooded into his eyes. "This is how it all ends."

Carlitos ran out of the house as Olga watched with tear-filled eyes.

"*Mi vida*, come back!," she called after him. "Manolín," she asked, "bring him back."

Her brother stood up to go, but Tina placed a hand on his shoulder. "No. Let him go. He'll be back soon enough. He knows it's not safe out there."

Carlitos rode the bus without a destination in mind. He stared out the window at the rolling scenes of chaos and violence. *Milicianos* were emptying houses, tossing furniture on the sidewalks as innocent men were shackled and led to an uncertain future. At one intersection a long bearded *miliciano* boarded the bus with a machine gun.

"Everybody out!" he ordered.

The bus driver looked at the soldier, hoping he could be relieved of his duty.

"Not you," the soldier said to the driver. "We need you to drive."

Carlitos and a dozen passengers stepped out, making room for rebel soldiers who stood in line to enter the bus. An empty truck was on the side of the road.

"Did you run out of gasoline?" a fellow passenger asked a soldier.

"What does it matter to you?" the soldier replied angrily and pushed the man to the floor. Carlitos and the other passengers froze in place as the soldiers entered the bus and left. Two men helped the fallen man, who was shaken by his brush with violence.

Carlitos walked alongside a diminishing group of passengers and soon found himself at the *Paseo del Prado*, the shaded promenade which at one time was full of hand-holding couples and families with exuberant children. He looked around and saw he was alone. Fear had gripped the city, and nobody dared to venture out for an afternoon stroll. At a distance, an elusive shadow wearing a long black coat quickly crossed the cobblestone street toward the rear of a building. Carlitos carefully approached the scavenger, who was opening garbage cans to peer inside.

"I'd buy you a meal, but I think all the restaurants are closed," he said.

El Caballero de París slowly turned and stood with a garbage can lid in his hand.

"Anything good in there?" Carlitos asked and took one step forward.

"The wolves are here," *el Caballero* said. "I need supplies."

"Yes, I've seen them, but I don't think you have anything to fear."

He rotated his eyes upward, as if searching through the archives in his mind, lowered the lid and raised his hand, a pose Carlitos had seen him strike before most recitals.

"My first word was 'brother,' and I served their hands," *el Caballero* intoned. "The lamb fell to their crimes, and in my soul died my brother's voice. I neared enough to examine with my own eyes, and wolves they all had become."

El Caballero paused for a moment, as if expecting a reply. Carlitos looked down and penitently said, "I'm sorry, but on this day, poetry is far from my mind."

"Hmm... Shame."

El Caballero returned to his scavenging, digging deep through discarded waste. He lifted a metallic bowl and placed it on his head.

"Mambrino's Helmet?" Carlitos asked.

"Invulnerable am I and with a mermaid I lay," *el Caballero* jumped and quickened his step. "Run, run as far as you can," he said as he disappeared into the night. "The wolves are coming. Their appetite will never sway."

A pickup truck with four rebel soldiers slowly passed by as it patrolled the street. Carlitos blended into the safety of the darkening afternoon as the madman ran into the shadows. He turned and journeyed toward the Capitol building, once in a while passing a solitary traveler, nervously trying to reach the safety of his home.

Rays of sunlight sped past the setting skies to glisten off the Capitol dome, which had marveled audiences for the thirty years of its existence. Now, it stood as a sad reminder of the democracy the island failed to defend. Carlitos stood at a distance, on the uneven cobblestone, admiring the beauty of the dome when a slow-moving car stopped, turned and approached him.

"*Gordo*," Cristóbal called out as he parked across from him.

Carlitos looked at his friend puzzled, "What are you doing here?"

"Looking for you."

Cristóbal turned the engine off, opened the door and walked toward him with the summer breeze blowing behind him.

"Olguita called. They're all nervous. It's not safe, you know."

"Do you remember when this was built? We must have been four? Three?"

"I was too young to know anything but the love of my mother."

"My earliest memory of this building is when Papá delivered his constitutional speech from those steps."

"I was there," Cristobal said and placed a welcoming hand on his friend.

"Were you?"

"Absolutely. I was among the many boys who sat on their father's shoulder and was told to admire the men who wrote our constitution."

Carlitos leaned back and looked down, "I'd be screaming bloody murder if it weren't so sad. We were so close. So close... I could feel it."

"C'mon. Get off the street. Let's go home."

"We told them, didn't we? We told those sons of bitches their support of Batista would cost us the country. They wouldn't listen."

"We told as many people as we could."

"Right? I mean, how many more times did we have to speak on a news program? How many more times did we have to implore business leaders and police captains to stop supporting an egomaniac? Did they not realize this would be the consequence of their blind support? And for what? A good economy?"

"*Gordo*, c'mon. This isn't helping," he lightly slapped his shoulder.

A nearby Tocororo chirped and a flock of seagulls flew towards the bay.

Carlitos looked up, trying to see the birds, but his eyes were swollen with tears. "This island was about to break out of its cocoon and fly."

"Come. Get in the car. It'll be nighttime soon. Let's get out of here."

They drove in silence, taking back streets and avoiding large intersections.

"Guess who I bumped into at the university?" Cristóbal asked.

"Who?"

"*El comemierda de* Fernandez."

"Is he still gloating over Fidel's triumph?"

"He stopped in front of me to say he didn't like the way things had turned."

Carlitos smacked his lips. "What did he think was going to happen?"

"Did you know he's part of the organizational meetings?"

"I heard."

"He whispered in my ear that Che Guevara is going to seize all bank assets."

Cristóbal stopped the car to look at Carlitos directly. The sun was rapidly setting, and the crickets began their disjointed chirping in celebration.

"I've already transferred my funds to a bank in Miami. You should do the same."

"I don't have any money," Carlitos confessed, "other than what I keep in the house."

"What about your relatives?"

"*Papá* is in Washington. I don't know about Manuel, but Belencita has jewels in a safety deposit box. I'll warn Tina and the Gutierrez clan. Thanks for the information."

Cristóbal softly accelerated while Carlitos looked at the passing scenery.

"This isn't looking good," Cristóbal said while scanning the empty streets. "I'm thinking of our South American history class. Most revolutions get bloodier before they get stable."

"You mean all revolutions. This one won't be any different."

"So, you know what else the *comemierda de* Fernandez told me?"

"He said more?"

"He's leaving on the next flight out."

"After he bad-mouthed my father and did everything possible to discredit the elections, the coward is leaving?"

"Says he's going to Miami."

Cristóbal stopped at the intersection where Oscar Jorge was shot. The blood stain was still on the street.

"We're leaving too," Cristóbal looked at Carlitos with eyes that glistened with moisture. "I've booked plane tickets for me, Marisa and the kids."

He looked down at the bloodstained road.

"Please don't wait too long to follow," he implored. "I'd hate to lose another friend to this damn revolution."

An eternal moment of silence passed. Cristóbal slowly drove up to Tina's carport, where Carlitos' MG was parked.

"God be with you," Carlitos said while hugging Cristóbal.

The moon was rising, and the cricket's sonorous chirping filled the evening air.

"*Coño,* I'm even going to miss these crickets," Cristóbal said and then drove away.

******

Olga stood outside her father's home, nervously hoping his wife wouldn't answer the door. Numerous young men in olive-green uniforms with newly grown beards populated the neighborhood. A busy energy was palpable.

"*¿Olguita, que paso?*" Manolo said in a concerned voice as he opened the front door.

"*Nada.* It's nothing," she said. "Are you alone? I need to speak with you."

Manolo turned to see if anyone was behind him. With the grace of a dancer, he stepped over the threshold while silently closing the door. He motioned her to follow and walked on his toes. Olga did as he, so her steps would softly land on the sidewalk. Two blocks later they reached a *bodega*, grabbed a shopping cart and walked down an aisle of canned goods.

"What's on your mind?" he whispered as he reached out for a can.

"We're leaving. Carlitos is certain they're coming for him."

Manolo paused to control his breathing. Without looking at his daughter, he reached over for her hand. Her breathing had become erratic.

"I've been worried for him... and you," he squeezed her hand and then placed the can in the shopping cart. "His last name is not going to win him any friends in this revolution."

"Papá, it can't stay like this, can it?"

He looked at her but did not offer an opinion. They took a few more steps down the aisle and stood in front of a row of evaporated milk.

"I think it's a smart move," Manolo whispered. "Get out of here and come back when things calm down." He reached for a can. "Right now, there's a frenzy. They want to get anyone who might be a threat to the revolution and throw them in *la Cabaña.*"

Olga bent over to examine the cans.

"I'm packed," she straightened up. "Just in case we need to leave in a hurry."

"It's going to be unpleasant," he said to her with swelling eyes. "Leaving the island is seen as an offense to the movement."

"What do you mean?"

"I attended some meetings with Jenny, and I've heard them make plans. Groups of people, in the hundreds, go to the airport with the sole purpose of humiliating the people who are leaving."

They walked a bit further and stared at the bags of cornmeal.

"Get ready for the insults. Lean on Carlitos and it'll be over before you know it."

"No, we won't be together."

"What do you mean?"

"We've decided to go on different days, just in case. My identification still reads Gutierrez, and he's going to use his mother's name, Dominguez."

"Alright. When will you go?"

"Soon, I think. But I need your help with one thing."

His eyes began to fill with tears. He turned to wipe them and then placed a bag of cornmeal in the cart.

"Can I give you my cross?"

"Your cross?"

"From the wedding. Agramonte's cross. I'm afraid they'll confiscate it at the airport."

"What do you want me to do? Sell it?"

"No. Keep it safe until I return."

They took a few more steps and saw the butcher behind the counter.

"*Hola,* Manolo," the butcher greeted.

"*¿Qué tal?* How are you?" Manolo replied and turned to continue walking. Olga, however, approached the butcher.

"How much for a couple of filets?" she asked.

"Prices are going up, I'm sorry to say. I can get you two, these here, for just under four *pesos.*" The butcher pointed at a short row of beef steaks.

"Papa?" Olga turned and called him back, "Do you mind?"

Manolo returned and smiled at the butcher who wrapped the steaks in paper. They continued shopping in silence, randomly placing food items in the cart.

Before leaving the *bodega*, Olga opened the wrapped steaks, took out Agramonte's cross from her purse and placed it between them. She then returned it to her father with a weak smile. From the living room window, Jenny watched Olga walk toward the bus stop as Manolo entered with a brown grocery bag in his arms.

"What did she want?" Jenny asked.

"Nothing. She was checking to see how I'm doing."

"Why?" Jenny's lip curled.

"I don't know. I think she's worried. You know, there's trouble."

"Not for us, but I can see why she thinks that. There's nothing but worms in that house."

Manolo placed the grocery bag down and turned to look at her.

"Don't talk about her that way."

Jenny saw Manolo's stern look and shrugged her shoulders.

"*Chico, por favor*, you can't be serious," Jenny said. "Your daughter married into a family of bureaucrats and worms. Must I remind you who fled the country?"

"I'm asking you to not talk about her that way, or any of them," Manolo raised his voice and stepped toward Jenny.

"Okay. Okay. If you insist, I won't talk about her like that."

"Promise me you will leave them alone."

"What?"

"Promise me you won't interfere with Tina and her home."

"I can't..."

"Promise!" Manolo loudly demanded. His daughters came out to see what was happening.

"*Mamá?*" the oldest daughter asked fearfully.

Jenny stood to approach her.

"*Esta bien*. I promise, but you realize this is much bigger than me. I'm just one of many." She took their daughter and walked into the room. "There are other comrades doing the work of the revolution, including Rubio," she said and then closed the door.

Manolo stared at the closed door, wondering if his wife had uttered a threat. He took out the wrapped package, opened it and saw Agramonte's cross. The diamonds glistened beneath the blotches of pooled blood.

******

Dust was everywhere that summer. Maybe it was the overabundance of trucks carrying rebel soldiers through the city; or the nearby training of new soldiers, marching and shooting rifles. Regardless of the growing uncertainty and chaos, Tina was determined to keep her house clean. She was sweeping the sidewalk when her neighbor, another housewife wearing an apron, approached.

"*Hola compañera,*" the woman saluted.

"*Buenos días*, Petunia."

"I see you're always busy keeping the neighborhood clean, comrade."

"Petunia, you know I like a clean house and it helps if I have a clean walkway."

"Yes, we all like a clean house," Petunia said, "and we must also do our part for the revolution."

Tina paused her sweeping and looked directly at her neighbor.

"Do you value the directives of our *comandante*? Didn't he say every young man needs to become part of the movement? I don't see your son wearing a uniform. Does he not want to support the revolution?"

Tina paused to consider the best response to the challenge presented and then quickly smiled, switching her broom from her right hand to the left.

"Absolutely, but you know there are many ways to be supportive. The *comandante* has a long list of publications that need to be printed and sent to every workplace, school and home. Those publications don't appear magically. Someone needs to set a printing plate, and that's what *Fotograbados Gutierrez* is doing. There are plenty of soldiers, but few engravers, and my son is serving where he is most needed. So, thanks for asking and giving me the opportunity to clear up any misunderstandings."

Tina stood with the broom in her hand and smiled at her neighbor, who looked down and backed away.

"*¡Gracias, compañera!*" Tina said loudly and then continued to sweep the sidewalk. "*Comemierda,*" she muttered to herself.

"What was that about?" Olga asked when Tina returned with the broom in hand.

"Another explanation to another nosy neighbor as to why Manolín is not in uniform." Tina slammed the closet door shut after tossing the broom inside. "And must they keep calling me *compañera?* Have they forgotten my name?"

A loud knock on the door startled Olga. Tina looked at it with annoyance.

"Now what?" she said as she opened it and Olga bit her lip.

A long-bearded man in an olive green uniform wearing sunglasses stood in front of her. The scar across his cheek disrupted the balance of his beard.

"Tina," he said as he removed his sunglasses.

"Rubio?" she replied and saw Jenny standing behind him several yards away.

"Please address me as captain."

Tina stepped forward and closed the door behind her. "How can I help you?"

"You still don't want me inside your house," he chuckled while looking her over. "Surely you can trust a hero who fought in the *Sierra* with *el Comandante.*"

Tina's face became flushed as she caught Jenny smiling smugly.

"What do you want?"

"Hmm... I think it would take less time if I consider what I don't want? How's Olguita? Do you think she remembers me?"

"Captain," Jenny stepped forward to make eye contact with Tina. "We should get moving."

"Yes," he answered but kept his eyes on Tina for a silent minute, as if listening to an internal argument that would decide her fate. "Hmm... I came to inform you the neighborhood in Boca Ciega has been confiscated by the 26th of July Movement. Your beach house no longer belongs to you and your personal effects are in temporary storage at the Boca Ciega station. You have one week to claim them."

He paused to run his eyes down her body and smiled at her. "But I wouldn't bother. Have a good day, *compañera*."

Tina nodded. Her bottom lip was shaking as Rubio turned and walked away with Jenny. She softly closed the door. Olga stood at the edge of the living room with terror in her eyes.

"Mima, that was him," Olga said while squeezing one hand into the other. "That was him, the man who... he's the one who.... *¡Ay Dios mío!* What did he want? Why is he here?"

Tina leaned on the door and locked it, but realized it wasn't strong enough to keep dangerous men out. She leaned on the wall, and knew it wasn't solid enough to keep the revolution out. Her vision darkened and her legs buckled as the floor spun beneath her. A burning pressure gripped her chest and tightened her lungs. The air was thick with fear. Her eyes widened as she flailed on the living room floor, unable to open her bronchioles and extract some needed oxygen.

"*¿Mima, qué te pasa?*" Olga cried and held Tina's head. "¡Carlitos!" she screamed. "¡Carlitos!" she called out again, forgetting he wasn't home.

A forced gulp of air made its way through her constricted airways, and then another. With every breath she relaxed, assured the gift of life was still hers. The room slowly stopped spinning and Tina was able to focus on her daughter, who held her head and torso while shedding nervous tears. Olga helped her to the sofa, placed a cool compress on her forehead and offered her a cup of *manzanilla* to calm her nerves.

"I've called the doctor. I told him you suffered an upset and he said he'll pass by later today," Olga said. "For now, drink some chamomile tea."

"Seeing that man again, after all these years," Tina said. "I'll be ready next time!"

"The tea should help."

Tina looked at her daughter and began to cry.

"*Pero* Mima, you can't get like this! What he did to me was a long time ago. He won't be able to do it again."

"It's not that," she said, wiping her nose.

"Then what is it?"

Tina lowered her head, unable to control her emotions.

"You have to leave," she said while wiping the tears away. "It's not safe."

"I know. We've had this conversation."

"I know, but before it seemed like a vacation. Now, it's real and the thought of it..." she started to cry again.

"*Ay*, Mima, I'll be back." Olga said as she reached for the cup of tea. "It won't be long. You'll see."

Tina took a few breaths and examined her house while sipping from the cup.

"How is it, any good?"

"Yes. It's fine. I need Carlitos to secure this house before he leaves."

That evening, Manolín returned to find his brother-in-law installing a deadbolt on the front door.

"What's going on?" he asked.

"Making sure your mother is safe before we leave," Carlitos replied.

"Why are you late?" Tina asked her son. "Dinner's been ready for hours."

"Working for the revolution. *El taller* is busier than ever. Everyday a *miliciano* walks in with an order and insists it has to be done right away," Manolín complained. "This revolution is producing more edicts and written material than five governments put together."

"I hope you're not complaining," Tina asked with concern.

"But they're not paying us," he raised his voice. "They treat us like slaves and act like they're doing us a favor."

"Manolín," Carlitos interrupted in a soft voice. "Let Pedrito handle the money."

"Yeah, let Pedrito be the one who talks about money," Tina said angrily.

"Just keep showing up for work," Carlitos continued in a soft voice. "Smile at the *milicianos* and survive this. Soon enough, things will change. They have to because nobody works for free. And whatever you do, don't let them hear your complaints or you might get classified as an enemy of the movement."

"Call everyone a *compañero* if you have to," Tina interjected.

"The goal is to survive this stage of the revolution." Carlitos sat down.

"What do you mean?" Olga asked. "This is a stage?"

"Revolutions go through stages," he explained without making eye contact. "This is the most dangerous one, especially for people like me. *Mierda le entró al piano.* The piano got full of shit, and people are not sure what to do. There's a lot of confusion. Nobody really knows what's coming next, and the rebels are itching for a fight. They want blood, because they think it will lead to success. They're eager to use their rifles and root out the resistance, but eventually somebody has to clean the piano."

Carlitos took off his glasses, leaned back and looked at his audience. "Do you understand what I'm saying? Everyone is a soldier until they realize the institutional work is needed. That's when the soldier will become the civil servant, and the revolution will become a series of departments to provide services for the people."

They looked at Carlitos with confused amazement as he lightly bit the leg of his glasses.

"So, you're saying Cuba is like a piano," Manolín asked. "And the revolution is the shit that got in?"

"That's exactly it!" Carlitos half smiled and sat up.

"Fidel is the piano player," Olga guessed.

"And not a very good one," Carlitos commented.

"And an election is when people choose which piano player they want to hear," Olga said proudly with a smile.

"Exactly! Do they want a master, like Ernesto Lecuona, on the bench, or a brute who will bang at the keys? Batista got on this piano and decided to stay on it. The man is full of faults, but he was able to play a little something. Every once in a while we were able to hear a semi-pleasant rendition of a recognizable tune. The problem came when the people decided they wanted to hear something different. But instead of turning his seat over to a master, Batista surrendered the bench to this *barbudo*, and now..."

"... he can't play because it's full of shit," Manolín interrupted and began to laugh.

Carlitos used his glasses to point at an imaginary screen where he painted his illustration.

"In order for the country to run, and for people to understand how to function in it, the chaos of the moment, of this stage, has to be cleaned up."

"Is this how they teach at the university?" Manolín laughed. "Because if it is, sign me up to be a university student."

"No," Tina interjected. "That's just the mind of your brother-in-law. Now, off to the shower, because you smell like something that got into the piano."

"The point is," Carlitos lifted his hand to emphasize a point. "Don't lose your cool. Hold on and persevere. At one point or another, things will settle."

"In the meantime, you need to leave," Manolín said to Carlitos with seriousness.

"If I don't, I'll be another casualty of this..."

"Shit," Manolín interrupted.

"I wish you would change the analogy," Tina said.

A small cockroach crawled alongside the floorboard. Tina got up, rolled up a newspaper and smacked it. The cockroach ran but Tina was faster. Olga gave her a look of disgust as her mother picked up the dead insect.

"How long before you can return?" Manolín asked.

"Not sure. Some revolutions have a short life span. I'm praying the Americans realize what is happening before it's too late. They have the means to put an end to this very quickly."

"And you're leaving with him?" Manolín turned to Olga, who was biting her lip and rubbing her hands.

"No. I'm going the next day."

"*Bueno, ya basta*, enough." Tina commanded with a broken voice. "I don't want to talk about this anymore. You," she pointed at her son, "off to the shower and get ready for dinner." Her voice began to crack. "God will look over us and one day we'll return to normal."

Carlitos looked at Tina and shook his head.

"What?" Manolín stood from his seat and asked.

"Nothing."

"No, really. What? Another shit in the piano analogy?"

"Go take a shower," Carlitos replied. "You don't want to know what I'm thinking."

"That's right. Go take a shower," Tina ushered Manolín to the bathroom.

Carlitos smacked his lips and made eye contact with his brother-in-law.

"The notion of God being normal, and society striving for normal," Carlitos said with annoyance. "It just..." he stopped mid-sentence and looked down.

"What about it?" Manolín asked.

"If you studied your bible a little," Carlitos spoke softly, "you'd know that God is far from normal. There's nothing normal about Noah and the flood. There was nothing normal about any of the prophets. Even Jesus wasn't normal. This idea that God will restore things to normal is absurd. God doesn't care for normal because God is not normal. Do you understand what I'm saying? And just what exactly is normal? Do you even know what you're praying for?"

"Now you're saying things that are blasphemous," Tina argued loudly, "and I will not allow that kind of talk in my house. I know my bible and I know what the church teaches. So, if you don't want to sleep outside, keep your atheist ideas in check."

"Mima, por favor," Olga defended. "He's not an atheist."

"I won't have it," Tina protested. "He can't say God doesn't want us to be normal and take away my beliefs like that. It's all that I have left."

Olga and Carlitos remained silent as Tina retired to her room, slamming the door behind her. Manolín held back a laugh.

"Looks like more shit got inside the piano," he said with amusement.

"Go take a shower," Olga ordered and waved him away. "Why did you have to say something like that?" she said to Carlitos.

"Because she lives in a fantasy," he answered loudly. "You all do!"

Manolín stepped out of the bathroom, no longer amused, concerned to where Carlos' temper might lead.

"In these four walls you all live a lie," Carlitos pointed at Tina's room accusingly. "You think you're able to keep dust and cockroaches out, but life is not a carport to be cleaned up. Fidel's revolution is happening because nobody wanted to face the truth, and now... guess what? The house is gathering dust and the cockroaches are out, running crazy."

He stood wide eyed as his wife stared back at him.

"There's only a few roaches in this house," Manolín complained.

Olga waved her brother back into the bathroom and approached her agitated husband.

"Come sit with me," she said to him. "Let's just sit on the porch and look at the stars like when you were courting me."

Carlitos resisted, but she reached for his hand and gently led him to the front porch, where they sat next to each other. The sound of palm trees swaying in the wind greeted them. The stars shone brightly, despite the moon's competition. She sat closer, tighter, and held his hand until the tension relaxed. Tina's garden dedicated a floral fragrance to the moon and surrounded the porch with an intoxicating aroma. Carlitos exhaled a long and repressed sigh. His jaw reluctantly softened. He turned to open his mouth and release an overabundance of words, but she placed her finger on his lips.

"No more talking," she whispered. "Just sit with me. Can you do that?"

"I..."

"No more talking," she ordered.

He surrendered to her wish, granting his shoulder for her head to rest on. Eventually, the rising and falling of their breathing became synchronized. The softness of her touch, the scent of her hair and even her perspiration, became sacred for their last night on the island.

******

At the airport, neighbors gathered to publicly shame those who were leaving the country, calling them worms and traitors. Carlitos held his breath as he faced the long walkway lined with Fidel supporters, who threw insults and spat at him. Inside, he was interrogated and inspected with offensive thoroughness. The luggage was opened, and his clothes strewn across a table. His money passed through several hands, each person taking a little for themselves. He caught sight of Robert Brown and a small group of *Americanos*. None of them seemed worried as inspectors threw their casino chips in the trash.

Carlitos sat in the back of the twin-engine plane, anticipating the bird's-eye view of Havana. The Hotel Nacional sat majestically over the city. The capitol dome stood out over the surrounding 19th century buildings, seemingly impervious to a new communist regime. He located *el Paseo del Prado* and traced it until he located the neighborhoods of *el Vedado* and *la Víbora*. Soon after, he saw the university with its famous staircase and the students eager to reach its top. The plane flew low over the *Malecón*, which was full of people waving farewell at the passing plane. Carlitos pressed his face against the window and thought he saw *el Caballero de París*, wearing his black overcoat and smiling up at him.

With tears streaming down his face he thought of a proverb taught in grade school, "The wise man, like the tortoise, may travel but will never leave home." From that day forth, Carlitos identified with the tortoise. "I am a turtle."

******

Two years later, Tina was planning her emigration from the island. Both Manolín and Olga were living in Miami with their spouses and had given her grandchildren. She longed to be reunited with them, but the thought of her house becoming a residence for a *barbudo* was unacceptable. Instead, she made plans to leave it with a cousin. She had just hung up the phone with that cousin, when Manolo knocked on her door.

She stood silent at the threshold, still unable to reconcile with the man.

"Tina, I'm going to Miami."

"Are you?"

"I don't know how much longer I can stand this."

"Isn't your wife a respected member of the revolution?"

"I'm not a communist."

"Really?"

"I heard about our new grandchildren and I want to see Manolín and Olguita."

"Hmm..." Tina tilted her head as if learning something new. "I didn't think you would ever say that."

"I have a problem, though."

She waited silently for him to continue.

"It's about Olguita's wedding cross."

"Agramonte's cross?"

"I don't know what to do with it. Can I give it to you?"

"I don't think so. I'll be leaving too, and there's no way of getting it out of the country."

Manolo stood silent and met her unwavering eyes.

"Is your wife going to give me any problems when I leave?"

"Hard to say," he said while looking down. "I'm trying my hardest to keep my departure a secret." He rubbed his hands and looked around to see if anyone was listening. "You may want to leave before I do."

Manolo looked at the empty carport and raised his eyebrows.

"What happened to Carlitos' MG?"

"Funny you should ask," Tina's tone grew in sarcasm. "Ask your new friends in the revolution, *compañero*."

"That's not fair, Tina. You know I'm not a communist."

"Do I?"

"I would never be part of something like this."

"I know," she conceded. "It was Rubio. He came back and took it. He also went inside and helped himself to my fine china."

"*¿Como?*" Manolo looked at the edge of the property and noticed small pieces of porcelain strewn down the walkway. "The blue set from Portugal?"

"Yes. Apparently, he thought it would look better shattered on the sidewalk."

"That son of a bitch!" He walked over and picked up a small, blue piece of porcelain.

"I don't sweep the sidewalk anymore," Tina shrugged her shoulders.

He paused and looked at her with empathy.

"I know how much you liked that porcelain set. I'm so sorry. Can I help in any way?"

"Help?" she almost laughed but couldn't. "I haven't needed your help in years. No. Thanks for offering, but my brother, Mario, is around. He checks in regularly."

Manolo stood quiet, realizing there was nothing for him to say.

"Hide it," she said to him.

"The cross? Yes. That's what I'm thinking."

"Hide it well, so we can retrieve it years from now, when all this comes to an end."

"All right, then," he said and stepped away. "I hope to see you in Miami."

"I hope so too. By the way, I think you got the wife you deserve."

He paused, looked at her blank stare and broke out in laughter. She stood there, not knowing what was so funny, but eventually his laughter made her chuckle.

Weeks later, under the cover of a moonless night, Manolo placed the cross in a brown paper bag, sealed in a jar filled with uncooked rice, inside a box, deep in a hole, which he dug in his backyard. It was never to be seen again.

CHAPTER 16

Post Exile

July 2021
Miami

From the balcony of my mother's Miami apartment we could see the congested traffic accumulating. Thousands of cars, seemingly stuck to each other, moving inches at a time in a frustrated effort to reach side streets where more cars were immersed in a slow-moving sludge. The monumental and historic traffic jam consisted of parents desperately wanting to reach their children, elderly who needed a toilet, sickly who had to get to the hospital, and laborers who were extremely late to work. As drivers lost their patience, a cacophony of honking horns angrily disrupted the Miami sky, normally filled with the sound of squawking parrots. My mother and I stood on the balcony relieved we had nowhere to go, and amazed as to how a local protest managed to become the rally of a decade, disrupting traffic for millions of commuters.

"*¡Ay, Dios mío!*" my mother exclaimed. "This is horrendous. Do you think Carlos Francisco is stuck in this traffic?"

"No. He's fine, but I'll call him to make sure," I replied and pulled out my cell phone.

"*Sí, sí, sí.* Call him. I need to make sure he's home."

I dialed his number, passed her the phone, stepped inside, and turned on the television to see what the local news was saying about the protest that jammed an entire city. I stopped my channel surfing at the image of a protester being interviewed. A well-groomed, middle aged, Cuban American man, wearing Ray Ban sunglasses and a blue Polo shirt, held a banner that read "#S.O.S. Cuba." He was standing in front of the Versailles Restaurant, one of several hubs for the exiled Cuban community to hold political demonstrations.

"We're here in solidarity with our Cuban brothers who are protesting on the island," the man said into the microphone. "I want them to know, they are not alone. We stand with you and together we will bring down the oppressive regime that has ruled over our motherland for the last sixty-two years."

"What are you hoping to accomplish with this protest," the reporter asked.

"It is our goal that President Biden hear our cry and denounce the many crimes of the Castro dictatorship. It is time to bring an end to this travesty."

The camera widened to show hundreds, possibly thousands, of protestors waving Cuban flags and chanting, "*Patria y Vida.*"

"Carlos Francisco is safe in his apartment with *el niño*," my mother said as she entered the living room and closed the sliding glass door behind her. "I told him to stay put and not go out. It's just too crazy out there."

"Have a seat, Mama, and look at this. It seems the traffic jam is city wide."

She sat next to me to watch the news report when another protester jumped in front of the camera to scream in a disruptive manner, "Viva Trump! Biden is a fucker!"

"*¡Ay, que pena!*" My mother exclaimed. "How embarrassing! This is a national moment of concern and look at how that man behaved in front of the camera, for the whole world to see."

"There's always one in every crowd," I shook my head.

"How can he say something like that, about the president of the United States of America? And what does Trump have to do with any of this?"

"Mama, the mob mentality always brings out the worst in people."

"*Pero*, of all the things to say, why insult President Biden? The situation in Cuba is not his fault."

"Well, hopefully, the president won't find out, and even if he does, he won't take it personally. I'm sure he understands that in every protest there are people who don't know what the real issues are. They're just releasing their pent-up anger and frustrations."

"The real fucker is Raul Castro."

"Mama, please, such language!" I reprimanded her playfully and chuckled. "Is this what it took for you to say that word?"

"No, no, no, no, no. If there ever was a time to call Castro a fucker, it's now."

"Let's put it on a T-shirt, 'Castro, the real fucker!' What do you think?"

We laughed together and then settled down to watch the images of protesters in Cuba filling up the streets of Havana and chanting in unison.

"Could this be a call for democracy on the island?" I asked.

"Well, I don't know about that. I don't think there's anyone left who knows anything about democracy. But maybe it'll be the first step toward some kind of change."

"Maybe this is the beginning of the end for the Castro regime," I said wistfully.

"I sure hope so. I'd like to think that God has kept me alive this long so I could witness the fall of that dictatorship. Maybe now, after sixty years, this country will help restore Cuba."

"Really? You still have that hope?"

"Why not?"

"Because no other American president has ever taken that step. Quite frankly, it hurts to see how much they care about the well-being of European countries while Cuba, just a few miles away, is falling apart. The discrepancy in foreign policy is so blatant that it's almost impossible to not consider racism as part of the equation."

"Guille, don't talk that way. This country has been very good to us. Look at the life we have. Look at how far you've gotten. Had we stayed in Cuba, I doubt you would even be alive today. No, no, no, no, no. We owe this country our lives and we should be eternally grateful."

"That's not what I'm talking about. Of course, we have a good life here. If there ever was a group of immigrants that was going to succeed in this country, it's us Cubans. We have flourished, but let's not be blind to the priorities of U.S. legislators, especially when it comes to foreign policy. They would rather go to war in Vietnam, Beirut, Iraq and Afghanistan before helping their Latino neighbors become politically and economically stable."

"You may have a point, but after living through the Cuba of 59', when I was in fear of being jailed, after being chased out of the island by my own neighbors, I look at this nation with very forgiving eyes. The virtues of this country outweigh her faults."

"I guess everything is subjective."

"I don't know what you mean by that."

"I mean that your life experiences will determine your judgment."

"Exactly! That's it. Go live in Cuba for a few months or years. I dare you. You'll come back kissing the ground. Where else can a person call the president a fucker and not fear any retribution? I'm ashamed of that young man for saying those words, but did the police arrest him? No, but what do you think would happen if you go to Cuba and call Diaz-Canel a fucker?"

"Mama," I protested, "stop saying that word. It sounds so ugly when you say it."

"Fucker, fucking fucker." She started laughing. "I think I like saying it."

"No! I can't take it."

Her laughter became a full body activity. She leaned back and partially covered her face as her belly jiggled with joy. It was infectious, and I also started to laugh uncontrollably as she blurted out, in between breaths, "Castro is a fucker." And then, as expected, she lost control of her bodily functions. She stood up in a hurry and ran to her bedroom. When she returned, wearing a different house dress, I was in the kitchen preparing a batch of coffee.

"You know, Guille, I was just remembering my first day as a refugee."

I looked at her as I vigorously stirred the sugar required for a foamy cup of espresso.

"You know that I don't like mine too sweet," she said with a concerned tone as she looked at the container of whipped sugar.

"I know. Don't worry. This is mostly for me."

"But that's a lot of sugar."

"It's the same amount of sugar I use for every coffee that I have ever served you. So, go on. You were saying something about your first day as a refugee?"

"*¡Ah, sí!* I realize that your father and I were running away from danger, but at that time I had no clue we were political refugees. I thought we were just going to wait a few months, and the whole Castro thing was going to blow over."

"What about Papa, what did he think?"

"Your father knew things in Cuba weren't going to change on their own, but I think even he was surprised to see the revolution last as long as it did."

I poured her a cup and we sat together in the living room, sipping hot coffee in silence and savoring the taste. I was daydreaming when I noticed tears building up in her eyes.

"What's the matter?"

"I'm so silly. I don't know why, but I have the urge to cry."

"Was it the TV, showing images of people protesting in Cuba?"

"I think so. It has me remembering so many things."

"Tell me. I think I want to hear it."

"No, *mijo*, no. It's just going to make me cry."

"It's okay. A few tears in this living room won't ruin the day. A little while ago you wanted to tell me about your first day here in Miami."

"*Sí,* well, I think I told you we had to leave the island on different days. I was so afraid..." her mind traveled to that fateful day sixty-two years earlier as tears accumulated in her eyes. I waited patiently for her to continue.

"People lost their sense of civility. If they thought you were against Castro, you better hide. Which is why your father left the island a day earlier."

"Were you nervous?"

"Of course I was! And then, when I got to the hotel, he wasn't there."

"Was this a hotel in Miami or Miami Beach?"

"No, it was the beach. Your father wanted to relive our honeymoon. I had to take a taxi to the hotel, but when I got there I couldn't find him. I started to think something happened."

"Could you have been at the wrong hotel?"

"No. Your father made the arrangements and I had it on paper, in his handwriting."

"And he wasn't there?"

"Well he was, but the hotel manager was looking at my passport, and it had my name, Gutierrez. So, he didn't see another Gutierrez on the list and said my husband hadn't arrived."

"What did you do?"

"The only thing I could do, I checked in. I remember the manager telling me I couldn't bring men into my room. And I told him that it was not my intention to bring men into my room. I don't know, maybe he thought I was a prostitute."

She chuckled and repeated the sentence, as if it were a punch line.

"So, what happened?"

"I went up to the room but after a few minutes I got hungry, so I stepped out to find a place to eat. It was the funniest thing. There I was, standing on the sidewalk, wondering where I should go, and standing just a few feet from me was your father, facing the other way. And I said to him, 'Carlitos!' He turned around, surprised to see me."

"He was there all along?"

"He was. I have to say, we were never so happy to see each other as we were at that moment. Can you imagine that? It was like something out of a movie."

Her eyes began to fill with tears again.

"So, we went back inside to my room and the manager gave me the dirtiest look. You should have seen him." Her laughter got louder. "The man had just told me I couldn't bring men to my room, and there I was holding hands with your father, going to the elevator."

We paused so she could laugh, giving me the chance to catch her infectious laughter.

"*Ay*, every time I think about the man's disapproving face..."

"And when was that? The date you arrived in Miami?"

"June 19, 1959," she said without hesitating. "That first week, we pretended to be on vacation, but soon we realized we were going to run out of money. So, we left the hotel and got a place over by the Orange Bowl."

"That area became Little Havana, right?"

"*Si, si, si*. You know it was a joke, right? The area was nothing like Havana. Guille, you have to remember, Havana was magnificent and Miami was ... well, it was depressing, especially around the Orange Bowl."

"I've heard," recalling all the conversations when my parents recited their favorite poem, "Everything Was Better in Cuba."

"Havana was so beautiful that people came from all over to see her," she said and then sighed. "There was no way that Miami could ever be like Havana."

"So, you and Papa moved out of the hotel and into an apartment?"

"Do you know how much we paid in rent those days?"

"Dirt cheap, I suspect."

"Eight dollars a week. Can you imagine that?"

"Was that a lot of money?"

"Not really, but we didn't have jobs and we were quickly running out of money."

"So, how did you find a job? Was there a Craigslist in 1959?"

"*¿Que es eso?*"

"It's a modern version of the classified section."

"No, the Catholic church got us the work. The church was very helpful. Had it not been for the church, I don't know what we would have done."

My phone rang and I excused myself to speak in private. One phone call led to another and I completely forgot about my mother and her refugee story. Over an hour had passed when I returned to the living room. She was seated in low lighting with the television off.

"Why are you here like this, sitting in the dark?" I turned on a lamp. "Don't you want to watch the news or something?"

"No, not now. Are you leaving in the morning?"

"You know I have to, but don't get sad. I'll be back. Are you sure you're okay?"

"Yes, I'm fine. Why do you ask?"

"I don't know. You seem... sad."

She half smiled and then looked as if I guessed correctly.

"What's going on? I asked.

"Nothing."

She caught my disbelieving eyes and confessed, "I was actually praying," she said and revealed a rolled-up rosary in her hand.

"Oh! Did I interrupt?"

"It's okay. I was thanking God," she paused and looked at the darkening sky. A pair of doves flew to a nearby tree. "I've had a good life. There were times when I thought my world was turned upside down, but maybe that's God's way of turning life right side up."

She paused, allowing me to think about the image she offered.

"Lord knows, my life could have been a lot worse," she said with a sigh.

"*Ay*, Mama, you have a great life. How many little old ladies have a son that makes them laugh so hard they have to change their underwear?"

"Hey," she protested, "who are you calling an old lady?"

I chuckled, knowing I got a rise from her.

"Do you want to continue praying?" I asked.

"If you don't mind."

"Not at all," I turned, to give her some privacy, and walked to my room.

As I opened the door, from the corner of my eye, I caught a glowing beauty enveloping my mother. I'm not sure if it was the reflection of the setting sun or something more ethereal, but my breath was momentarily suspended as I gazed on her light-filled countenance. Time stood still and then I blinked. Her glow vanished and a darkening reality filled the room, yet the feeling that I witnessed something beautiful remains with me to this very day.

The End.

As a Cuban-American, Guillermo Márquez-Sterling has witnessed the trauma Cuban exiles suffered after fleeing from the Castro dictatorship. He is a direct descendant of Carlos Márquez-Sterling, a political figure responsible for ratifying the Cuban constitution and who actively advocated for democracy while the island slipped into dictatorship. Márquez-Sterling is a pastor, activist and teacher whose love of the written story has led him to write several books: *Rise of the Spiritual Activist* (2012), and the trilogy *Praying for an Eclipse* (2017). He currently lives in Arizona with his life-long partner and wife, Maria.

NOTE TO THE READER

Killing the Butterfly is the story of two families, connected through marriage, living in Havana during the 1950s. Their drama unfolds while the most economically advanced Caribbean country slid into the most oppressive authoritarian model of governance. As a descendant, I have taken the liberty of writing their story. Authors everywhere will recognize the dilemma I face: How to narrate a remembered past in an appealing and literary style that doesn't compromise the basic, historical realities.

Do I include every name and person, as minor as they might be, and risk turning this story into a 1000-page novel with too many characters to follow? Or do I combine and fuse into a few characters' core traits and points of a larger population so that it might be easier to read? I chose the latter.

Killing the Butterfly bears the hybrid category of historical fiction for reasons that uphold both the historic and literary value of the book. The people and events described are based on undisputed facts. There were people in Havana during the turbulent 1950s who advocated for fair and clean elections, for the constitution to be upheld, and for a peaceful transition of power. Those men and women comprised a vocal minority and risked becoming targets of both the Batista regime and the Castro revolution. Sadly, the overwhelming majority of the population were either politically indifferent (and easily manipulated) or knowing actors whose actions compromised the sustainability of democracy. For more on this subject, please visit www.killingthebutterfly.com.

ACKNOWLEDGMENTS

Writing is a solitary experience. Many an early morning, I sit alone with a blank screen that is waiting to be filled by images and dialogues swimming around in my head, but at some point in time, I need someone to read what I've placed on that screen. Blanca Mesa, thank you for serving as my first editor and for the suggestions that led to my first rewrite. Patty Shillington, thank you for always being willing to read what pours out of my mind and for brainstorming ways to improve it. Beth England, thank you for your words of encouragement. You'll never know how timely and needed they were. I want to thank Conrad Kanagy and the staff from Santos Publishing. You are keeping the literary art alive.

Special words of gratitude are due to the following people: my wife, Maria, whose love provides the space I need to write. My three amazing children, Karina, Carlos Andres, and Natalia, thank you for listening to your ancestral stories and making them your own. My aunt, Uva de Aragon, for serving as a historical reference and whose works of literary art motivate me to make new metaphors for this life of ours. I must thank my brother, Carlos Francisco, whose creative genius inspires me to create. And, of course, to my mother, Olguita, whom I am eternally indebted to and will never be able to sufficiently express how much I love. Thank you, Mama, for being the easy laugh, nurturing love, and wise counselor in my life.

Finally, thank you, my reader. This is, after all, worthless without you.

Killing the Butterfly
Genealogy up to 1959

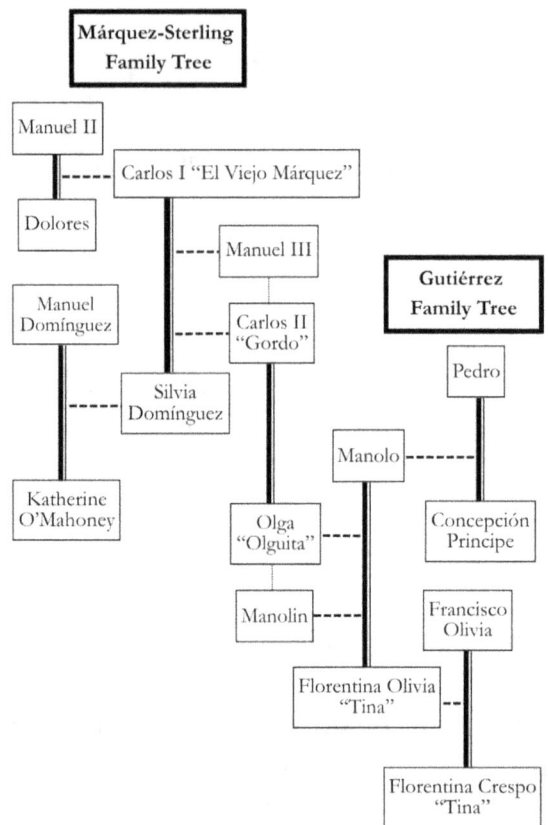

Márquez-Sterling Family Tree

Manuel II

Carlos I "El Viejo Márquez"

Dolores

Manuel III

Gutiérrez Family Tree

Manuel Domínguez

Carlos II "Gordo"

Pedro

Silvia Domínguez

Manolo

Katherine O'Mahoney

Olga "Olguita"

Concepción Principe

Manolin

Francisco Olivia

Florentina Olivia "Tina"

Florentina Crespo "Tina"

Manolo Gutierrez (circa 1952)

Olga and Tina (circa 1950)

Olga (about age 15)

Manolo, Olga, Manuel (standing) Carlos Jr.

El Caballero de Paris

Carlos Marquez-Sterling Sr. (circa 1954)

Carlos Marquez-Sterling Sr. (circa 1958)

Wedding photo of Olga (wearing Agramonte's cross)

Wedding photo at the reception (Tina standing)

Olga Gutierrez (at her grandson's wedding--2023)

www.ingramcontent.com/pod-product-compliance
Lightning Source LLC
Chambersburg PA
CBHW060138150626
46550CB00015B/1462